EASY FIXES
FOR EVERYDAY THINGS

EASY FIXES

FOR EVERYDAY THINGS

1,020 Ways to Repair Your Stuff

Reader's Digest

New York | Montreal

CONTENTS

INTRODUCTION

What do you do when your washing machine won't spin, when you spill hot coffee on your keyboard, or when your phone freezes? If your first instinct is to call a repairman or to go shopping for a replacement, think again. There is another—better—way. Many common problems with household technology and objects can easily be fixed with a few basic tools, a little ingenuity, and some sound instructions.

FIX YOUR LIFE

The fixes described in this book are simple and quick. When something goes wrong in your kitchen, laundry room, or car, they'll get you up and running again without fuss, and without the need for technical knowledge. Many of the fixes here are inventive and fun, using tools and materials in new and unusual ways. They'll put you back in charge of your environment without spending much money or valuable time.

It's not as hard as you think

True, some things are best left to the professionals. If your furnace fails or your car's brakes lose their bite, you will need expert help. But many fixes are really easy and can be done with stuff you already have in your home. A squirt of shaving cream will lift a juice stain from your carpet and a sink plunger can fix a dent in your car. All you need is a can-do attitude, some patience, and the advice contained in this book.

Count the benefits

Fixing things yourself isn't just about saving money. Think of the time and hassle involved in taking your broken wheelchair to and from the repair shop—why not try a home fix first? It's not only you that benefits; home repairs are much kinder to the environment than buying replacements or calling for professional help.

Take charge

While it's true that modern technology can be very complex, it doesn't follow that it's difficult to repair: many of the things that go wrong with sophisticated electronic devices, such as PCs, smartphones, and games consoles, are easy to put right. Fixing such things puts you back in control at home, at work, and at play, and it gives you a real sense of achievement when a job's done well.

Be prepared

Once you gain the confidence to fix things, you'll become more familiar with the essential systems that make your home work—your electrical systems and plumbing, for example. So when they do go wrong, you'll know what to do to avert disaster. Learning to maintain and care for your things will make them last longer, look and feel better, and it gives you a sense of pride that you can't buy.

HOW TO USE THIS BOOK

The scope of this book is as wide as everyday life itself. The quick fixes described on its pages are divided into four chapters covering almost every type of simple, but annoyingly common, problem—a computer that's running slowly, a flickering light bulb, a blocked vacuum cleaner hose, or a flat wheelchair tire. Whatever the trouble, you're likely to find an easy solution right here.

Quick and concise solutions

Easy Fixes for Everyday Things is intended to be practical, no-nonsense, direct, and easy to follow. The problems you are most likely to encounter are stated simply, then the solutions are given clearly and in detail. Some fixes are accompanied by step-by-step illustrations that show you exactly what to do; others have informative photos that demonstrate the fix in action. Major systems and more complex appliances, including home plumbing, desktop computers, car engines, and washing machines, are introduced by features that provide an overview of the most common problem areas and their fixes.

As you flip through the book, you'll also see the symbols opposite. These identify additional tips that'll help you resolve your problems safely, sensibly, and economically, and explain any technical terms.

Chuck it

When a fault is serious, you'll see this symbol. The text beneath it will help you weigh whether it's worth trying a repair or if you'd be better off upgrading to new equipment.

Tools of the trade

Some repairs are hard to carry out without some special, but often inexpensive, gear. The text under this symbol will tell you what you need to make your fix as easy as possible.

Jargon buster

It's hard to avoid technical terms, especially when fixing high-tech equipment, such as computer networks. The text under this symbol will explain any jargon used by repairmen and manufacturers.

Warning

If carrying out a repair presents any hazards or risks damaging whatever it is you're trying to fix, you'll see this warning. Read the text carefully—safety is your first priority.

Make it last

Prevention is always better than cure, so dotted throughout the book are tips on how to look after your essential gadgets and appliances. This "Make It Last" advice will help keep your belongings in top condition longer, saving you time and money.

Working within your limits

The aim of this book is to encourage you to give it a try and solve your problem. But *Easy Fixes for Everyday Things* doesn't pull any punches—if something is tricky to do, it'll advise you to respect the limits of your know-how and call in a professional or admit defeat and buy a replacement.

Protecting expensive devices with covers and cleaning equipment after use will help extend its life and make it perform better.

It's worth trying to diagnose and fix a problem yourself if the guarantee on the faulty appliance ran out a long time ago.

START HERE

When something goes wrong in your home, step back and think before reaching for your toolbox. The solution may be easier than you think—and sometimes it's better to do nothing at all.

Guarantees and your rights

Anything you buy new in a shop is protected by consumer law. You have rights if it does not work or if it fails within a certain period. A retailer or manufacturer may also guarantee the goods for a set time, or may sell you a warranty—an insurance policy that covers the cost of repair for a year or more. Make sure that you and the retailer complete and send off any documents needed to register a manufacturer's guarantee, and keep your receipt and guarantee documents in a safe place.

If your goods fail and they are still covered by the terms of the guarantee or warranty, don't try to fix them. Return them to the retailer or manufacturer for professional repair. If you attempt a fix, you are likely to invalidate the guarantee. Even if your guarantee has expired, you may still be covered by consumer law, especially if the goods were bought relatively recently. Get to know your consumer rights; contact the retailer or manufacturer and try to negotiate a reasonable solution.

Check the obvious

Repair professionals will tell you that a very high percentage of their house calls are for problems that have an extremely simple solution—a blown fuse, a tripped circuit breaker, a tap not turned on. So before you pick up the phone and pay a service charge or try a home repair, check the obvious. If your washing machine won't switch on, is it properly connected to a working power supply? Does the electrical socket work? Has its circuit breaker tripped? Has its safety been turned off? Does water come out of nearby taps?

Switch on and off again

Computers and many other electronic devices can "crash"—stop working because their built-in software has developed a temporary glitch. Such appliances can usually be reset by turning the machine off and on again. If it is plugged in, remove the plug, wait for two minutes, then put it back in and attempt a restart. If the gadget has batteries, take them out for at least 30 minutes, put them back in, and switch on. Try recharging or replacing the batteries.

Restore the original settings

If one of your gadgets dies, try the "reset" or "restore" button— usually a recessed switch on the appliance or a combination of buttons. Pressing this takes the device back to its original factory settings. You may lose stored information, but building that up again will be easier than getting a repair and cheaper than buying a new device.

Check cables and connectors

Is the space behind your computer, TV, DVD player, or game console a mess of wires and cables? It's easy for these connectors to get tangled, work their way loose, or get mixed up. If a device that relies on connections is acting up, test all the wires first to make sure they're all intact and fitted securely in their correct sockets.

Consult the instruction book

Fewer and fewer of us these days bother studying instruction manuals. Check the back of the manual (or the final page or so of the PDF version on your computer) for a "troubleshooting" section. It will list the common problems and tell you how to go about solving them. Keep all your instruction manuals in one place, together with the receipt and warranty for each appliance.

Search the Internet

Search for the make and model of a faulty appliance, adding a brief description of the problem—chances are that if you've had the problem, so have many others. You may be able to find step-by-step instructions for the fix you need. But be wary—look for a consensus of opinion between trusted websites.

Keep a maintenance diary

Regular maintenance and seasonal storage will help prevent problems with machines and fixtures. Make diary entries for activities like furnace servicing, clearing gutters, cleaning air conditioners, and so on, so you don't forget to get the jobs done.

A hard or soft reset of an electronic gadget will often get it working again without the need for costly repair.

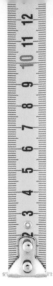

YOUR HOME REPAIR ESSENTIALS

Most simple repairs don't require a fully stocked workshop, but a few basic tools will make any job easier. If you don't have the right tool, don't rush out and buy a cheap multipiece tool kit—it's always a false economy. Invest in good-quality tools as and when you need them. Look after them, and they will last a lifetime.

Measuring tool

A 16-foot tape measure is essential. Make sure you also have a small spirit level and a T square for drawing straight lines.

Cutting tools

The most useful cutting tools are a craft knife with a retractable blade, a small hacksaw, and a tapered wood saw.

Hammer

There are many different kinds of hammers. For most jobs you can get by with a mid-weight claw hammer (weighing around 1 pound). It should have a fiberglass or steel handle and a cushioned grip.

Screwdrivers

Most fixes can be handled with 3/16, 1/4, and 5/16 in. slotted screwdrivers, and no. 1 and 2 Phillips-head screwdrivers. If you have limited storage space, buy a screwdriver with interchangeable bits.

Gripping tools

Invest in a pair of engineer's pliers, which have flat and rounded gripping surfaces. Fine-tipped needle-nose pliers are extremely useful in a variety of jobs. Make sure you have an adjustable wrench and team it with a mole grip—ideal for gripping and stabilizing nuts and pipes.

Electric drill

A modern drill may be the only power tool you will ever need. With the right bits and accessories, it can be used to make holes, grind, sand, and polish.

Lubricants, solvents, and adhesives

To get the best of the fixes in this book you will need some commercially available chemicals. These fall into three categories: lubricants, solvents, and adhesives. The basic lubricants are WD-40, which drives out moisture; 3-in-One, which is a light engine oil suitable for metal components; silicon lubricant for use on rubber; and perhaps a specialist cycle lubricant. The main solvents are mineral spirits, which shifts grease; isopropyl alcohol, for cleaning electrical contacts; and acetone, which is a stain remover. As for glues, contact adhesive is best for plastics, rubber, and leather; PVC cement is designed for pipes and guttering made of polyvinyl chloride; epoxy resin makes a strong bond on metals, ceramics, and some plastics; and then there is superglue, which is perfect for fixing small breakages.

Keeping Safe

Working safely is a mostly matter of common sense: don't rush, don't take risks, and heed the warning boxes throughout this book. There are a few other obvious safety measures that you should take: wear goggles when appropriate; always use an GFCI (ground fault circuit interrupter) when using electrical tools. If you are working on electrical appliances, make sure they are unplugged; and if you are working on the electrical systems in your house, first switch off the power at the electrical panel or fuse box.

A word about ladders. Falls from ladders are one of the most common causes of injury in the home. First, wear nonslip shoes. Place the ladder on a firm and even surface—never on top of another object. If the ladder is leaning against a wall, its base should be moved 10 inches away from the wall for every yard of height. Always face the ladder when going up and down. Never lean so far to the side that your belt buckle is outside the ladder's uprights.

YOUR "MAGIC TOOL KIT"

Many common problems can be fixed in minutes without any conventional tools. The solution might already be waiting in your storage closet, bathroom cabinet, or even your fruit bowl. These tools are magic because they are invisible until you know what to look for, and because they work in astonishing and unbelievable ways. Among the tools in your magic tool kit are pencils, bananas, candles, aluminum foil, and modeling clay. These can be used to solve plumbing problems, free caught zippers, repair scratches on phones and furniture, or reduce ironing time.

Microfiber cloth

Conventional cleaning cloths are made from cotton fibers which—at microscopic scale—are large and smooth. Synthetic microfibers are more than 100 times thinner than a human hair. When woven into a cloth, these fibers have immense cleaning power. They pick up dirt very effectively without the need for detergent or other nasty cleaning agents, and they don't leave behind traces of lint. They're perfect for cleaning delicate electronics and screens, as well as for hundreds of other jobs around the home.

Aluminum foil

Foil is just about the most versatile tool in your kitchen. Its surface is covered with a layer of oxide, which is an abrasive, so crumpled sheets of foil are perfect for scrubbing off corrosion and dirt. Foil reflects heat, conducts electricity, and can be molded into almost any shape so it can be used to bridge broken battery contacts or make your iron work more efficiently.

Pencil and eraser

You can do so much more than write with this double-ended tool. The eraser on the end of the pencil is perfect for cleaning hard-to-reach surfaces, and the graphite in the "lead" of the pencil is an effective oil-free lubricant. That's why it's used by locksmiths to ease lock mechanisms and keep keys turning freely.

Baking soda

The cleaning power of baking soda was well known by the ancient Egyptians, and it is still one of the best environmentally friendly cleaners you can use, especially when mixed with water into a lightly abrasive paste. Chemists call it a "buffer" which means that it neutralizes both acids and bases, so it will also absorb and get rid of nasty odors from your shoes, bins, fridge, and drains.

Hair spray

The holding agents and solvents in hair spray give it some remarkable properties. It is a liquid when it is propelled from the can but quickly sets into a film that gives a water-resistant toughness. Spray it on polished shoes to protect them, or on your kids' drawings to stop them smudging. Or use it as a quick-setting glue.

White vinegar

Distilled vinegar is a great cleaning agent and disinfectant that kills most molds and bacteria, due to its high acidity. It dissolves lime and other mineral deposits on glass and chrome, making it ideal for shining up bathroom fixtures and cleaning sinks, though it should be diluted with water before use. Try it on rust—it will often restore corroded metal surfaces. Vinegar is an inexpensive, natural nontoxic product that you can use safely around the home—and it is biodegradable too, so it won't damage the environment.

Candles

When you need to silence a squeaking door or free a reluctant drawer, there's no need to buy a special lubricant. Rubbing candle wax on the stuck part will do the trick. Wax is ideal for filling chips and gouges in wooden furniture too.

Hair dryer

When you need a source of heat that you can aim and control, reach for your hair dryer. A blast of warm air will help lift spilled candle wax or sticky labels off furniture, fix a dented table-tennis ball, or reshape the plastic arms of your eyeglasses for a better fit.

Plastic bags

Don't send your old plastic bags to landfill when they have so many uses around the home and garden. They make handy disposable gloves when working on a kitchen or bathroom spill or spreading wax over furniture, and they double as waterproof socks if your rain boots leak. If you've amassed a lot of bags, try using them as packing material to pad and protect delicate items that you're sending by mail.

Fruit

The citric acid in a lemon makes it a natural cleaner. The same acid means that lemons are great at dissolving the lime that builds up on faucets and bathroom fixtures. As a bonus, you get a naturally fresh lemony smell when you're done cleaning. Bananas contain oils and waxes that make them infamously slippery, but also excellent for filling scratches in smartphone screens, CDs, and DVDs.

Length of hose

Hose is tough and waterproof and so makes an effective temporary splint for a cracked pipe. Splitting a piece of hose lengthwise opens up lots more uses— try wrapping split hose around the metal handle of a bucket to make it more comfortable to carry, or protect the blades on your garden tools and saws by pressing a split hose over their sharp edges.

Tape

Duct tape was famously used to save the lives of the astronauts on board the ill-fated Apollo 13 lunar module, and no home—or spacecraft—should be without it. This tough, cloth-backed tape has hundreds of uses, from making temporary splints and sealing cracks and holes to catching flies on its sticky surface.

Steel wool

This handy abrasive comes in grades ranging from superfine (which is labeled #0000) to coarse (labeled #4). It can be shaped into almost any form, so it is great for getting into tight crevices. Use it to clean electrical contacts, polish up stainless steel, or even as a makeshift filter to stop debris from washing down a drain.

Toothbrush

Don't chuck that old toothbrush—it's a valuable addition to your magic tool kit. Use it to remove dust and grime from those hard-to-reach places, such as the cooling fans inside your computer or the corners of your oven or grill. Team it with white toothpaste to polish up your headlights or jewelry.

Modeling clay

Children love oil-based modeling clay, but its special properties make it a great help around the home too. It is waterproof and workable, so you can use it to temporarily stop leaks, and it stays flexible over time, meaning that you can use it as a shock absorber—for example to silence a rattly window or buzzing loudspeakers. And you can use it to firmly hold any fiddly objects (such as jewelry) while you fix them.

1

Digital
Living

KEEPING IN TOUCH

ENTERTAINMENT ON THE GO

HOME ENTERTAINMENT

COMPUTERS

KEEPING IN TOUCH

Most of us still make use of a home landline, where the telephone is connected to the network through wires. These phones may have a wired handset or a cordless handset, which links to a wired base station through radio signals. Mobile, or cellular, phones work in a different way, sending and receiving signals directly to and from nearby cell towers connected to the network. Many problems that arise with communications devices are simple to diagnose and solve, but some will require professional knowledge or help from your service provider.

WIRED PHONES

Home phones that use traditional lines are generally reliable and provide high-quality voice calls and—crucially—a link to broadband Internet services. Faults with these phones can often be traced to incorrect setup and can be fixed quickly and without much expense.

The phone line is dead

Isolate the problem

If you pick up the receiver and there's no dial tone, the problem may lie with your equipment or your phone company's network. First, unplug every device connected to a phone socket (including computers, fax and answering machines, and broadband routers) from its wall jack.

● Buy or borrow a hardwired—not cordless—phone that you know works. Plug it into your master phone socket—this is usually located at the point where the phone line enters your home. If this phone works, the problem lies with your phone or extension wiring; if it doesn't, contact your phone company to report a fault. Wait an hour or so before calling them—many network glitches last only a short while. Check your phone's symptoms—you may be able to make calls, or the phone may ring when receiving a call; you'll need to describe the nature of the fault when you call the phone company.

● If you have extensions in your home, a problem in one phone may cause all the others to appear dead. Plug all phones back into their extension sockets and make sure they are on the hook. Next, disconnect one phone at a time from its socket and test if the others in your home work. If unplugging one phone makes the others come back to life, then your problem lies with that phone.

WARNING

If you use a cordless phone as your primary phone, always have a "wired" or mobile phone on hand. Cordless designs won't work when there's a power outage, because the associated base station is powered by the grid. This could leave you out of contact in an emergency.

Check the connections and charge

Once you have narrowed down the fault to one of your phones, try a few simple checks.

● Unplug the cable that joins your phone to the wall jack. Do this at both ends of the cable so that it is completely free. Depending on the type of connector on the cable, you may need to press down on a small plastic tab with your fingernail to release the plug or you may need to use a small flat-head screwdriver. Replace the cable with an extension that you have checked and know is working. Make sure the plugs are firmly inserted in the phone and socket, and check the phone again. If the phone works, buy a replacement cable from your local electronics or phone shop.

● If you use a cordless phone, check that its batteries are fully charged or try a new set of batteries. Next, try making a phone call closer to the cordless phone's base station—you may be out of range. The maximum range specified in the manual may be reduced by metal framework in walls or sources of potential interference (such as microwave ovens, fridges, and Wi-Fi networks). If your Wi-Fi router allows, change the band on which it operates (see page 85).

● Cordless phones sometimes contain circuits that switch off the phone if there's a buildup of static electricity. Reset the phone by removing then reinserting its batteries.

● Clean the metal plates through which the cordless handset receives power from the base station. Wiping them with a cotton swab dipped in isopropyl alcohol (also known as rubbing alcohol), or even the end of a pencil eraser, will do the job.

My phone won't ring
Is your line overloaded?

First, check that the phone is connected to the wall socket and line power (if it is a cordless model).

● Check and adjust the ringer volume setting. On wired phones, this is usually a slider switch on the base of the phone; see if it has been inadvertently moved to a minimum setting. On most cordless phones, you can change the volume on the ringer and handset through the menu on the handset itself.

● How many telephones do you have on your home network? Depending on where you live, a home phone connection will support only three or four ringing devices (phones and fax machines)—any more on your line and the phones will not ring. Try unplugging any additional devices and test your line again.

A quick wipe of a cordless phone's contacts with rubbing alcohol is often enough to get it charging again.

No one can hear me on the phone
Check and untangle your handset cord

Some phones have a "mute" (or "secrecy") function accessed through a button on the handset or base unit. Ensure that this isn't active.

● If you are using a wired phone, unplug the cable connecting the handset to the telephone base unit; there's usually a transparent plug at either end and you'll need to depress the small plastic lug to free the plug. Clean the metal contacts on the plug and socket with a swab soaked in isopropyl alcohol.

● Try untwisting the handset cable. In use, this wire may become coiled up like a spring, pulling on the socket, and so temporarily breaking the connection. Simply unplug the cable at the base unit and hold the plug, with the handset dangling beneath. Allow the cord to spin and untwist itself. If this doesn't work, replace the cable or the phone.

● Are you using a cordless phone? Check that you are within range of the base unit when making calls.

The line crackles and hisses
Cut the noise

To help diagnose the cause of a crackly line, first unplug all your phones and plug a wired phone that you know works into your master phone socket. If your line still crackles, contact your phone company for help. If not, plug in all your extensions, then unplug each phone (or answering machine or fax) one at a time, and test the quality of the line on the master phone. If the static disappears when a certain phone is unplugged, then that phone is the probable culprit. Check and clean its connections to the phone socket and between the base and receiver (see above) or remove the phone.

● Check that any phone cables are at least 3 feet away from power cords, speaker wires, transformers, and other electronic devices.

● If you're using a cordless phone, try switching its operating channel. This easy procedure retunes the phone to a slightly different frequency and may cure a noisy line. Consult your owner's manual for instructions.

● Does your telephone line also carry your broadband Internet service? If so, you'll need to fit a small box called a DSL filter between every phone (as well as fax or answering machine) and the telephone socket (you don't need to fit them to extension sockets that are not being used). A microfilter is usually supplied by your Internet provider, but additional units can be bought cheaply from any electronics or phone store.

JARGON BUSTER

DSL (digital subscriber line) filter or microfilter
Broadband Internet uses the same phone line as ordinary voice calls. The job of the DSL filter is to split the frequency being sent through your phone line into two separate signals, a low-frequency analog voice signal and a high-frequency digital broadband signal.

I'm barraged by nuisance calls
Take steps to reduce the annoyance

Unwanted sales calls can ruin your evening or even become intimidating, but there's no need to tolerate them.

• Register your phone number on the FCC's national Do-Not-Call List. Telemarketing companies are then prohibited from calling you.

• Contact your network provider—they may offer services that bar specific numbers, such as international calls (the location of many telemarketing centers) or display the caller's number on your handset so that you can choose which calls to answer.

• Only give your phone number to those who need it; think twice before publishing it on websites, social networks, or bulletin boards, because your number could be "harvested" and passed on to unscrupulous businesses!

• If you are caught by a telemarketer, never press your keypad if requested—it could put you through to a premium rate line. Be polite, but insist on being removed from their call list before ending the call.

CHUCK IT?

Cordless phone handsets communicate with their base stations using either analog or digital signals. If you have a crackly old analog handset (these usually have long extending antennae), consider replacing the phone with a newer digital model, which offers better call quality. These phones are usually designated DECT 6.0 (Digital Enhanced Cordless Telecommunications).

Make it last
WIRED PHONES

Check your wiring to ensure that phone cables are well secured to walls and baseboards and that they cannot get trapped in door jambs.

Clean your phone once a month with a cloth moistened with mild disinfectant.

Replace the batteries in your wired phone once a year (right)—if they die, you'll lose any numbers stored in the phone's memory.

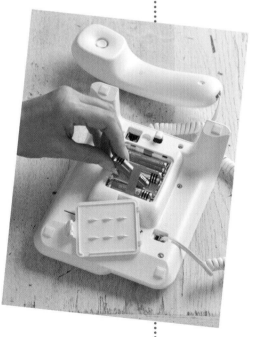

CELL PHONES

Cell phones range from basic models, capable only of voice and text communication, to smartphones. These are pocket computers that can run a variety of programs—or apps—via sophisticated operating systems, such as Google's Android and Apple's iOS. There's a lot you can do to optimize your use of this advanced technology, thus solving common problems yourself before you contact a professional for help.

JARGON BUSTER

SIM card
A Subscriber Identity Module, or SIM card, stores data, such as your user identity, phone number, and contact lists. It can be removed from your phone and used in another on the same network, making your important data easy to transfer when you buy a new phone.

My phone is showing no signs of life
Clean the contacts and reset

If the phone has been idle for a few weeks, charge it for at least 4 hours. If recharging doesn't work, try the following:
● Remove the battery (if possible) and SIM (see left) according to the manufacturer's instructions. Clean the metal contacts of both using a cotton swab dipped in isopropyl alcohol; wait for 30 minutes before replacing both and restarting the phone.

- If your handset is still dead, try a spare battery borrowed from a friend with the same phone. If the phone comes to life, buy a replacement—batteries for even the oldest models can still be bought on eBay or elsewhere online.
- Try a soft reset—your manual or manufacturer's website will tell you how to do this. A soft reset is equivalent to shutting down and restarting a computer—it will close any programs (apps) that you are running but won't delete any of your stored data.
- If that doesn't work, try a hard reset. This will restore the phone to its factory defaults, meaning that your stored contacts, settings, and data may be lost. Always back up your data (if possible) before performing a hard reset.
- Try updating (also called "flashing") the phone's "firmware" (see right), which may have become corrupted. To do this, you'll need to link your phone to a computer using the supplied cable, connect to the manufacturer's website, and then download the latest compatible firmware.
- Has the phone been in water? If so, try the fix on page 28, then seek professional attention.

JARGON BUSTER

Firmware The computer code that controls how a phone works is called firmware. It is different from software in that it is very closely tied to the hardware components of the device. Firmware is stored in a dedicated part of the phone's memory, away from data such as pictures and music.

My batteries keep dying
Change your charging and usage habits

The vast majority of cell phones are powered by lithium-ion batteries, which deteriorate from the day they are made. A typical lifetime is 500 to 800 charging cycles or around four years, whether they are used or not. You can extend the long-term life by following a few simple rules.
- Recharge the phone when its screen "bar graph" registers between 10 and 15 percent of capacity remaining. You may be able to achieve a longer-lasting charge by carrying it out in a cool environment.
- Never leave the phone fully discharged for a long time. If your phone is a spare or used just for emergencies (for example, if you keep an old phone in the glove box of your car), fully charge the phone and then remove the battery.
- Avoid leaving the phone charging overnight; depending on the quality of the charger, the battery may overheat. This will shorten its useful life.
- Replace your battery after three years. Some phones have accessible battery compartments for ease of replacement, but many smartphones have built-in power packs. You can buy kits from independent phone shops containing all the tools and instructions to carry out battery changes on sealed phones, but it can be difficult and it is usually better to have the work done by a professional.

A toothpick is the perfect tool to remove dust and lint from a cell phone's charger port.

My phone doesn't charge
Clear out its USB port with a toothpick

A phone that lives in your pocket or handbag will inevitably attract dust and lint. If this makes its way into the charger port (usually a micro-USB port), it may make your phone charge intermittently or not at all when plugged in.

● Gently use a toothpick to fish out any lint that has accumulated in the port. If you find you need a finer point, sharpen the toothpick by running one end along a sheet of sandpaper.

My phone's speakers don't work
Use a cotton swab to clean the jack

If a piece of grit works its way into your headphone socket, it may fool your phone into thinking that headphones are connected even when they are not. This will automatically mute your phone's speakers. To remedy the problem, try pushing a cotton swab into the headphone socket and twirling it around to dislodge and remove any trapped particles.

The headphone jack has snapped off
Pull it out with a hot needle

The plug that connects your headphones to your cell phone is fragile. It is prone to snapping off if you drop your phone while it is connected, leaving a stub inside the socket that effectively disables your phone's sound output. First, switch off the phone and remove its battery (if possible) and try prying out the broken jack stub using a pair of fine tweezers or a needle.

● There is another solution that relies on the fact that most headphone jacks have a plastic core within its banded metal contacts. First, pick up a needle at its blunt end with a pair of long-nose pliers. Carefully heat the pointed end of the needle in a flame; when it glows red, push the needle into the exposed plastic core of the broken jack. Hold it in place while it cools and sets in the melted plastic. Using the pliers, gently pull the needle and hopefully the stub will come out with it. Take extreme care when using a hot needle.

There's a scratch on my smartphone screen
Fill and polish the screen

Smartphone screens are usually made of glass topped with a special coating that helps your fingers glide across the screen. Even a small scratch on the phone's screen can be annoying—sometimes it creates a rainbow effect on everything that you view. If your screen is affected, try fixing it with a banana. First, check the depth of the scratch: if you can't run a fingernail across it without it catching, you'll need to learn to live with the scratch or replace the screen.

● Try filling shallower scratches with a banana. Lay your phone on a clean, firm surface, screen upward, and gently wipe off any dust with a clean cloth. Peel a banana and break off the tip. Place the banana tip to one side of the scratch and drag it slowly and firmly over the scratch, applying gentle pressure as you go. Wipe across the scratch in the same way with a microfiber cloth; repeat the process until the scratch has faded.

● Polish the scratch away using an abrasive, such as a non-gel toothpaste or metal polish applied with a cloth, and buff it with a microfiber cloth. Use masking tape to cover the other parts of the screen and phone. Note that polishing is likely to remove the screen's coating, leaving it looking dull. To prevent future scratches, attach a screen protector as soon as possible.

The natural oils in a banana can fill small scratches in a glass screen. This unusual fix also works for scratched DVDs and CDs.

My phone has cracked
Keep the casing comfortable and dustproof

If your cell phone's plastic body cracks in a fall, check that you can still make and receive calls.

● If the phone still functions, simply buy a close-fitting silicone case designed for your make and model—it'll do a good enough job keeping water, dust, and dirt away from the insides of the phone. You can smooth out any deep scratches on the plastic body with fine sandpaper. The phone will no longer look its best, but it will work until you are able to replace it.

Replace the screen

There's no fixing a cracked screen. The cracks are also likely to spread with use, and you may end up with a pocket full of glass splinters. Screen-replacement kits for most phones can be bought online, but if you don't feel confident about carrying out the work yourself, send the phone for professional repair—it may be cheaper than you think, or at least less expensive than a new smartphone.

Help! I dropped my phone in water
Dry it out in a jar of rice

If you drop your phone in water, it's not necessarily a disaster. But time is of the essence, so act fast. If the water was clean, or you've left your phone in the wash:

● Switch off the phone and remove the SIM, memory card, and battery pack (if possible); dry them with a lint-free cloth and put them in a warm room.

● Dry the phone as much as possible with a lint-free cloth, then place it in a jar of uncooked rice, burying it under the rice. Seal the jar and leave it for 24 hours—rice is a desiccant and will draw water out of the phone. Replace the SIM card, battery, and memory card and try restarting the phone. If you're lucky, it'll jump back to life.

● If you dropped the phone in dirty or salty water, remove the SIM, memory card, and battery pack. Fill a sink with clean water, submerge the phone and move it to and fro gently to rinse out the dirty water. Then follow the steps above.

TRY USING THE DRYING PROPERTIES OF RICE TO SALVAGE YOUR WET PHONE

My phone's keys stick
A quick cleanup will get you texting again

Dirt and grime can work their way into the gaps between your phone's keys and its body, making the keys slow or "sticky."
● Switch off your phone, then dip a microfiber cloth into isopropyl alcohol and press it down onto the sticky key. Rub the key in small circular motions while keeping it firmly depressed. Don't use cotton wool to clean the phone—its fibers may themselves get trapped down the sides of the keys.

I've got no more space on my smartphone
Purge unwanted files

However much memory originally comes with your smartphone, it is likely that you will soon fill it up with photos, apps, music, films, ebooks, and video clips. As the memory approaches capacity, its performance drops, slowing everything down, so it's worth spring cleaning your phone from time to time.
● The easiest way to manage all the files on your smartphone is to connect it to your computer via the supplied cable and use the manufacturer's software to move files on and off your phone.
● Review your apps and uninstall any that you haven't used in the last few months—some apps may take up 1GB or more of memory.
● The biggest files kept on most smartphones are photos and videos. Back them up to cloud storage, such as iCloud or Google Drive (see box, right), then delete them from your phone to free up lots of memory. When you want them again, you can simply view them online or download them onto your phone again.
● If you subscribe to online newspapers or podcasts, old issues can quickly clog up your phone's memory: use your phone's software to delete unwanted issues.
● Be ruthless with emails—delete old messages that you're never likely to need again.
● The memory in many phones can be easily expanded by fitting an inexpensive micro-SD card into a slot on the phone. Some smartphones—notably iPhones—are not expandable in this way because their memory is built-in.

JARGON BUSTER

Cloud storage
Instead of copying data to a physical storage device, like a hard disk or CD-ROM, you can back it up to a "cloud," which is actually a series of huge data storage centers around the world that you access seamlessly via the Internet.

Ten ways to boost your phone's battery life

Smartphones are power-hungry devices, often using up a full charge in less than a day. There's no need to get stranded with a dead phone—follow these tips to make your battery go further.

SMARTPHONES ARE ALL-PURPOSE MACHINES; SWITCHING OFF FUNCTIONS YOU DON'T NEED WILL SAVE BATTERY POWER AND MAKE YOUR PHONE FASTER

1 Go to your phone's "Settings" menu and switch off the Bluetooth, Wi-Fi, and GPS functions if you don't use them regularly.

2 Reduce the brightness of the phone's screen to the lowest usable level, or set the brightness to adjust automatically to ambient light.

3 Set a dark background, rather than a photo, as your wallpaper.

4 Switch off your phone's vibrate alert and turn down the volume of its ringer.

5 Keep your phone cool—don't leave it in direct sunlight or inside a hot car.

6 Quit any apps that you are not using—keeping them running in the background uses up battery life.

7 Many phones come supplied with a power-management app that optimizes battery use—turn it on and configure it to your needs.

8 Switch your phone off or set it to "airplane mode" if you're in an area where there is no signal. Otherwise, the phone will keep trying to connect to a network, using power.

9 Use Wi-Fi instead of 3G, 4G, or 5G. Wi-Fi uses 40% less power when surfing the web. By using Wi-Fi instead of your cellular data you'll save battery power and if you have limited data per month, you'll help manage that data.

10 Buy an external battery. These are available for many phones in the form of a case that adds hours of battery life, though at the cost of some extra bulk and weight.

How do I recycle my old cell phone?
Be environmentally aware

Every year millions of cell phones are discarded, potentially releasing toxic materials into the environment.

● In most cases, recycling a cell phone means donating it to a worthy cause. Next time you upgrade, free up some storage space and bring that drawer full of older models to your local wireless retailer (AT&T, Verizon, T-Mobile, LG, Sony, Best Buy) or big box office supply store (Staples, Home Depot).

● Many charities and local government offices also accept cell phone donations.

● You can also consult these websites for more information on recycling mobile devices: Earth911.com and call2recycle.org.

The photos I take with my phone are blurry
Most phones give you a choice

Most phones include a camera capable of recording still and video images. Camera phones are constantly improving, but most lack the controls of a conventional camera that enable you to get crisp images in a variety of conditions.

● Clean your lens with a lint-free cloth before you take a shot. Phones live in pockets or bags, where the lens will soon get dirty and covered with fingerprints, resulting in hazy images.

● Camera phones tend to have small sensor, which means that images taken in low light tend to look grainy; move your subject to a well-lit area or switch on room lights. Use the camera's flash as a last resort— its light is rarely flattering—and remember that it will not reach a subject more than a couple of yards away.

● Keep your phone steady by wedging it against a door or wall— camera phones may set long shutter speeds that will otherwise make your images look shaky.

● There's often a short delay between pressing the shutter and the phone taking the picture. Don't move the phone for a second or so after you've pressed the shutter or it may be in motion when the picture is recorded, resulting in blur.

● Set your camera to maximum resolution and avoid using its digital zoom function (if you have this option). Carry out any image editing or cropping on your computer later.

Phones usually have wide-angle lenses, so at a distance of 5 yards, a person will look very small in the frame. Get closer to your subject for more interesting and dynamic shots.

My smartphone bill is sky high
Keep an eye on your data use

Smartphones give you access to a wealth of information and media, but many plans put a cap on the amount of data that you can use each month. A typical phone contract includes an allowance of between 250MB and 20GB per month; the more data that's included, the higher the monthly cost. If you exceed your data limit, you'll pay a high price. Your data use can mount up surprisingly quickly: watching a film through your network, chatting on Skype for an hour, or listening to an hour of streaming music can use 200MB or more of data.

- If possible, wait until you can connect to free Wi-Fi before using your phone's data features.
- When you are on the road, use your car's GPS, not your phone, to find your way. The phone has to download map data as you move, but maps are preloaded in a GPS, making this free to use.
- Be careful of how many "free" games you play on the move. Many of these are funded by advertisements that pop up on your screen during play. Every advertisement has to download through your network, using up your data allowance.
- If you regularly use more data than your plan allows, go with an unlimited plan. Look for discounts that my be available, many companies offer ones to military families and folks 55 and older.
- When you go abroad, your phone will switch over to use a local network provider. Calls and—especially—data can be charged at extremely high rates. Call your home network provider before you leave to check if they can put you on a lower tariff in your destination country, and establish exactly what the charges will be. Alternatively, you can disable data roaming on your handset (you'll be able to select this option in the phone's "Settings" menu). You'll then need to use free Wi-Fi hotspots (provided in public areas, such as cafes, restaurants, and libraries) to access data.

Using your phone on vacation can be very costly. If your phone is unlocked, you can buy a local SIM card and fit this into your phone while you're away. Alternatively, buy a cheap pay-as-you-go phone locally—it may be worth the expense if you plan to make lots of calls.

Make it last CELL PHONES

Equip your phone with a high-quality screen protector and a robust case (below) to protect it against physical damage. Don't keep the phone in the same pocket or bag as loose keys or coins.

Update your phone software with the latest downloads—you'll usually be prompted to do so. The latest software will contain fixes for bugs and known security issues. Do this when you are connected to a free, secure Wi-Fi network.

Regularly back up the data on your phone to a "cloud" (see page 29) or to your computer.

How do I keep my phone secure?

Set a password and be wary of downloads

Your smartphone holds a great deal of personal information, such as lists of your contacts and emails, so it makes sense to protect it from prying eyes.

● Almost all phones have some form of password protection. Once set up, this requires you to enter a PIN before you can use the phone. You should activate this feature through the phone's "Settings" menu—it is a simple and effective first line of defense.

● Be careful what you download. There are hundreds of thousands of apps available for smartphones, some made by reputable publishers, some not. Download apps only from trusted sources, and be sure to read user reviews before installing them.

● Don't click on suspicious links sent to you by email, text, or on websites, and consider installing antivirus software on your phone. This can be downloaded in the same way as other apps—just search your app store for "mobile security" or similar key words.

● Don't carry out transactions using any of your passwords, PIN codes, or credit card numbers on a public Wi-Fi network—it's too easy for criminals to eavesdrop and steal your details. Wait until you can connect to a secure Wi-Fi network at home or elsewhere.

● Check your cell phone bill carefully. Look out for calls to premium-rate numbers and for unusually high amounts of data downloaded. Contact your network provider immediately if you spot anything suspicious.

ENTERTAINMENT ON THE GO

Portable media players, such as tablets, MP3 players, and e-readers, are one of the fastest growing and most rapidly changing areas of consumer technology. These devices rely on sophisticated electronics housed within sleek cases that are not designed to be opened easily, but there are still many things you can do to put things right when they go wrong.

TABLETS AND MEDIA PLAYERS

Tablet computers are affected by many of the same problems as smartphones—such as cracked screens, slow running, and short battery life. If your device has frozen or only works at a snail's pace, start by carrying out a reset according to the manufacturer's instructions—this will often solve the problem.

My MP3 player won't turn on
Try a sharp tap to free the hard disk

If you have an MP3 player that uses a hard disk rather than flash memory to store music and video files, you can sometimes bring it back to life with a sharp tap from a magazine. Before trying any of the following, charge the player for 3 to 4 hours.

● To find out if your MP3 player has a hard disk, search its make and model on the Internet. If you're still not sure, place it close up to your ear. If you can hear a whirring or clicking sound, it almost certainly contains a hard disk.

● Place the player face down on a towel on a flat surface, and give it a few sharp taps with a rolled-up magazine or newspaper; this is sometimes enough to temporarily free a stuck hard disk.

● Try resetting the player: this usually involves toggling a switch or pressing and holding a combination of buttons. If this doesn't work, you may need to reformat the hard disk of your MP3 player by connecting it to your computer. How you carry out resets and formats depends on the exact make and model—consult your user's manual or seek advice online. Be warned that reformatting will erase the disk, so you'll need to reload your songs, videos, and images afterward.

My tablet seems to lag
Cut down on widgets and live wallpaper

Does your tablet seem slow when starting up apps, or is there a delay between typing and characters appearing on your screen? You can reduce this lag by following a few simple tips.

● If your tablet runs the Android operating system, start by disabling any live wallpaper you have running; these animated, interactive backgrounds on your home screen may be fun, but they can introduce lag and will also reduce battery life. To do this, open your "Settings" menu and navigate to "Applications Manager." Tap on the icon of the live wallpaper you have running, then press "Uninstall." While in this area of the menu, uninstall any apps that you don't plan to use. Close apps that you're not currently using—simply select the app and press "Stop" to shut it down.

● Android tablets and phones may be installed with widgets—icons that appear on your home screen that act as shortcuts to an app, or display information directly (for example, a widget may show you weather conditions at your location). If a widget isn't useful, remove it by pressing and holding on its icon, then dragging it to the top (or sometimes bottom, depending on the model) of the screen until it turns red. It will disappear when you lift your finger.

The touch screen is unresponsive
Software or hardware could be to blame

Start by cleaning your screen. This has a special coating that repels oil from human skin and so needs careful treatment, so avoid using any solvents or domestic glass cleaners on its surface—any moisture may cause damage.

● Switch off the tablet and unplug it from the charger. Use a blower brush (sold in camera stores) to remove any grit or lint on the screen or lodged between the screen and the case. Then rub the screen gently in a circular motion with a microfiber cloth, such as that used for cleaning eyeglasses.

● Try resetting the tablet. If this doesn't work, you may need to restore it to its factory default state. This usually involves pressing a certain combination of keys and connecting the device to your computer. Consult the manufacturer's website or your user's manual for instructions for your make and model of tablet.

Use a microfiber cloth—never a paper towel or tissue—to clean the screen of your tablet.

The sound I get from my MP3 player is poor
Try changing file format

If you're unhappy with the quality of sound delivered by your tablet, MP3 player, or phone, there are a few steps you can take.

● Most audio players have a built-in equalizer, which allows you to balance the audio frequencies that occur in music—enhancing or reducing bass and treble and tones in between. Most players also have a number of presets suited to different genres of music. The equalizer is usually found in the "Settings" menu—it's worth spending a little time experimenting with it.

Use a USB cable to connect your MP3 player to your computer; software such as iTunes (Mac) or Device Stage (Windows) allows you to sync your music between the two. Many alternative software packages are available.

● Invest in better quality headphones—those supplied with media players are usually not the highest quality. A good retailer will let you try before you buy.

● If you have a high-end stereo system, you may find that music fed into it from your MP3 player sounds dull compared to when it is played directly from a CD. The process of copying music from a CD to your computer, and then onto your MP3 player, is called "ripping." Changing some settings in your ripping software (iTunes or Windows Media Player, for example) will let you create cleaner files, close in quality to the originals on the CD.

● If you use iTunes, navigate to **Preferences ▶ General ▶ Import settings**, then select the "Apple Lossless Encoder." If using Windows, click on the arrow on the "Import CD" tab that appears when you insert a CD into your computer. Select the "Import Using" option from the menu and choose the "Apple Lossless Encoder" option. Bear in mind that the music files made from ripping your CD will be higher quality, but up to ten times larger than those made using the default setting, so you'll be able to fit far fewer onto your audio player.

WARNING !

When you charge any portable electronic device, make sure to remove it from its case to minimize the danger of overheating.

My iPad won't connect to my computer
Check your software and USB

Connecting your iPad, iPhone, or iPod to your Mac or PC should be simple. But what if the device doesn't show up when it is plugged into the computer?

● Try charging the device for at least 3 hours and then reconnect it to the computer.

● Use a different USB port on the computer and another compatible cable if you have a spare or can borrow one.

My headphones are tangled

Flag them with tape

To listen to music or films as intended, you need to put the correct earphone into the correct ear. This can be difficult if you're using earbud-style headphones, where the only indication of the correct orientation is a tiny "L" and "R" printed onto the body of the earphones. Just wrap a single turn of colored electrical tape around the cable of the right ear as a reminder.

Stop the tangles

Thin headphone cables tend to get badly knotted when stored in a pocket or bag. Keep them tangle-free after use by winding the cable loosely around one hand. Use the clip (supplied to secure the cable to a lapel) or a small binder clip to pinch the bunched wires together. Next time you use the headphones, remove the clip and you'll be able to unwind the cables easily.

My e-reader has frozen

Try a reset

If you can't get your e-reader to respond, first make sure the battery is fully charged. Switch it off fully (not into sleep mode) and restart.
● To reset a Sony e-reader, use the tip of the stylus or an unfolded paper clip to press the recessed "Reset" button on the back and then slide the power switch. To reset a Kindle, hold the power switch for 15 seconds before releasing it, then restart.
● Kindles are automatically updated by Amazon every month or so. While this is underway, the device is unresponsive. Wait for a while, and then restart.

I can't read my old books on my new e-reader

Convert your files

The digital books market is changing fast, and books are sold in a variety of file formats. Amazon sells books for its Kindle reader in proprietary formats, while most other suppliers use the EPUB format.
● To read EPUB files on a Kindle, or Amazon's proprietary files on devices other than a Kindle, you'll need to convert the files first on your computer. There are numerous free programs that can carry out this conversion; the best known is Calibre, but you should search the Internet for the most current options.

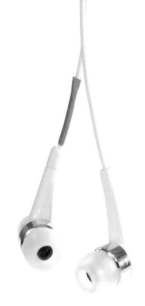

Wrap colored tape around one of the headphone cables to distinguish left from right at a glance.

TOOLS OF THE TRADE

Kindle for tired eyes

If reading long articles from the Internet on your computer screen strains your eyes, you can send them to your Kindle with a single click. You'll need to be using either the Chrome, Safari, Opera, or Firefox browser; navigate the browser's website and download the "Send to Kindle" extension. Follow the instructions to activate and use the extension.

HOME ENTERTAINMENT

Digital technology is increasingly blurring the boundaries between familiar devices, such as TVs and radios, hi-fi, and recording equipment. But many basic components—screens and speakers, connectors and cables—remain central to any home setup and can be kept in top condition without the need for professional help.

TV AND HOME VIEWING

Optimizing your TV set's picture and sound, and configuring it to work seamlessly with other equipment, such as a DVD player, home theater system, and satellite receiver, can be taxing. A few simple tips will help you achieve the best viewing experience.

My TV won't turn on
Check the power and the inputs

If the TV's power indicator is not illuminated, make sure the set is connected to a working power outlet (test it with a table lamp or other small appliance).

• Try selecting a channel or switching on the TV using the controls within the set rather than those on your remote. If this works, you probably need to change the batteries in your remote control.

• If the TV appears to have power but there's no picture or sound, it's possible that someone has set the TV to receive its input from an attached DVD player or another source. Select the correct source using your remote control: the button you need may be labeled TV/VIDEO or INPUT, though this varies from model to model. If your remote control doesn't work, you can sometimes access the TV's on-screen menu by simultaneously pressing the "Volume up" and "Volume down" buttons on the set itself. Then use the P+ and P- buttons on the set to navigate through the menu until you reach the input control. Select the correct input and press both volume buttons together repeatedly until you exit the menu system.

• The cables that connect your TV to your DVD or satellite box can come loose—check that all the plugs are firmly connected.

The TV strains my eyes
Set up a light behind the TV

Eye strain or headache is sometimes the result of watching TV in a darkened room. This is because your TV's two-dimensional image appears to "float" in the darkness, and your eyes and brain work harder trying to deal with this odd perception.

• You can reduce the problem by adding just a little ambient lighting to the room. Place a lamp near your TV screen, or even behind it. Fit the lamp with a daylight-balanced bulb (available from electrical stores). Choose a low-wattage bulb, so that the intensity of its light around the screen is a little lower than that of the screen itself.

The image on my TV looks squashed
Correct the aspect ratio

Do actors appear too fat or thin on-screen, or is part of your picture or text obviously missing? If so, you have probably selected the wrong aspect ratio for the input. You can change the setting easily, usually through a button on the remote control labeled "Aspect" or "Ratio."

The picture on my TV is garish
Change the default settings

TVs in a showroom compete against one another for your attention, and for this reason, many manufacturers produce them with default settings in which the image is bright and colorful. When you buy a TV and take it home, it's easy to adjust its settings for a truer picture.

● Set up the lighting in your room for optimum viewing (see page 39).

● Using your TV's remote control, navigate to the on-screen menu and select "Picture Settings." On modern sets you'll usually find a number of preset options, such as "Vivid," "Standard" and "Movie." "Movie" mode usually reduces color saturation and brightness and is ideal for watching DVDs or Blu-ray disks; "Standard" mode is a reasonable compromise for watching normal broadcast TV; while "Vivid" mode boosts colors, and may be a good choice if you use the TV primarily for playing games.

● Tweak the defaults or create your own unique picture quality by changing the "Brightness," "Color," "Contrast," and "Sharpness" settings. Set the brightness so that pure black tones on-screen appear black, but you can still discern detail in shadowy areas. Reduce the sharpness so that halos do not appear around objects on screen, and try turning down the contrast, which is typically set far too high by default. Color is more subjective, but try to set the TV so that skin tones and foliage appear realistic—if these colors differ widely from nature, the image will look "wrong."

● Make any changes gradually and let your eyes get accustomed to the new settings before further tweaking.

● A more objective way to adjust the picture quality is to use a tool such as THX Optimizer on your DVD player (see box, left).

The TV's picture and sound break up
Carry out a reboot and check the antenna

Your TV may be connected directly to the aerial, but it is more likely that the antenna first enters a satellite box, a free-to-air box, or a cable box, which in turn links to the TV and other components, such as a DVD player or home theater system. Any interruption in this daisy chain of boxes can cause the picture to stutter, break up, or disappear completely.

● Make sure all the cables between the components and to the antenna are fully connected.

● Do a little housekeeping—untangle the cables that carry electrical power to the components from those that carry signals between the components or from the antenna. This will help minimize any possible electrical interference. Make sure that cables run straight, with no kinks along their length.

● Check with your neighbors; if they also lack TV reception, it may be that your satellite or cable supplier is carrying out tests or work that is affecting your signal.

● Reboot your TV. Press the menu button on your remote control and navigate to the tuning section. Most sets will automatically tune in to the strongest signals for each channel.

● Check the antenna or satellite dish on the outside of your home for damage—birds may have nested on the antenna, it may have been knocked out of alignment, or its connecting cable may have been damaged. If so, call a professional.

The picture is fuzzy
Use the best connectors for optimal performance

If the image on your TV is consistently blurry, first check and adjust the picture settings (see opposite). If these measures don't work, you may need to look at the way your equipment is connected. Turn your TV around and you will see numerous sockets that allow you to connect to a DVD or Blu-ray player, satellite box, surround-sound system, and games console. Some of these ports support the most up-to-date digital standards, such as high-quality audio and high-definition TV, while others are "legacy" connectors that allow you to hook up older equipment, usually at the cost of picture and sound quality.

● Always choose the most modern connector possible (listed in descending order below and pictured, right) to link together two pieces of equipment.

● The latest flat-screen TVs will have HDMI connectors, which allow high-quality digital signals (including high-definition TV) to pass through a single cable; if it is available, use this option to connect your audiovisual components.

● If you don't have HDMI connectors, the next best standard for video quality is Component Video; here, the video signal is carried by three cables (colored red, blue, and green). A separate connection is needed for the audio signal.

● Older sets lack HDMI connectors, but may have an RCA connector that requires three cables—a yellow cable to carry the video signal, and red and white cables to carry stereo sound.

HDMI

Component Video

RCA

Identify the connectors fitted to your TV set and other equipment, and use the most recent standard available to maximize picture and sound quality.

Glasses for active 3-D TV systems contain a small battery that will need to be replaced when it runs down.

My 3-D TV images look ghosted
Master the settings and that extra dimension will be yours

At present, there are two main systems available for 3-D TV—one is termed "active," the other "passive." With active 3-D, the user needs to wear quite heavy glasses containing electronic "shutters" that let light pass into one eye at a time. In passive systems, users wear lighter polarized glasses. If your 3-D images look ghosted or unclear, there are a few steps you can take.

● In your TV menu, switch off the ambient light sensor (this makes the TV screen brighter if the room is well lit, and darker if light levels fall). Then, toggle through the TV's picture settings (see page 40) while wearing your glasses and select the mode that gives the best 3-D image. You'll probably need to set your TV to a brighter level than for 2-D, because the glasses absorb some light.

● If you have an active system, check that there is nothing blocking the infrared emitters that tell the glasses when to flip their shutters. These emitters often take the form of a "wand" that plugs into the TV, or they may be built into the TV itself.

● Make sure that the batteries in the glasses are fully charged. Some recharge via a port on the TV; others employ a button-type lithium battery, which you'll need to replace once in a while.

I find it hard to hear dialogue on the TV
Reposition the set and tweak the menu settings

If you rely on your TV's built-in speakers, you may find that their sound is muddy or faint—especially when it comes to reproducing dialogue in movies. That's because movie sound is often designed to be listened to on a surround-sound system and suffers in quality when forced through a TV's small stereo speakers.

● Using your TV's remote control, navigate to the on-screen menu and select "Sound Settings." Most modern sets will have a number of options suited to different types of sound (movies, sports and so on). Try these first, and choose one that suits your ear.

● You can then tweak the settings to refine the sound: reduce the bass level—excessive bass can cause cabinets to rattle and introduce unpleasant distortion at higher listening levels. If the sound lacks "sparkle," try increasing the treble.

● Some TVs have a "Virtual Surround" mode that attempts to emulate the sound of a multi-speaker home cinema system. Unfortunately, these modes often tend to muddy the sound, so try switching them off and listen for an improvement.

- Try positioning your TV in the corner of a room, rather than flat against a wall. This creates an effect similar to cupping your hands around your mouth when speaking, and may help to intensify the TV's sound.
- If you have a hi-fi system in the same room as the TV, try routing the TV's audio signals to the stereo for superior results. Many TVs (and set-top boxes) have audio output ports. Connect an RCA cable of appropriate length from this to one of the spare auxiliary inputs of your hi-fi system.
- Buying and installing a surround-sound system will give you the best audio experience when watching TV, but these systems are expensive and include multiple speakers, which make them unsuitable for small rooms. A cheaper and neater solution is a "soundbar"—a narrow array of speakers that fits neatly beneath a TV and gives you some of the benefits of a full home theater system.

The keys on my remote control are sluggish
A quick cleanup will get it working like new

Do you have to push harder on the buttons of your remote control to change channels? Over time, grease and gunk build up under the keypad. Fortunately, there's a simple fix.

Time needed **30 minutes**
You will need **screwdriver, blunt flat-bladed knife, cotton swab, isopropyl alcohol, detergent, damp cloth**

1 Remove the batteries from the remote and undo any screws holding the two halves of the unit together. Keep the screws in a bowl to stop them from rolling away. Insert the blade of the blunt knife into the joint between the upper and lower plastic casing and gently pry open the unit (see below, left).

2 Remove the rubber key panel and, using a cotton swab dipped in alcohol, clean the contacts beneath

each key (see below, center). Work gently so you do not damage the delicate contacts. Clean the upper surface of the key panel with a damp cloth and mild detergent.

3 Now clean the circuit board by gently wiping it with a damp cloth and mild detergent (see below, right). Wipe with a clean cloth and leave both halves to dry completely. Reassemble the remote by reversing the previous steps.

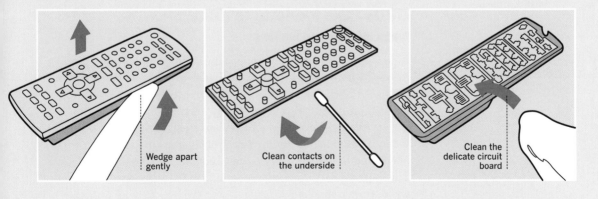

Wedge apart gently

Clean contacts on the underside

Clean the delicate circuit board

My remote control doesn't work
Check it with your phone

If pressing keys on your remote control doesn't have any effect on your TV, the problem could lie with the remote unit or the set. There's a simple way to check if your remote is working.

● Switch on your cell phone's camera and point the remote control toward the camera's lens. Press a button on the remote, and you should see a blue glow from the remote's emitter on the camera's screen. This is because digital cameras pick up the infrared radiation of remote handsets.

● If the remote doesn't work, first try changing its batteries and cleaning the battery contacts. You can do this by rubbing the contacts with a pencil eraser or some fine-grade sandpaper.

● If the remote does work, the fault may lie within the TV set. But before you call for a repair, turn off any room lights and try again. Some types of fluorescent bulbs can interfere with the signal from a remote. Try repositioning the light or consider replacing its bulb with one of another type (see page 133).

My TV screen is dirty
Wipe it with a microfiber cloth and vinegar

Today's LCD and plasma TVs have screens faced with plastic that is easily marked by abrasive cloths and chemicals, so try this low-tech cleaning method.

● First, switch off the TV, then wipe the screen with a microfiber cloth, which won't leave behind traces of lint. Don't press too hard. If marks remain on the screen, moisten the microfiber cloth with a fifty-fifty mixture of white vinegar and water and lightly rub any spots. Dry the screen immediately with a clean microfiber cloth to avoid smudge marks.

DVDs take too long to load
Clean the disk and the lens

A dirty disk is the most common cause of slow loading. Try cleaning the disk with a dry microfiber cloth; wipe gently from the inner hole out to the edge, not around its circumference. If this doesn't work, moisten the cloth with a little window-cleaning fluid and wipe as above. Allow the disk to dry before inserting it into the DVD player.

● Buy a cleaning disk from an electronics shop; insert it into the DVD player and follow the on-screen instructions to clean the player's lens. This is particularly important if your DVD player is used in a room where people smoke.

The DVD skips
Polish out any scratches

When your viewing is interrupted by a skipping DVD, first try cleaning the disk (see opposite). If this doesn't do the trick, check for scratches. Hold the disk up to a bright light—if the light passes through the scratch, it's probably too deep to fix, and if the scratch runs around the circumference of the disk you may be out of luck, too. However, if the scratch is radial, try the following fix.

● Cover the disk's playing surface with a thin layer of furniture polish; wipe it on gently with a microfiber cloth, working outward from the center. Using a clean microfiber cloth, buff the surface until it is dry—then try your disk again.

WORKING SOME FURNITURE POLISH INTO A SKIPPING DVD WILL HELP FILL ANY SMALL SCRATCHES AND GET THE DISK TO PLAY SMOOTHLY

My home theater system has no picture
Change the way you start up your equipment

Home theater systems integrate a high-definition TV, DVD or Blu-ray player, a satellite box, and a surround-sound system. If you have set up your system and used HDMI cables to connect between the components, it should work perfectly—but sometimes it just doesn't. That's because each component must recognize all the others before it makes a connection in a process called the "HDMI handshake." If the handshake fails for any reason, the components won't talk to one another and you'll have no picture or sound.

● Try changing the sequence in which you switch on the individual components of your home theater system. For example, try turning on the TV first, then the DVD player, then the surround-sound system. If this doesn't work, experiment a little and you'll probably find a sequence that works for you.

● Still no picture? You may need to update the firmware (the instructions embedded in the components' circuits). You can usually do this via your system's connection to the Internet. Consult your user manuals for detailed instructions.

Make it last TV AND HOME VIEWING

Keep your equipment cool by giving it enough space to breathe and by adding ventilation holes if it is kept in a cabinet. The hotter it runs, the shorter its operational life; plus there's an increased risk of fire. Turn down the bright and garish default settings on your TV—these will cause it to run hot.

Position your TV so that it is not exposed to extremes of temperature (such as above a radiator) and sources of dust and water. Keep it away from strong magnets (such as those in speakers).

Close the front flap of your TV once you have finished using the controls beneath. These covers are often flimsy and can snap off if bumped.

Disconnect the antenna and power supply from your TV or system if a thunderstorm is expected—a lightning strike can damage your equipment. Consider buying a surge protector; many of these units also contain circuits that cut electronic "noise" to give you a cleaner picture on your TV.

Buy the best quality blank DVDs if you record TV programs on a DVD recorder—they will have a much longer useful life than budget alternatives.

GAMES AND CONSOLES

As with all complex digital devices, serious faults in games consoles will require professional repair, but there's much you can do at home to address some basic problems.

The console keeps freezing
Check the disk and controllers, and keep it cool

A common cause of freezing during game play is a dirty or scratched disk. Try cleaning the disk and examine it under indirect light for scratches; shallow scratches can sometimes be filled with furniture polish (see page 45).

● Disconnect your wireless controllers and substitute a wired controller that you know works. If this fixes the problem, try changing or recharging the batteries in your wireless controllers.
● Make sure there are no obstacles (such as shelves or game disks) between the wireless controllers and the console. Try switching off any appliances that may interfere with the signal from the wireless units—these include fluorescent lights, microwave ovens, cordless phones, and wireless routers.
● Turn off the console and leave it to cool for 30 minutes. Move your machine to a better ventilated position and never place it on a carpet—its fibers could block the cooling vents. Use a vacuum cleaner with a brush attachment on a low setting to clear away any dust from the ventilation holes on the console's casing.
● Don't use a "chipped" console (one that has been modified to sidestep copy protection) or play pirated games.

Try changing the batteries in an unresponsive wireless controller; clean the recessed battery contacts using the eraser on the end of a pencil.

My console won't read a disk
Check the controllers and keep it cool

Make sure the disk is clean and scratch-free. If this doesn't help, you need to check the console.

● Turn off the console for 15 minutes, then restart and check if the problem is resolved.
● Make sure that the console's parental controls allow the playing of the disk—you'll find these settings in the console's menu; they allow you to restrict disks based on their age rating.
● Game disks are made for sale in a particular region of the world—check that the disk's region matches that of your console.
● Check the connections between the console and the TV, ensuring that the plugs are firmly inserted.

My game console is running slow
Clear the system cache

If your games load or run slowly, try clearing the system cache—this is the console's store of data, such as game updates and pictures of your friends' game avatars. Select the "Memory" option from the console's "System Settings" menu, and press the "Y" button on your controller, then choose "Clear System Cache."

● Keeping your console up-to-date with the latest system software will help it to run smoothly. If you are is connected to the Xbox Live service, press the "Guide" button on your controller, then navigate to **Settings ► System Settings ► Network Settings ► Wired Network** (or the name of your wireless network) ► **Test Xbox Live Connection** and then choose to update the console software if prompted. You can also update the software from a new game disk or by downloading it to a computer and transferring it to the console via a USB flash drive.

● If you have a PlayStation®3 or PlayStation®4, update the system software online. Navigate to **Settings ► System Update ► Update via Internet.** The console will check if you have the latest version. If not, it will download and install it for you.

The disk won't eject
Use the manual override

If pressing the eject button on the console does nothing, it's still possible to remove a disk. There's no universal fix for this common problem—much depends on which model of disk reader your machine came with. You'll need to search the Internet for the solution that applies to your model number.

● If you have a PS3, try this first. Turn off the power rocker switch at the back of the console. Place your finger on the eject button and hold it down. Turn on the rocker switch at the rear; when you hear the console's cooling fan start up, repeatedly press down on the eject button—the disk tray should open.

● Some PS3 consoles, such as the "slim" type, require a different approach. Switch off and unplug the console, then turn it upside down. Find the rectangular black plastic tab over the disk drive and pull it off to reveal two holes—one with a blue screw head. Insert a small Phillips-head screwdriver into the other hole, pushing through any protective tape; turn the screwdriver counterclockwise and the disk should emerge from the console. Pull it free when one-third of the disk protrudes.

● If you have an Xbox, first switch it off and unplug it from the outlet. Then remove the faceplate from the console by pulling it away

Press repeatedly on the PS3's eject button after restarting to free a stuck game disk.

from its retaining clips. This will reveal a number of small holes just below the disk drive. Pushing a straightened paper clip into one of these holes will make the tray open slightly; when it does, use your fingers to gently pull the tray out completely. You'll need to check on the Internet which hole to use for your model number—it is not consistent across all machines.

• To avoid problems in the future, never stick labels onto disks and don't move the console while there's a disk inside.

To eject a disk stuck in your Xbox, remove the console faceplate, then use a straightened paper clip to release the tray.

I can't get any video from my PS3
Change the settings

If you move your PS3 from one TV to another, you may find the screen is blank or displays a "No signal" message when you switch it on. The solution is simple: shut down the console, and then restart by holding down the power button until you hear two beeps. You can then select the correct display mode for the TV you're using.

My PS3 can't detect its wireless controllers
Synchronize your hardware

Blinking lights on a controller mean that it's not linking with the console. Try joining it to the controller via a USB cable; allow it to connect and then unplug the cable. It should remain connected wirelessly.

• Reset the console by holding down the power button on its front panel and then press the "Reset" button on the back of the controller using a straightened paper clip.

• If that doesn't work, switch off the console and controller; restart the console before turning on the controller.

My Wii seems to lag behind my movements
Set your TV to "Gaming" mode

If the on-screen action lags behind your movements with the controller or if the picture on your screen is blurry when you connect it to your Wii, try the following fixes:

• Navigate to your TV's menu and select its "Gaming" mode, if it has one.

• Try using Component Video cables (see page 41) to connect to the TV rather than the Wii's yellow video cable.

COMPUTERS

Since the launch of the first mass-market computers in the late 1970s, the power of PCs has risen exponentially, and today's machines are fast and reliable. Any problems with the computer's circuits and power supply will probably need expert repair, but there are a few hardware fixes—and many software tweaks—that can be carried out at home for a better computing experience.

GETTING UP AND RUNNING

Computers are logical machines, so you need to think logically to fix any glitches—diagnosing an issue is often a process of patient elimination. On the following pages are instructions for Windows and Mac computers. Since operating systems change rapidly and the instructions may differ on your machine, search the web or your manual for newer steps to resolve issues.

WHAT YOU CAN FIX YOURSELF

Computers vary in design. Tower computers usually have hinged sides for easy access to the hardware, while all-in-one designs and laptops are easier to get into. What you can reasonably achieve inside the machine is limited—always call an expert if you feel out of your depth.

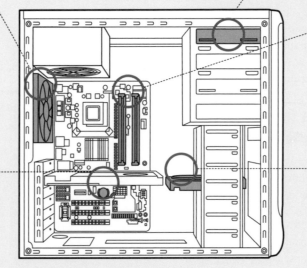

CD/DVD drive
Disks stuck in the drive can be removed without damaging the mechanism (see page 54).

Cooling fans
Fans and heat sinks stop your computer's processor, cards, and power supply from overheating, but dust quickly builds up on their surfaces. A simple cleanup will keep them running well (see page 55).

Random Access Memory (RAM)
The computer's memory cards can become loose, causing crashes, but these are easy to adjust (see opposite). Upgrading the cards will boost performance.

Backup battery
The tiny lithium cell on the motherboard can be removed to reset memory or replaced when it runs out after a few years (see page 52).

Hard disk
The hard disk, which stores your files, programs, and operating system, should be defragmented to prevent crashes (see page 57).

Tower computers allow easy access to the circuits within—simply remove the screws or thumbwheels on the side panel.

Remove RAM cards by pressing down on the levers on either side of each card. Reinsert the cards by pressing down on the middle of the card.

JARGON BUSTER

Hardware The "physical" parts of a computer system—the electronics, as well as electromechanical items like printer mechanisms, keyboard, and disk drives.

Software The coded instructions, held as magnetic dots on the computer's hard drive, that tell the machine how to perform a huge range of tasks—from word processing to video editing.

Operating system The software that enables your computer to manage files and run other programs. It processes inputs (from your keyboard, for example) and controls outputs (to your screen and printer).

My computer won't start
Check the external connections

A computer that refuses to start up is frustrating, in part because it provides you with few clues about the cause of the problem. Don't panic—it is unlikely that your precious files are damaged.

• Press the "Caps Lock" key on the keyboard—its light should come on, indicating that the computer is receiving power. If the light does come on and there's nothing on your screen, your monitor may be switched off (see page 69).

• Check the power source by plugging in another appliance to the wall socket. Make sure all the computer's switches are on and ensure its power cable is firmly plugged in.

• Tower computers may have a switch on the back that allows the operating voltage to be changed—make sure it is set to the mains voltage for your country.

• Computers can fail to start because cards that plug into the main circuit board, such as RAM cards, have come loose. Try removing and reinserting the RAM cards—this will often fix the problem (see above, right).

• If your PC still fails to start, it is likely that the power supply (a unit within the computer that distributes the correct power to different components) has failed. Power supplies can be replaced fairly easily and cheaply by your local computer repairer.

WARNING

If your computer doesn't switch on but instead emits a high-pitched whine or smells of burning wires or ozone (a metallic, acidic smell), switch it off immediately and call a professional; the computer's power supply may be compromised.

The computer switches on but the operating system doesn't start
Troubleshoot your startup

By far the most popular operating systems on home PCs are Windows and macOS (the latest version is Mojave). These essential pieces of software manage your computer and start up (or "boot") when you switch on your computer. If they fail to load correctly, you'll see a blank screen or error message or hear an audible warning.

● Do you get a "Missing operating system" message (Windows) or a blinking globe or question mark (macOS) when your computer starts up? Eject any CD or DVD that you may have left in the drive and disconnect any external hard drives, flash drives, and devices, such as scanners and printers, connected to the computer. Try restarting the machine.

● Make sure nothing is resting on the keyboard. Try unplugging and reattaching both the keyboard and the mouse.

● Does your computer beep when you start up? These beeps are the audible result of a self-test routine and indicate some kind of problem—a failed memory card, for example. Make a note of the number and duration of the beeps (short or long) and, armed with this information, talk to an expert: the nature of the beeps is a very useful clue to what's wrong, but it needs skilled interpretation.

The operating system still won't start
Jog your computer's memory

If Windows or macOS still refuses to boot when you restart, your computer may have forgotten the correct startup sequence. The part of the computer's memory responsible for this is located on the motherboard—usually the largest circuit board in the computer, which holds the processor, as well as slots for the RAM cards and graphics and sound cards. The memory is powered by a small battery that maintains the memory even when the machine is switched off.

● Turn off the computer and unplug the power cable. Open the computer's case and locate the battery on the motherboard. In most PCs, this is a CR2023 coin cell that resembles a watch battery (see left). In some computers, it may be a small, barrel-shaped cell. Remove the battery and wait 20 minutes before replacing it, closing the case, and attempting a restart.

● If you are a macOS user, try restarting the computer while simultaneously holding down the following keys: **Command+Option+P+R.**

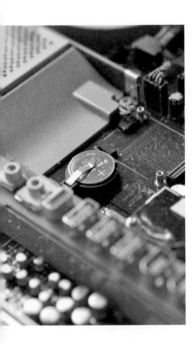

Computer batteries are easy to remove—simply slide the battery out from under its sprung retaining clip.

I get a blue screen at startup
Use safe mode to fix the problem

PC users have an apt name for the alert displayed on screen when Windows fails to start up correctly—the "blue screen of death." Mac users see a spinning colored ball (sometimes called "the pizza of death"). The message is the same—there's a problem with startup, which can happen for a variety of reasons. You're most likely to see it after you have installed a new piece of software or hardware that causes a conflict with the operating system.

● Restart your computer in "safe mode": this is a shortened form of the operating system that allows you to perform maintenance and restore full function. To enter safe mode in Windows, restart the computer while holding down the F8 key. If using a Mac, restart while holding down the shift key. Starting in safe mode can take a while.

● If Windows now starts, you can restore the system to a previous, working configuration. Go to **Control Panel ▶ System and Security ▶ System** select System Protection and click on System Restore. Reboot your PC after the recovery process is complete.

● When your Mac restarts in safe mode, start up the installer you used to install the new software. You'll usually get an option to "Uninstall"; check this and run the software to remove the recently installed application and hopefully fix your startup problems.

The computer stalls during startup
Switch off the startup items

Still getting the blue screen or spinning ball at startup? Or does your computer take a long time to get going? When you fire up your computer, Windows/macOS isn't the only application to load. Other programs, called startup items, may launch too, and switching some of them off can give you a speedier startup.

● Using Windows? Restart in safe mode (see above), go to the Task Manager by pressing **Alt+Ctrl+Delete** and select the **Startup** tab which will reveal a list of all the programs that launch when you start up your computer. Research each item on the web to find out what it does before you change it from enable to disable. Restart your computer.

● If you are a Mac user, restart in safe mode (see above), then go to **System preferences ▶ Users & Groups** and click on the **Login items** tab list for a list of all the programs that launch when you start up your computer. Research each item on the web to find out what it does before you delete it from the list. Restart your computer.

WARNING

Always back up your valuable data before carrying out any significant changes to your hardware or to installed software (see page 58).

Trap a stuck disk between two flexible plastic cards and ease it out. Have a friend grab the disk in their fingers once it protrudes sufficiently from the slot.

My CD is stuck in the CD/DVD drive
Use a paper clip to eject the disk

A CD or DVD stuck in the drive is a pain. If pressing the eject button on your PC (or dragging the disk icon to the trash can for Macs) has no effect, you have a couple of options.

● If your computer's CD/DVD drive is a tray-loading design (usually found in tower PCs), you'll find a small circular hole just beneath the drive's loading tray. Straighten a paper clip and push the wire into the hole to engage the manual drawer release.

● If you are using a PC or laptop with a slot-loading drive, pick up the computer and turn it so that the slot faces down. Press eject and let gravity help dislodge the disk.

● Still stuck? Insert two credit cards into the slot—one beneath the disk and one above. Press them together, and gently pull the disk out of the computer.

● Be careful what you put into the computer. Disks that are scratched, cracked or have paper labels are likely to get stuck.

My computer is really noisy and hot
Reduce its workload and improve ventilation

When your computer gets too hot, its cooling system kicks in. Most computers have one or more cooling fans that circulate air within the casing to carry heat away and protect delicate circuits.

● Close down some programs, especially those that demand a lot of processing power (and so generate heat), such as graphics-intensive games or videos.

● Make sure that air can circulate around the computer, especially near the fan vents at the rear. Don't enclose the computer in a cabinet or push it up too close to a wall.

The fan is noisy and the computer is slow
Calm down your machine with some software therapy

In normal use, your computer runs hundreds of mini-programs, or processes, in the background. Sometimes, one of these processes will get stuck—as if in an eternal loop. Your computer responds by slowing down, crashing, or running its cooling fans to cool its circuits. You can stop a looped process to resume normal service.

● If you are running Windows, first save any files you have open if possible. Press **Ctrl+Shift+Esc** simultaneously to bring up a new window called the Task Manager. Click on the **Processes** tab; this shows all the processes that your computer's CPU (see right) is running and what percentage of your computer power they are using. If a process is out of control, it will be taking up close to 100% of the power. To turn off a suspect process, just double-click its name in the list, then click the "Stop" button.

● You can do the same thing on a Mac. Navigate to **Applications ▶ Utilities ▶ Activity Monitor**. Locate the suspect process and click on it to open a new window. Click on **Quit** at the bottom of the window.

● If the problem recurs and the same process is to blame, seek expert help—you may need to reinstall part of your software.

The fan is still loud
Clean off the dust for quiet cooling

If the fan remains noisy—and if your computer shuts down when it's been on for only a short while—the computer's cooling fans or its heat-sink vents may be clogged with dust.

● Switch off your computer and open the case. Locate the fans and the heat sink—they are easy to spot. Use a can of compressed air to blow dust from their surfaces; an old toothbrush or fine paintbrush will dislodge more persistent dust.

Heat sinks are assemblies of metal fins designed to radiate heat away from sensitive components. Brush dust from their surfaces with an old toothbrush to maintain their efficiency.

WARNING

Always back up your valuable data before carrying out any significant changes to your hardware or software (see page 58).

My hard disk is chattering
Be safe—back up your files

If you hear a high-pitched whine or a faint chattering sound from your computer, it is probably coming from your hard disk. It could simply indicate that your hard disk is busy, but if you hear it constantly, your hard disk may be under stress or even about to fail.

● Don't take any chances. Back up your files immediately (see page 58). It is usually possible to retrieve files from a "dead" disk using a specialist service (search the web for local data-recovery services), but it is far better to keep your files backed up regularly.

● Defragment your hard drive or upgrade your RAM (see opposite).

My computer has become very slow
Empty your trash

You have probably noticed that your computer is more sluggish today than when it was new. It's not your imagination: computers get slower as their hard drives get filled up and cluttered with old files. Keeping at least 15% of the space on your hard drive empty will help prevent the worst of these slowdowns.

● First, check how much space is available on your drive. In Windows, go to **Start ▶ My Computer or This PC.** Click on the hard drive named **Windows C.** You'll then see how much space remains on the disk. Mac users can click on the hard disk icon and then go to **File ▶ Get Info.**

● Empty the bin. Any files you delete from your computer first go into the Recycle Bin (Windows) or Trash (Mac) and remain on the hard disk, occupying valuable space, until you empty the bin. In Windows, right-click the **Recycle Bin** icon and click **Empty Recycle Bin.** If using a Mac, go to right-click the **Trash** icon and click **Empty Trash.**

Declutter your drive

Spring-clean your files and applications. Sort through your work, pictures, music, videos, and emails. Be ruthless—delete anything you don't need (especially large video files) and move anything you might need onto an external disk.

● To do this in Windows, go to **Start ▶ Control Panel ▶ Programs and Features.** Select the program to delete and click **Uninstall.** Then, clean out any unnecessary files by running "Disk Cleanup": go to **Start ▶ Control Panel ▶ Administrative Tools** click on Disk Cleanup from menu.

● Mac users should drag unused applications from the **Applications** folder into the Trash, then right-click the **Trash** and click **Empty Trash.**

CHUCK IT?

Computers are built up from modules, each of which can be replaced if it fails. However, it's probably not worth spending much—if anything—to repair a machine built before 2010 because it will probably be incapable of running new versions of the most popular software.

Defragment your drive

Over time the data on your hard disk gets broken up into ever smaller "chunks" so that when you open a file, your computer needs to do a lot of work to piece it together. A process called defragmenting puts the chunks of data back into order and can improve performance. Defragmenting the drive is easy: do it regularly to prevent problems.

● In Windows, go to **Start ► This PC.** Right-click to see menu. Click on and click on **Properites.** Open **Tools** tab and click on **Optimze** drive.
● Mac OS does not require regular defragmentation.

Carry out a security scan

If spring-cleaning your hard drive doesn't boost your computer's performance, scan your disk for viruses and spyware, both of which can seriously compromise operating speeds (see page 78).

Boost your computer's RAM

If you have an older computer, some new programs may run very slowly. This may be because your computer has insufficient RAM to handle the latest applications. In such cases, your computer will use part of the hard drive to do the job of the RAM—this is called "virtual RAM"; many of your applications will slow to a crawl and you may hear your overburdened hard drive spinning frequently. The solution is to upgrade the RAM cards—you'll notice an improvement in performance and your hard drive will last longer too. Fitting new RAM is easy (see page 51), but choosing the right cards to buy can be tricky. Seek advice from your local computer retailer or repair center.

TOOLS OF THE TRADE

Antistatic strap

The components of your computer are delicate and can be damaged by static electricity stored in your body. When doing any work inside your computer, use an antistatic wristband strap. This bracelet is available at low cost from computer stores. Attach one end to your wrist and the other (usually terminated with an alligator clip) to a ground—the chassis of the computer or a nearby radiator, for example (see below).

Attach an antistatic wristband to either hand when working on the inner parts of your computer.

Five ways to back up your files

Do you worry about losing precious files and photos? There's no need—just back up your data. There are many ways to do this—some free, others cheap—so choose a method that suits your way of working.

HARDWARE WILL FAIL—IT'S ONLY A MATTER OF TIME UNTIL YOU LOSE SOME VITAL DATA—SO START BACKING UP TODAY!

1 Copy, or "burn," your files onto DVD-Rs—they are inexpensive, available in most supermarkets and offer a moderate 4.7GB of storage. DVD-RW disks are a little pricier, but can be rewritten hundreds of times, making them more flexible.

2 Transfer your files to an external hard drive. Choose a drive that is as big as your computer's hard drive so you'll never need to choose which files to back up—simply copy them all. You can manually drag and drop files to copy them, or use backup software (see below).

3 Use backup software to copy the contents of your hard drive to an external disk. You can download free or paid-for versions of such software, which offer differing degrees of sophistication. Some allow you to schedule automatic backups of selected files, or will update only those files that have changed since your last backup. Backup software is constantly updated—search the Internet for backup software to find the latest versions.

4 Use a remote backup in the Cloud. This copies selected files (which may be encrypted to ensure privacy) over the Internet to a secure data center. You'll need an Internet connection for this to work. It is usually a subscription service, but is sometimes offered free by Internet providers. Use it for your most valuable data.

5 Try a cloud backup service. There are many advantages to backing up to the cloud including that the backup is in a separate location from your computer and you can back up multiple devices into one account. An example of such a service is IDrive (www.idrive.com).

Help! I just deleted a vital file
Act quickly to recover it

It happens to everyone—instead of dragging a file into a folder, you drop it into the bin instead.

● Immediately go to the Recycle Bin (Windows) or Trash (Mac). The file should still be there. If using a Mac, just drag it back to its desired location. If you're a Windows user, right-click on the accidentally deleted file in Recycle Bin and choose **Restore** from the menu.

● If you have already emptied your trash, the file may still be on your hard drive. Stop using the computer immediately—any activity might write over some or all of the accidentally deleted file. Get advice from an expert about file-recovery programs that might be able to retrieve your file.

● Always back up your data (see opposite). That way, you'll at least have an earlier version of the lost file.

I can't copy files onto my flash drive
Free up some space on the drive

Flash drives are gadgets that allow you to store files temporarily or move them from one computer to another. If your flash drive doesn't respond, here's what to do.

● If the flash drive is new, it may require formatting by your computer. First, plug the stick into your computer's USB port; in Windows, go to **My Computer** and right-click the USB drive on the list. Select **Format** from the menu. In Mac OS, navigate to **Applications ▶ Utilities ▶ Disk Utility**. Select the flash drive and click on **Erase**.

● The flash drive may be full. If using a PC, drag any files you don't need from the flash drive to the Recycle Bin to create more space. Be aware that the files will disappear for good—there's no way to retrieve them later. If using a Mac, drag the files into the Trash; you then need to go to right-click on the Trash icon and select **Empty Trash** to get rid of the files and create more space on the flash drive.

My computer's date and time are way off
Replace the battery

If your computer tells you it's January in 1949 or some other crazy date, it's time to change the battery on the motherboard (see page 52). Don't be tempted just to live with the incorrect date—all the files you work on will be "stamped" with this wrong information, making them impossible to sort in date order later.

USB flash drives are a convenient way of carrying data and can be rewritten thousands of times. Be careful when using them to transport sensitive data— they are easily misplaced.

My computer's clock is inaccurate
Set it with atomic precision

The clock within your computer is little more than a cheap wristwatch that relies on a quartz crystal to keep time. Its long-term accuracy is usually poor. However, if you have an Internet connection, it's simple to set your time and date to synchronize with the most accurate atomic clocks in the world.

● In Windows, click on the clock on your screen to bring up the **Date and Time Properties**. Click on the **Internet Time** tab and check the **Automatically Synchronize** box. Mac users should click on the clock on screen, then select open **Date and Time Preferences ► Date and Time** and check the **Set date and time automatically** box.

As I get older, I'm finding it harder to use my computer
Get some help from your computer's accessibility features

If you find it hard to read text on the screen, to manipulate the keyboard and mouse, or if you can no longer hear audible alerts, your computer can help through its accessibility features. These will allow you to make changes to the way you communicate with your computer and it with you. For example, you can reverse the screen colors (black to white and vice versa) and increase text size for better legibility; you can set your computer to "read" your text out loud; or you can make your screen flash in place of audible alerts.

● If using Windows, navigate to **Start ► Control Panel ► Ease of Access ► Ease of Access Center**. Here you'll find access to a range of features and tools to make using your computer easier. Mac users can find these features in Mac OS by going to **System Preferences ► Accessibility**.

TOOLS OF THE TRADE
Make the Internet your friend

Many computer problems are specific to a particular combination of software and hardware; unfortunately, there are millions of permutations! Try searching the Internet for solutions to your problems; there is much wisdom out there, but also misinformation. Look for a consensus between different sites, and give most weight to established sites.

My computer has crashed
Retrace your steps to find the problem

Crashes, when your computer freezes or displays the blue screen of death, seem to occur at the worst possible time. Crashes can occur for many reasons, but it is possible to pinpoint the problem.

● Review what you were doing just before the crash. Was the crash triggered by a certain task or a particular program? Restart the computer and try to replicate the exact circumstances of the crash to confirm the cause. If you have experienced this crash, so will have many other users, so use the power of the Internet to find a fix (see left).

Make it last COMPUTERS

Keep your original software disks and all the documentation that came with your computer. You may need to reinstall the system software at a later date. Many modern computers, especially laptops, are not supplied with such disks. They instead exist as disk images, hidden away in a secure area of the hard drive. The machine's manual will explain how these images can be transferred to a blank CD or DVD. Do this now, if you haven't already.

Note the product key—the code that comes with your system software disk. You'll need this if you ever have to reinstall your system software. It is often printed on a label attached to your computer or on the sleeve of the system software disk.

Shut down safely and correctly. In Windows, go to **Start ► Turn Off Computer**; in Mac OS, select **Shut Down** from the **Apple** menu. Only then should you turn off the power. If you routinely shut down by killing the power, you may corrupt the data on your hard disk.

● Make sure your system software is up-to-date. Apple and Microsoft issue regular updates that can be downloaded for free. Set Windows to download and install recommended updates automatically: go to **Start ► Control Panel ► System and Security ► Turn Automatic Updating On**. Mac OS will periodically prompt you to download updates; review the list presented and download what you need.

● Download the latest software drivers for your computer's internal cards and peripherals, such as hard disks and scanners (see page 72).

● If you have recently installed new software onto your computer, it may be that your machine isn't equipped to run it. Check compatibility on the Internet; enter your make and model of computer, plus the software and its version number, as terms into a search engine, such as Google. This should reveal any problems other users have had with this particular hardware/software combination. You may need to upgrade your RAM (see page 51) to remedy the problem.

LAPTOPS AND NETBOOKS

Laptops and netbooks are constantly being moved and taken in and out of bags, and so are subject to knocks, scratches, and spillages. Their screens and keyboards are especially vulnerable, but damage can be repaired and disaster averted with a little know-how. Batteries can also die or run down prematurely, but there's no need to find yourself stranded without power.

I've scratched my laptop screen
Reach for the petroleum jelly

All but the deepest scratches can be filled and disguised. First, clean the affected area using a fresh lint-free cloth dipped in water. Wipe it dry with a second lint-free cloth.

● For shallow scratches, lightly rub the affected area with a clean, soft pencil eraser, following the direction of the scratch. You might need to repeat this several times before the scratch disappears.

● Fill deeper scratches with petroleum jelly. Press the jelly into the scratch with a clean finger, then wipe away the excess with a lint-free cloth. The jelly left within the scratch has similar optical properties to the screen material, making the blemish less noticeable. In time, when the jelly wears off, simply reapply as above.

My laptop screen is broken and I urgently need to get at my files

Hook up to an external monitor

A broken screen will need a professional repair, but in the meantime, you may still be able to access your vital files. Put your laptop to your ear; if you can hear whirring, then there's a good chance that it is still operational. If so, try connecting the laptop to an external screen.

● Look on the rear and side panel of your laptop. Most models have a socket through which you can connect the laptop to a monitor. In most cases, this will be a VGA socket with 15 holes (five holes in three rows), but could also be a DVI socket (see page 69). You'll now need to buy or borrow a compatible cable through which to connect your laptop to an external monitor.

● When connected, copy all your important data to a USB flash drive, removable hard drive or CD/DVD (see page 58) and send your faulty laptop for professional screen repair.

My laptop battery barely lasts an hour

Set up your system for maximum life

Short battery life is the curse of all laptop users, but there's lots you can do to boost your machine's stamina.

● Eject CDs and DVDs when they're not in use. If you need to access data or programs on a CD or DVD, copy them onto your hard drive rather than accessing them directly from the disk.

● Disconnect unused USB devices (such as mice, external hard drives, and scanners)—they all draw power from your laptop battery.

● Run only one program at a time; for example, don't play music while working on a spreadsheet.

● Add more RAM (see page 51)—it'll make your computer faster, too.

● Set up your laptop to save energy; your computer's hardware and system settings can be configured to cut power use or improve performance. If running Windows, go to **Control panel ► Power options** and select a set of options that best fits the way you work. Mac OS users can find these controls at **System preferences ► Energy saver**.

● Turn down the screen brightness.

● Regularly defragment the laptop hard drive (see page 57).

● Switch off your laptop's Wi-Fi connection if you don't need to be online. In Windows, go to **Control panel ► Network and Internet ► Change adapter settings ► Disable wireless network connection**. If you are using Mac OS, in the Apple menu go to **Systems preferences ► Network ► Turn off**. Repeat with bluetooth.

My battery stores less power each time
Prevent the memory effect

Laptops from the 1980s and early 1990s use Ni-Cd batteries, while newer models usually use Li-ion technology (see box, left). If you have a Ni-Cd or Ni-MH battery, you can slow down its gradual loss of power over time.
● Charge your laptop battery fully, and then discharge it completely at least once every two weeks. Avoid topping off the charge too often between complete discharges.

My charger cable is fraying
Play it safe and reinforce your connection

Moving your laptop when it is charging puts strain on the charger cable at the point where it plugs into your computer. The cable may become loose or even begin to fray—but it's easy to reinforce this vulnerable area.
● Visit your local electronic components shop and ask for a length of heat-shrink sleeving. Buy the smallest diameter that will fit snugly over the cable plug—it will cost very little. Cut off a 2 1/2 inch length and poke the plug through it so that the sleeve end is flush with that of the plug's barrel. Carefully heat the tubing using a lit candle, cigarette lighter, or heat gun. It will contract, fitting snugly around the plug's body and cable.

My netbook is getting really hot
Improve your ventilation

Netbooks are low-cost laptops designed for portable Internet use. Many lack a cooling fan, which makes them especially vulnerable to overheating. A few simple steps will help prevent this problem.
● Use the machine on a solid, flat surface, not on a carpet or on bedclothes—fabrics can block its cooling vents. Consider buying a laptop stand to lift the machine up and improve air circulation.
● Use the netbook in the shade or in a cool place.
● Try not to "multitask"; close programs and windows you're not using. Avoid games and high-definition video playback—these make intensive use of the processor and generate lots of heat.
● Clear dust and debris from around the air vents using tweezers and a swab soaked in isopropyl alcohol. Don't use an air blower as this will push dust back inside the netbook's case.

I've spilled water on my laptop
Power down and act quickly

The biggest danger posed by spilled liquids is that they cause short circuits that permanently damage delicate circuitry.

● Unplug the charger immediately, if it is connected. Your machine should revert to battery power.

● Shut down the laptop. If your machine's battery is failing, keep the charger connected—but only for the time needed to shut it down safely. If the charger is wet, though, unplug it immediately.

● Disconnect any attached hardware, such as storage devices, network and audio cables, and so on.

● If possible, remove the battery pack. You'll usually need to release one or more catches on the base of the computer. In some machines, the battery cannot be removed easily, in which case, proceed with the battery in place.

● Open the screen at right-angles; hold the laptop upside down and sway it from side to side to encourage water to drip out.

● Place a dry towel on a table. Set the laptop keyboard-down on the towel, with the screen hanging over the side of the table. Leave overnight in a warm, well-ventilated place.

● Next day, hold a hair dryer about six inches above the keyboard, and blast warm air into the machine for 15 minutes. Constantly move the hair dryer to avoid creating hot spots.

● Contact Apple.com for additional advice for a Mac.

Use a hair dryer to dry the keyboard only when most of the water has drained from the computer's casing.

Make it last LAPTOPS AND NETBOOKS

Carry your laptop or netbook in a padded bag and never leave it in hot place, such as in a car on a warm day.

Hold the laptop by its base, never by the screen, and always work well away from liquids.

Before closing the screen, check that there are no objects (such as pens and paper clips) on the keyboard: closing the laptop with an object on the keyboard is almost guaranteed to crack the screen.

Never force connectors into USB or other ports on the laptop and always remove plugs and memory sticks when not in use.

Don't stick labels onto CDs and DVDs—they can peel off in the warm environment of a laptop and jam the mechanisms.

KEYBOARDS, MICE, SCREENS, AND SOUNDS

The earliest computers communicated with their users through punched cards or paper. Nowadays, computer interfaces include technologies such as touch screens, voice control, and video-enabled glasses. Most of us, however, still interact with computers through familiar devices—keyboards, mice, screens, and speakers—which get a lot of day-to-day punishment and need a little care to keep them working efficiently.

My keyboard is not responding
Test and fix your connections

If selected keys don't work, a quick cleanup may resolve the issue (see below). If whole blocks of keys don't work, the keyboard probably has an electronic fault that will need professional attention. If no keys work, check your keyboard's connections.
- If you have access to another computer, borrow its keyboard and connect it to your machine. If the new keyboard works, you know that your original keyboard, or its connection, is to blame.
- Reconnect your original keyboard using a different USB port on your computer. Reboot the computer and try again.
- Wireless keyboards use a lot of power. Try replacing the batteries in the keyboard before rebooting. Make sure that the wireless keyboard is "linked" to your computer via Bluetooth—your computer will prompt you to set up this link on startup.

My keyboard is filthy
Keep it in top condition with a few cleaning tips

Dirty keyboards and sticky keys not only affect your productivity, they're a health hazard too, harboring harmful bacteria.
- Turn the keyboard upside down and give it a few taps to shake out any loose dust and dirt, then use a small vacuum cleaner nozzle attachment to suck out debris from between the keys.
- Use a wet wipe to remove everyday grease from the keys.
- For congealed dirt, remove the key caps by gently prying them off with a small flat-bladed screwdriver. Take a photo of your keyboard first so that you can see where to replace them. Soak a cotton swab in isopropyl alcohol (see box, left) and wipe away any residue beneath and around the key caps before snapping them back into place.

I've spilled coffee on my keyboard
Act quickly and rinse away the problem

● Immediately shut down the computer and disconnect the keyboard. Run cold water from a tap over the keyboard to remove as much of the sticky liquid as possible.

● Shake off the water, turn the keyboard upside down and place it on a towel. Follow the instructions for dealing with a water spill on a laptop (see page 65).

● If all else fails, place the keyboard on its own, facedown in the top tray of a dishwasher. Run a short cleaning cycle with no detergent and allow the keyboard to dry thoroughly.

DISHWASH YOUR KEYBOARD AS A LAST RESORT—YOU HAVE LITTLE TO LOSE!

Greasy deposits on your mouse can be removed using isopropyl alcohol.

My computer mouse is jumpy
Take control over your pointing tool

There's little more that's as frustrating as trying to select a word or an image onscreen with a jumpy mouse. Skittish movement can come down to software or hardware, but it is usually easy to tame.

● Some devices work best on a mouse pad on a solid, flat surface. Wipe the pad clean from time to time to remove grease and grime.

● Most modern computer mice are "optical"—light is emitted from the base of the unit, allowing sensors to detect its movement relative to the surface. The sensors can be fooled by debris on the underside of the mouse, and the movement of the mouse can be impeded by dirt on the "running tracks." Clean the underside with a cotton swab soaked in isopropyl alcohol (see page 66) to get rid of the grime.

● An older computer may have a "ball mouse" that contains a rubber ball that rolls against spring-loaded rollers as the mouse is moved. This, too, is easy to clean. Twist the retaining ring on the base of the mouse to release the ball. Use a pair of tweezers and a cotton swab soaked in isopropyl alcohol to clean the two rollers that make contact with the ball. Wash the ball in soapy water, then dry and reassemble.

● Your mouse can appear jumpy if your computer's processor is busy doing other work in the background. Close any programs that you are not using and try again.

My mouse is moving really slowly
Tweak your system for extra speed

If you need to drag your mouse halfway across your desk to move the cursor by an inch, or if your cursor flies across the screen when you touch your mouse, follow a few simple steps to get back on track.

● In Windows, go to **Control panel ► Mouse ► Pointer speed** and adjust the speed until it is comfortable.

● Mac OS users should go to **System preferences ► Mouse ► Tracking speed** to make the same adjustment.

My screen is dirty
Get a clear view without scratching

Older glass-fronted CRT (see box, left) screens are tough and resilient, but most computers today have LCD or LED screens. Cleaning these with paper towels is a no-no—paper towels are abrasive and can cause scratching. Also, avoid alcoholic solvents (such as isopropyl alcohol), which can attack the plastic material used in LCD screens.

- Rub the screen with a dry, lint-free cloth. Use the smallest amount of pressure that works.
- If the dirt proves stubborn, don't rub harder. Instead, soak a cloth in screen cleaning solution and rub again. You can buy this readily from stationery and computer retailers, or you can mix an effective substitute from equal parts of white vinegar and distilled water.

My screen worked fine yesterday, but now it doesn't come on at all

Check that you're connected

Look for signs of life in your monitor—can you see a glowing power light, a faint glow from the monitor or a "no signal" message on screen?
- If the monitor is on, the chances are that your computer is switched off or has gone into power-saving mode. Press its standby button, move the mouse, or tap a key to "wake it up."
- If the screen shows no signs of life, push its power plug in fully and check its connection to the computer. Ensure VGA or DVI plugs (see box, right) are tight in their sockets: most have screws that can be hand tightened to ensure a good connection, so check that they are firmly in place (see below, left).
- Check that the pins of the VGA plug are straight—one can easily get bent out of shape when the screen is plugged and unplugged from the computer. If a pin is bent, use a pair of long-nose pliers to restore its shape (see below, right)
- Still no luck? Try connecting the monitor to another computer. If it works, the problem may lie with your computer's graphics card, which may have come loose or may need to be replaced.

JARGON BUSTER

VGA Video Graphics Array is a type of video connector designed in the 1980s that uses an analog rather than digital signal. Its plug has 15 pins arranged in five rows of three.

DVI Digital Video Interface is a more recent connector designed to carry digital signals. Its plug is a large rectangular connector with as many as 28 pins.

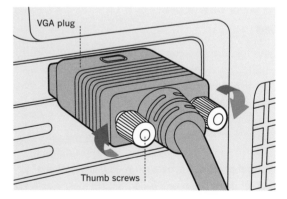

Make sure that the thumb screws on the VGA cable are tightened to ensure a good connection.

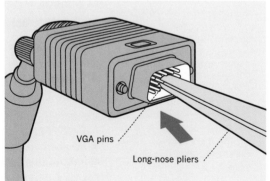

Use a pair of long-nose pliers to straighten any bent pins on the VGA plug.

Massage a reluctant pixel with the end of a pen, cushioned with a soft cloth.

There are tiny spots on my screen
Try massaging your pixels

● The pixels of an LCD screen can sometimes become stuck on—showing up as an annoying bright dots of color—or they can die, appearing as equally irritating black spots.
● Use online software that can identify and deal with affected pixels, such as www.flexcode.org/lcd2.html. The software will "massage" faulty pixels, applying a quick-changing pattern to affected parts of the screen. After a few hours of "exercise," the pixel may be restored.
● If this doesn't work, press down gently on the faulty pixel with the rounded end of a pen, cushioned with a soft cloth (see left). Restart your screen while maintaining pressure. This may "free" the stuck pixel.

The icons on my desktop are tiny
Take control of your display settings

Every computer display has a fixed number of dots (pixels) across its length and height; a screen with 1600 pixels across its width and 1200 along its height, is said to have a native resolution of 1600 x 1200. For best screen legibility, set your computer to the screen's native resolution; you can find out what this is by checking the model number on the screen manufacturer's website.
● If you're using Windows, go to **Control panel ▶ Appearance ▶ Personalization ▶ Adjust screen resolution**. Set your computer to the display's native resolution. This will automatically adjust the text and graphics to a readable default size.
● Mac users have the same controls at **System preferences ▶ Displays**.

It's still hard to see the text
Zoom in for a better view

If you're constantly squinting at the screen or reaching for your reading glasses when you go online, get relief with some extra magnification.
● Temporarily zoom in for a closer view using the magnifier tool. In Windows, you'll find this in **Start menu ▶ Accessories ▶ Accessibility**. Macs have similar settings at **System preferences ▶ Display ▶ Accessibility** and change resolution from default to scaled and select.
● You can also permanently zoom in on desktop items. If you're a Windows user, select **Control panel ▶ Appearance ▶ Personalization ▶ Display ▶ Make text and other items larger or smaller**. Set the best size for your eyes. Mac users can do the same by selecting **View ▶ Show view options**.

Ten ways to boost your productivity and comfort: setting up your workstation

Sitting in front of a screen for long periods puts stress on your body and mind, but it's easy to tweak your environment so that using your computer becomes a pleasure not a pain.

1 Remove your hands from your mouse when not using it to reduce static muscle work.

2 Use your arm, not just your wrist, to move the mouse if you find this more comfortable.

3 Position the keyboard so that your forearms are near horizontal and your wrists are straight when you type.

4 Keep commonly used items, such as the keyboard and phone, within comfortable reach.

5 Regularly modify your posture to reduce fatigue, but avoid twisting your body.

6 Adjust the height of your seat so that your elbows are approximately level with the desk and your lower back is supported by the back of the chair.

7 Position your screen so that you can focus on it without leaning forward. The top of the screen should be just below eye level.

8 If your feet dangle and don't reach the floor, use a footrest.

9 Reduce the screen brightness to a comfortable level.

10 Cut glare from windows by changing the screen angle or fitting suitable blinds.

GIVE YOUR EYES A BREAK BY LOOKING AWAY FROM THE SCREEN FREQUENTLY

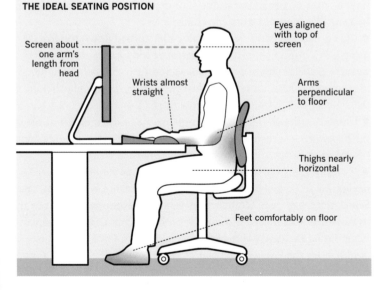

THE IDEAL SEATING POSITION

Screen about one arm's length from head

Eyes aligned with top of screen

Wrists almost straight

Arms perpendicular to floor

Thighs nearly horizontal

Feet comfortably on floor

Is it my eyes? The text on websites is too small to see

Adjust text size through your web browser

It's simple to set the size and appearance of the font that appears on websites to suit your own preferences.

- Using Microsoft Internet Explorer? Select an appropriate text size directly from the **View** option on the menu bar.
- For Google Chrome, click on the arrow at the upper right of the screen r and select **Settings ▶ Appearances**, then choose a larger font size.
- Firefox is a little different. In the **Tools** menu bar, go to **Options ▶ Content ▶ Fonts and colors** where you can specify the desired font size.
- Mac users browsing with Safari can find similar controls in the menu bar at **Safari ▶ Websites ▶ Page zoom**.

My computer's speakers are silent

Troubleshoot and fix the most common audio problems

Your computer has several volume controls. If one of these controls is turned down, your computer will make no sound even if the others are set to full volume. Find and adjust all the computer's volume controls before considering other causes.

- If your computer has external speakers, check that they are connected to a power supply and that their external volume controls (if present) are turned up. Make sure that the speaker cables have not become disconnected from the computer.
- Check that the main audio output isn't turned down too low. If using a PC, go to **Control panel ▶ Hardware and sound ▶ Audio devices and sound ▶ Sound ▶ Adjust system volume** and turn the main volume up to its maximum. Mac users can adjust the volume by simply clicking on the speaker icon in the Menu bar or the F11 or F12 keys.
- If there's still no sound, the volume may be turned down or off in the program or website that you are running. Find the volume control (its location varies with each program) and turn it up.
- If you're using a PC, check the status of your sound card by navigating to **Control panel ▶ System and maintenance ▶ Device manager ▶ Sound, video, and game controllers**. A yellow question mark next to the name of the sound card indicates a problem. This can often be solved by updating the card's software driver (see box, left). To do this, double-click the name of the sound card, then click on **Driver ▶ Update driver software**. Your computer will need to be connected to the Internet in order to update successfully.

JARGON BUSTER

Driver Software that allows your computer to recognize and interact with a specific piece of hardware, such as a printer, scanner, graphics or sound card, is known as a driver. Drivers are updated frequently by the manufacturers of the hardware; updates may eliminate bugs and add new features so are always worth installing. It's worth visiting the manufacturer's website every few months. If new drivers are available, download and install them following the instructions given by the manufacturer.

SCANNERS, WEBCAMS, AND PRINTERS

Printers and scanners—like all mechanical devices—are prone to jams, blockages, and worn parts. And along with other computer peripherals, such as webcams, they are subject to software glitches, and connection and compatibility issues. But it's always worth checking for simple mechanical faults before delving into software for a solution.

My scanner won't scan
Make sure it's recognized by the computer

First, check that you have power. Does the power light on the scanner body come on? If the scanner is part of a combined scanner and printer unit, can you still print? Make sure the unit is switched on and connected to a power source.

● Check the connection to the computer; try using a new USB cable and plugging into a different USB port. Restart both the scanner and the computer and attempt another scan.

● Most scanners have a transit lock—a physical switch that locks the scanner bed in place so that it can be transported safely. Make sure that this is disengaged.

● Download and install the latest software driver (see box, opposite) to ensure that your computer can recognize and communicate with the scanner. You can find the latest driver software by visiting the scanner manufacturer's website.

I keep losing cables behind my desk when I unplug my computer
Improvise a cable clamp with a bulldog clip

Is the area behind your computer an ugly tangle of cables? Does all the wiring fall to the ground when you unplug and move your computer or laptop? Get a little order in your computing life with some simple fixes.

● Use large bulldog clips to secure the cables to your tabletop.

● Wrap Velcro around each cable and attach a corresponding strip of Velcro to your desk to hold the cables in place.

● Run the cables through slots cut in a block of compressed foam to keep them together and prevent slippage.

SMOOTH THE
JAGGED EDGES OF
A SCRATCH ON A
PLASTIC SCANNER
PLATE WITH A
PENCIL ERASER

I've scratched the surface of my scanner

Smooth away the marks with an eraser

The clear scanner plate may be made from plastic or glass—check before you begin work. First, drag your fingernail over the scratch. If it catches, the scratch is most likely too deep to repair.

• If the plate is plastic, gently clean it with a fresh lint-free cloth soaked in water and wipe dry with a second cloth. Smooth over the scratch with a pencil eraser.

• If the plate is made of glass and the scratch isn't too deep, try erasing the scratch with a mild abrasive. You could buy an eyeglass scratch repair kit but simple toothpaste is a good substitute.

• If the scratch on the glass isn't deep, apply a normal (non-gel) toothpaste over the scratch using a lint-free cloth. Allow the paste to dry and harden for a few minutes. Wipe off the toothpaste and gently buff the scratch with a clean, lint-free cloth. Hopefully, your scratch will have vanished.

My webcam won't work with Skype
Set up quickly for video calls

If your webcam isn't built into your computer, check that it is plugged into the power supply and connected to your computer. Try swapping the USB port used, then restart both the computer and webcam.
- Check that Skype is set up to use your webcam. In Windows, launch the Skype application, and then navigate to **Settings ▶ Audio & Video ▶ Webcam settings**. Select the webcam you have from the drop-down menu—you'll see its live feed on your screen. If your webcam isn't listed in the menu, you'll need to download and install its software driver (see page 72). In Mac OS, go to **System preferences ▶ Audio/Video ▶ Camera** and select your webcam.

My webcam makes a blurry image
Sharpen up your image

Launch Skype and check the live feed from your webcam (see above).
- If the image appears fuzzy, clean the webcam lens (see page 41).
- Many webcams have a discrete focus ring set in around the lens—try turning this until the image is clear.

My laser printer's output is blotchy
Experiment with your paper

Use the printer's software to ensure that the toner levels are OK—most printers have lights or alerts to warn you when supplies are running low. Try experimenting with the paper you use. Some papers are too coarse, giving uneven prints, while others are too smooth or thick for the toner to bond with the paper.

WARNING

Laser printer toner is nasty stuff. If spilled, pick it up with sticky tape immediately.
- Avoid breathing in toner. It poses a health risk, particularly if you suffer with bronchitis or asthma.
- Don't use a vacuum cleaner to pick up spilled toner—its fine particles can cause the motor to catch fire.
- Do not wash your hands or surfaces with hot water. The toner particles will melt and be much harder to remove. Use cold water.

Nine smart ways to save on printer ink

Running an inkjet printer can be an expensive business, but follow these tips and you'll conserve ink and make savings that will really add up over time.

PRINT WEB PAGES IN BLACK ONLY AND SAVE ON COSTLY COLOR INK

1 Printing family and holiday photos will quickly run down your ink supplies. Instead, use online or drugstore photo-printing services—they will work out cheaper than home prints and be better quality, too.

2 Use a smaller typeface (or font) and reduce the line spacing. You'll fit far more text onto a page and so save ink.

3 Site your inkjet printer or spare cartridges in a cool place. If you keep them near a radiator, or next to your computer's fan, they will heat up and clog much sooner.

4 If possible, print your documents or photos in batches, all at once, rather than spreading out the printing over a period of days or weeks. Every time you restart the printer, it runs a head-cleaning or maintenance cycle that uses valuable ink. According to some studies, changing your printing habits in this way can cut your ink use by half.

5 Download ink-saving software to your computer. There are many free programs that help to optimize ink use. Try www.inksaver.com and follow the on-screen instructions.

6 Avoid switching off the printer mid-cycle—always let the print head return to its resting position.

7 If color isn't critical, print web pages and documents in black only. Black ink is often less costly than colored inks. You can usually opt to print in black only whenever you send a document to print.

8 The manufacturer's own ink cartridges can cost nearly as much as the printer itself. Look out for cheaper versions made or refilled by other companies. Don't mix brands as inks from different manufacturers may not combine well on the page.

9 Always think twice before you print—is a paper copy really necessary?

Help! My ink has run out
Trick your printer into delivering that vital document

Cartridges may still have ink stuck to their sides even though their built-in sensors indicate that they are empty.

● Remove the "empty" printer cartridge and find its sensor, which is usually a gold-colored chip on its exterior (see right). Cover the sensor with a piece of insulating tape, pop the cartridge back in and try printing again.

● Shake the cartridge from side to side.

● Reset the printer—shut it down and then switch on again.

● Remove the cartridge and heat it up gently with a hair dryer—this can help to loosen the thick ink within.

My printouts are ruined by ugly bands!
Clean the print head

The business end of your inkjet printer—the print head—can become clogged, especially if you use the printer infrequently.

● Try running the printer's built-in head-cleaning option. If you're using Windows, go to **Control panel ▶ Printers and other hardware**. Click on your printer's name to launch its software and select and run the head-cleaning utility. If you have a Mac, go to **System preference ▶ Print and scanners** and select your printer to activate its software.

● If the problem persists, try cleaning the print head manually. Remove the cartridges to get to the print head—the unit that shuttles back and forth across the printer. Gently wipe it with a soft lint-free cloth, moistened with isopropyl alcohol.

The paper's getting stuck again
Prepare your printer to beat the jams

A few simple checks to your paper, paper feeder, and rollers will guarantee perfect results each time.

● Make sure the guide rails of the paper feeder are spaced correctly for your paper size. If not, the printer may misfeed and get in a jam.

● Before loading paper into the printer, fan out both ends of the ream to stop sheets sticking together and causing a pileup.

● Check the paper you've loaded into the printer. It should be dry and flat, with no rough or crumpled edges.

● Switch off the printer. Open all the panels on your printer and shine a flashlight on the rollers inside. Using a pair of tweezers, remove any paper scraps, sticky labels, paper clips or other debris.

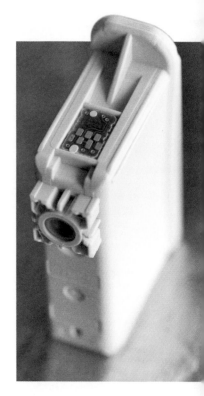

The electronic chip may tell the printer that the cartridge is empty, even though ink is still present.

TOOLS OF THE TRADE
Fresh ink for great prints

Inkjet cartridges have a finite life, regardless of how much or little you use them. They dry out after a few months, so don't stockpile—only buy and install them when they're needed.

COMPUTER AND INTERNET SECURITY

Keeping your computer safe from theft and your files protected from prying eyes and malicious damage is essential in today's connected world. But you can minimize the risks with a little common sense—plus some software and hardware tools that are often supplied with your computer.

How do I stop others from looking at my files?
Set up separate accounts for each user

If your home computer is shared by several members of the family, it's wise to set up a user account (see box, left) for each person. This keeps each user's files—including emails—separate, and restricts which programs can be accessed by each user.

● To do this on a PC, go to **Control Panel ▶ User Accounts and Family Safety ▶ Add or Remove User Accounts**. If you are a Mac user, go to **System Preferences ▶ Users & Groups** and click on the "+" button to create a new account.

● Make sure to create a unique password for each account—you'll need to enter the password every time you log into your account. This prevents other users of the computer from accessing your data without your permission.

● Even if you're the only user of the computer, set up a standard account alongside an administrator account. Use the standard account for all your work, including sending emails and browsing the web; only use the administrator account when making changes to settings or installing new software. Using a standard account for your everyday work will prevent you from accidentally deleting software needed to keep the computer running smoothly.

● Don't forget to log out of your account when you've finished using the computer.

Encrypt sensitive information

Some of your personal and financial data is highly sensitive. You can give it high-level protection by using encryption software, such as BitLocker. Download the program from the Internet (it's free) and follow the installation instructions. This will set up a part of your hard drive where all the information stored is "scrambled"—completely unreadable without your preset password. So, even if your computer is stolen or maliciously hacked, your data will remain safe. Be sure not to forget your encryption password—it is near impossible to access your protected data without it.

I'm worried that my laptop is easy to steal

Lock it down

If you use your laptop in a library or café, you won't want to leave it unattended. But a built-in feature on most computers can greatly reduce the chances of theft. Most laptop computers have some type of security slot—a rounded rectangular hole on the back or side, usually identified by a padlock symbol. A special cable (available at low cost from computer stores) will fit into the slot and can be locked in place with a key or PIN. Loop the other end of the cable around a heavy object or fixture for peace of mind—it's like padlocking your machine to the desk.

Laptops can be physically secured using inexpensive locks that deter all but the most determined thieves.

Can I protect my computer when I'm online?

Set up a firewall

Whenever you are connected to the Internet, your computer sends and receives data to and from other computers located all around the world. Most of this is data you have requested, but it is possible that some is malicious, allowing others to view and change your files or even take full remote control of your computer.

● You can greatly reduce these risks by setting up a firewall. This can be either a program (software) or a piece of hardware (electronic circuits) that examines each "packet" of data as it enters or leaves the computer and blocks any data that seems suspicious. Windows and Mac OS X have built-in firewall software, which should always be enabled. If you have Windows, go to **Control Panel ▶ Security ▶ Windows Firewall** and check the "On" button. For Mac OS, navigate to **System Preferences ▶ Security & Privacy ▶ Firewall** and select Turn on Firewall.

● Many broadband routers have a hardware firewall. Check your user manual to make sure it is enabled. You can usually enable both the hardware-based firewall in your router and the software firewall in your computer at the same time.

● Using a firewall isn't a guarantee against unauthorized access to your computer via the Internet. You need to develop safe habits when using email and visiting websites (see pages 95–97) and treat all offers and enticements you receive with measured suspicion—if something appears too good to be true, it probably is!

Malware
Malicious software is a
term that encompasses
viruses as well as other
types of destructive or
annoying programs.
These include: worms,
which spread through
a network choking
communication speeds;
spyware, which gathers
your private data;
adware, which diplays
unwanted ads on your
screen; and keyloggers,
which record all of
your keystrokes.

Treat a computer that you
suspect is infected with a
virus by running antivirus
software loaded onto a
USB memory stick.

My computer is slow: do I have a virus?
Install antivirus software

If you start to notice programs loading very slowly, or if scrolling around documents on screen becomes sluggish, your computer may have been infected by a virus. Viruses have many other possible symptoms: they can cause your computer to freeze, they can wipe out data, or even send themselves to friends and colleagues in your contact book using your email account. A computer virus is a program that has been maliciously hidden within another program—a game or other application, for example—that you may have innocently downloaded from the Internet. If you run that program on your computer, the virus will make copies of itself that attach to other programs, causing them to operate oddly. Viruses are just one type of "malware" (see box, left).

● Protect yourself—and others you communicate with—by installing antivirus software. There are numerous products available online (search for "antivirus software"), many of which are free and address not just viruses but also other forms of malware. You can set the software to scan your computer files regularly and to intercept viruses carried by incoming email.

● If you suspect that you have already been infected with a virus, immediately disconnect your computer from the Internet by unplugging its connection to your broadband router. Then use a different computer to download antivirus software. Save the antivirus program onto a USB flash drive and then insert this into the infected machine. Run the software by following its on-screen instructions to remove the virus from the affected computer.

● Be sure to update your antivirus software regularly—hundreds of new viruses and new forms of malware emerge every week. Most commercial packages will download updates automatically.

Avoid infection by viruses

The best way to deal with malware is to avoid it in the first place.

● Never open an unexpected email attachment—it may harbor a virus file. Be aware that malicious senders will do whatever they can to tempt

you into opening the attachment: for example, the email title may read "Your account has been cancelled" and invite you to open the attachment to "remedy" the problem, resulting in infection by a virus.

● Make sure your system software is up-to-date, or set your computer to update it automatically (see page 61). Updates are issued regularly to fix known security issues.

● Carry out regular backups of your most important data. This precaution means that if your files are corrupted by a virus, you will have "clean" copies to restore once you have removed the virus from your machine.

I get hundreds of spam emails every day
Use a spam filter

Spam, or junk email, is a fact of Internet life. Some of it carries malware as an attachment, but the main problem with spam is that it is annoying because it swamps your email inbox with pointless messages.

● Most email clients (programs such as Outlook and Gmail) have built-in spam filters that will recognize unwanted messages and divert them into a junk folder. You can configure the filter to "learn" what you consider to be spam as you use the email client, or to block or permit certain senders.

● Avoid publishing your email address on websites—spammers "trawl" the Internet for email addresses. Be careful who you give your email address to; don't needlessly copy (cc) your emails to many recipients; if you need to send out multiple copies of an email, use blind copy (bcc) instead to mask the other recipients' addresses.

● Delete spam emails without opening them. Look out for bad spelling in email headers, suspicious sender addresses, or emails sent at odd hours—these are all signs of possible spam. If you do open a spam mail, never reply to it or click on any ads, pictures, or links it may contain—it will only confirm that yours is a live email address.

● If you receive an unexpected email purporting to come from your bank, credit card company, or other supplier, be very wary. If the email asks you to respond by clicking on a link, don't do it! Instead, contact the bank or other organization yourself by calling their authenticated telephone number, or by navigating independently to their official website.

● Consider setting up a second email address—it's free from Google, Yahoo, and many other providers. Keep one address for your personal correspondence and another for your online transactions.

● Report repeated spam to your Internet service provider (ISP)—they should be able to block it.

Deleting spam emails without opening them is the safest way to deal with a cluttered inbox.

How can I keep my kids safe online?
Be alert and use software filters

The Internet is an amazing learning resource, but it is also full of unsuitable material that is all too easy to access, deliberately or accidentally. Children and teenagers are often more computer-literate than adults, so keeping them away from this material is a challenge, but not one you should ignore.

● Talk regularly to your children about their use of the Internet and make them aware of the dangers. An open dialogue with a caring adult is the most effective tool in keeping them safe online.

● Place the children's computer in a living area, not in their bedrooms. Make sure the screen is visible as you go about your daily business.

● Don't allow the use of Wi-Fi enabled devices (such as tablets and phones) in bedrooms.

● Set up standard (not administrator) accounts for the children (see page 78). Use the parental controls that come with your operating system. These can be configured to limit the programs accessible to each user, set time limits on computer use, and restrict access to certain types of websites. To set up parental controls in Windows, go to **Control Panel ▶ User Accounts and Family Safety ▶ Set Up Parental Controls (or family safety) for Any User**. Using Mac OS X, navigate to **System Preferences ▶ Users & Groups** and fcheck enable parental controls.

● Try a proprietary web-protection program—there are many available to download, some of which are free.

Can I trust my details to a website?
Look out for the signs of a fake site

Never enter any personal details, usernames, or passwords into a form on any website unless you're absolutely sure that you can trust the site and that it is authentic.

● Take precautions when you visit any website that requires you to log in with your details. Enter its web address (called a URL) carefully into the browser. Don't enter a website from a link provided in an email or other site—it may take you to a phony site designed to replicate the original and steal your login details.

● After you arrive at the website, check and recheck the spelling of the URL in the address bar. It should exactly match what you typed into the browser. Does the website look and feel authentic? Look for a postal address, telephone number, and email address—all signs that a website is likely to be genuine.

• If you are carrying out any kind of transaction on a website, check that the letters https:// appear at the start of the address. The "s" that appears after the letters "http" indicates that your connection to the website is encrypted. An address that begins with just http:// is not nearly so secure.

I keep forgetting my password
Use poetry and song to make it stick

Passwords control your access to the online world—you need them to access email accounts, online banks, and much more. You should never write your passwords down on paper or store them on your computer, so how do you choose and remember a secure password?

• A good password should have at least seven characters—the more the better. It should contain upper and lower case letters and numbers, and ideally other characters, such as punctuation marks. It should not be a recognizable word, contain any readily available information about yourself (your birth date, for example), or use any predictable patterns, such as QWERTY or 1234.

• It's much easier to remember a phrase than a random assemblage of characters, so one technique for generating memorable passwords is to take the first letter of each word from the lines of a favorite song or poem. For example, the first two lines of the poem *Kubla Khan* by Samuel Taylor Coleridge are:

> *In Xanadu did Kubla Khan*
> *A stately pleasure-dome decree:*

This produces an unguessable password that reads IXdKKAsp-dd:

• You shouldn't use the same password for more than one account. Try appending the name of the service to your password to create a unique string of characters for each account. For example, the password to your Facebook account could become IXdKKAsp-dd:fb or IXdKKAsp-dd:face

• Change your password regularly—simply choose a different poem or song as the "key."

• Never share your password with anyone or send it by email, which is not secure.

• Consider using a password manager. This is a program or web-based service that will safely store passwords and even create strong and unique passwords for multiple accounts: all you need to do is remember one master password. If you forget this, however, you're likely to lose access to all your accounts!

Don't carry out any type of financial transaction on a website unless the address in the browser begins with https:// or displays a padlock symbol.

BROADBAND AND WI-FI

At the center of most home broadband setups is the router. The router receives data that arrives through the broadband connection, deciphers it and delivers it to your computer, tablet, or other connected devices, usually via localized radio signals or Wi-Fi. It's usual for all these functions to be combined in one box that plugs into your home phone socket.

I can't connect to the Internet

Check your phone line

Fixing your computer's connection to the Internet can be a complex job, because the problem may lie with your Internet service provider (ISP), your phone line, your router, your computer, or the way that these components "talk" to one another. If your connection is suddenly interrupted, take the following steps before seeking technical help.
● First, check that your phone line is working—can you still make regular calls? If not, contact your phone company to report a fault.

Check that your computer is on the network

● Your computer (or tablet or phone) can sometimes drop off your wireless network for no apparent reason. Check that you are connected to your Wi-Fi system, not another one (belonging to your neighbors, for example). Try restarting the computer and the router—this will often reestablish the link.

Read your router's indicator lights

Take a close look at the router. It will usually have a number of lights on its face that indicate the status of its connections. The power light should be illuminated: if not, make sure it is plugged in securely to a live electrical outlet. Check that the cable is firmly inserted at both ends.
● One of the lights on the router will be labelled "DSL" or "ADSL" (see box, left). This should be steadily lit. If it is flashing or not illuminated, the router is not connected to a broadband service. Make sure that the router is plugged into your home's main phone socket, or modem via an Ethernet cable. Try disconnecting any other devices from your phone line (such as phone extensions, digital TV and set-top boxes, if you have them), then switch off the router. Wait for 2 minutes, then switch it back on again—this is often sufficient to reset the connection.
● The light on your router labeled "Internet" should be steadily lit or flashing. If it is off, and the DSL light is on, it means that you cannot

connect to the Internet even though you have broadband. Restart the router as described above: if this doesn't work, contact your ISP.

- The light labeled Wi-Fi should be on solidly or flashing; if not, this indicates that the Wi-Fi signal is not functioning properly. Try restarting as above. If this doesn't work, you may need to change some settings on your router.

My connection has become very slow
Ration your Internet use

Routers allow multiple computers, tablets and phones to connect to the Internet simultaneously through one broadband line. The more devices that use the line, the slower each individual connection becomes—especially when users are downloading big music or video files, or playing online games.

- The best solution is to upgrade to a faster connection by buying extra bandwidth from your Internet provider.
- Depending on where you live, upgrading to a faster connection may not be possible. If that's the case, you could have another phone line installed at home and add another DSL connection on the new phone line, though this is a costly option.
- A simple solution is to ration your family's Internet use, spreading it more evenly over time. Avoid streaming movies if there's an option to download them. Start your download just before you go to sleep—the movie will be ready to view the next day. Have a family meeting and agree on time slots for individuals to use the Internet—for example, limit online gaming to a certain hour and viewing catch-up TV to another.

My Wi-Fi signal doesn't reach every room
Move your base station and reduce interference

If you cannot connect your laptop or tablet to your home Wi-Fi network in some rooms of the house, or if your Wi-Fi connection regularly drops off, relocating the Wi-Fi base station may help. The base station needs to be connected to both your home's phone socket and a power source, so this may not be possible.

- Site the base station upstairs or high up on a piece of furniture. Keep it away from possible sources of radio interference, such as cordless phones, microwaves, and halogen bulbs.
- Change the radio channel on which your Wi-Fi operates to avoid interference from your neighbors' Wi-Fi network. You can do this through your router's interface.

JARGON BUSTER

Bandwidth
The amount of data that can be carried on a connection in a given amount of time is called bandwidth. It is usually expressed in terms of Mb of data per second. DSL connections can range from as little as 1Mb per second to more than 95Mb if you're lucky enough to have a fiber-optic, rather than a conventional wire-based, connection to your home.

Wireless routers work best when positioned high on a shelf for a better signal.

2
Home
Works

PIPES AND PLUMBING

HEATING, COOLING,
AND VENTILATION

POWER AND LIGHTING

DOORS AND WINDOWS

HOME SECURITY

PIPES AND PLUMBING

The combination of pipes, tanks, and valves that makes up a plumbing system is the arterial network of your home. And like the human body, it can suffer from wear, blockages, and cold. Most problems develop slowly and can be fixed with a little know-how, but others can cause a sudden failure and a big spill of water. Prevention is better than cure, but a level head and an understanding of your system will minimize damage if a catastrophe occurs.

WATER EMERGENCIES

A little forward planning pays huge dividends in case of a major water leak. Get familiar with the location of the stopcock in your home so that you can find it in an emergency. Consider how you'd access the water tank and locate the stop valves on the hot and cold water tanks so that you could shut them off quickly.

My floor's under water
Move fast to minimize flood disruption

Turn off the electricity supply to your house at the fuse box or electric panel before trying to find the source of the leak.
● Close the main stopcock, shut the stop taps from the hot and cold storage tanks and open the taps on your bath, sink, and basin to drain all the water from the system quickly.
● Collect the water in buckets until you can stop the flow and scoop water off the floor with a dustpan or mop. Put down old towels and sheets to absorb any standing water and so prevent damage to flooring materials. Lift carpets and floor coverings if possible and spread them out to dry.

The water's dripping from above
Save your bulging ceiling from collapse

If your ceiling is bowed by the weight of water above, push a screwdriver into the ceiling to let the water drain out. Have a bucket or two handy to catch the water.

WHAT YOU CAN FIX YOURSELF

Most homes have direct water systems where all faucets and tanks are fed directly from the water main. Common problems, such as dripping faucets and overflows, blocked sinks, and toilets that don't flush properly are jobs you can usually tackle yourself.

DIRECT WATER SYSTEM

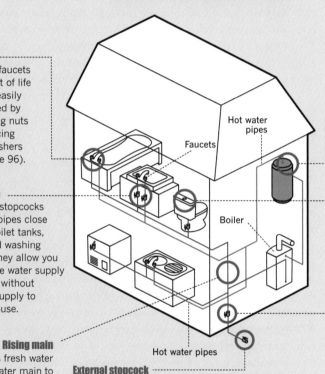

Faucets
Leaking faucets are a fact of life but are easily addressed by tightening nuts or replacing worn washers (see page 96).

Service valve
These small stopcocks are fitted in pipes close to faucets, toilet tanks, showers, and washing machines. They allow you to turn off the water supply to the fitting without cutting the supply to the whole house.

Rising main
This pipe carries fresh water from the water main to various parts of the house. Branches usually go to the cold faucet in the kitchen and the cold water tank in the attic. The rising main can be a site of condensation, leaks, or blockages.

Hot water pipes

Faucets

Hot water pipes

Boiler

External stopcock
Turning this tap isolates your home from the water main. It is typically found near the border of your property with the street, beneath a metal or plastic plate, or adjacent to a water meter (see page 90).

Hot water heater
This insulated tank is where water is heated and stored. Noisy cylinders in your boiler can sometimes be cured (see page 123).

Fill valves
Present in toilet tanks, fill valves allow water to flow in when the tank is emptied and stop the flow when the water reaches a given level. They can be adjusted to stop overflow (see page 111).

Main stopcock
This tap—usually in the kitchen, cellar, or under the stairs—shuts off the water to the house. Keeping the tap in good order lets you stop the flow fast in an emergency (see page 90).

Help—the stopcock won't turn
Ease the stopcock or head for the external tap

With water leaking onto your kitchen floor, you rush to stem the flow at the stopcock, only to find that it has seized open.
● If the leak is manageable, try spraying a little WD-40 or easing oil onto the spindle of the stopcock. Leave it to soak in for a few minutes, then gently ease the tap back and forth. This may be enough to free the stopcock.
● Don't use a wrench to force the stopcock open—it could snap, leaving you in a worse situation.
● Shut off the water before it even enters your home using the external stopcock. In many properties, this tap is below ground level and is accessed through a small hatch outside your home. The stopcock can be closed using a long-handled "key," which can be bought from any hardware shop. If you don't have a key, reach down to close the tap by hand; wear thick rubber gloves to do so.

Water is leaking from a joint
Tighten up and seal a compression joint

Plumbers often join two pipes together using a brass compression fitting (see left). This consists of a brass body with a nut at either end. The nuts are tapered, and when tightened will compress a ring of copper, or "olive," against the outside of the pipe to form a watertight seal.
● Try tightening the nuts slightly. Hold the body of the joint with a clamp and turn the nuts clockwise using an adjustable wrench. Take care not to overtighten.
● If this doesn't work and the joint still leaks, you'll need to shut off the water supply using a service valve or by turning off the main stopcock (see page 89). Undo the nuts to reveal the olives, which will be pressed against the exposed ends of the two pipes. Wipe their surfaces clean and wrap the olives with one or two layers of PTFE tape to seal any small gaps. PTFE tape is a low-friction tape that can be bought for very little from a plumbing supply or DIY store. Replace the nuts and restore the water supply.

Fix a leaky soldered joint

Soldered joints are harder to fix permanently, but you can make a temporary repair by wrapping the joint with self-amalgamating tape. This is a black tape that has no glued side, but which bonds to itself when stretched and overlapped. This fix may not be strong enough to stop the flow from pipes under pressure from the water main.

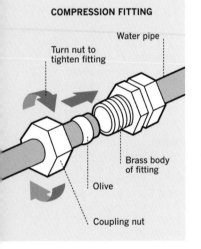

COMPRESSION FITTING

Water pipe

Turn nut to tighten fitting

Brass body of fitting

Olive

Coupling nut

The nuts in a compression joint have tapered threads, so when you tighten the nut, you compress the copper olive against the pipe to form a watertight seal.

Water is leaking from a split pipe
Stop the flow with a temporary patch

Freezing conditions can cause pipes to split open, giving you a problem when temperatures rise and the ice melts. You can make a temporary repair with a home-made clamp—it'll keep you dry until the plumber arrives.

Time needed **10 minutes** You will need **a sharp knife, two garden hose clips, a length of hosepipe or inner tube, steel wool, screwdriver**

1 Turn off the water supply using a service valve or by turning off the main stopcock (see page 89). Empty the pipe of any remaining water by opening the tap or appliance that it feeds.

2 Using a sharp knife, cut a length of inner tube, garden hose, or old washing machine hose—the more flexible the better (see below, left). It must be long enough to cover the split plus at least another inch at each end.

3 Clean the pipe with steel wool to get the surface as smooth as possible.

4 Split the hose or tube lengthwise and trim it so that it can wrap at least three-quarters of the way around the pipe (see below, center).

5 Secure the patch over the split with two hose clips, one either side of the damaged area (see below, right). Tighten the clips with a screwdriver and turn the water back on to test.

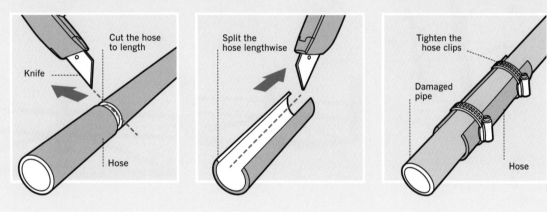

Cut the hose to length · Knife · Hose

Split the hose lengthwise

Tighten the hose clips · Damaged pipe · Hose

My tap water has turned a strange color
Diagnose the problem, and deal with it

Work on the water main or treatment plants in your area can sometimes affect the appearance and smell of your water supply.
- If the water looks cloudy, fill a glass and let it stand for a few minutes. If it turns clear, and stays clear if stirred, the cloudiness is almost certainly caused by air bubbles and the water is safe to drink.
- If the water is red or brown and contains some fine sediment, it's probably the result of iron particles dislodged by work in your area. Use a coffee filter to strain water for drinking, but avoid running dishwashers or other hot water appliances until the water runs clear again.
- If the water smells strange or you have any doubts about its safety, contact your water supplier for information.

My pipes have frozen
Thaw your system safely

Has your house been empty for a while in cold weather? If so, frozen pipes may be the cause of your lack of water. First, find the frozen area.

● If none of your taps work, the ice is likely to be on the rising main adjacent to an external wall. Look for signs of freezing (ice on the exterior of a pipe) and feel along its length for exceptionally cold sections.

● Close the main stopcock and fully open any taps near the frozen section of pipe. Use a hot-water bottle or a hair dryer to gently warm the suspect pipe. Don't use any type of extreme heat, such as a heat gun—the steam created could make the pipe explode!

There's no water

Identify problems with your water supply

If water isn't coming out of the cold tap at the kitchen sink, there's
a problem with your main supply.

● Check that someone hasn't turned off the stopcock. Ask neighbors
if their water is on—the supply may be off for maintenance.

● Are puddles forming in your front garden? The supply pipe between
your house and the stopcock in the street may have burst. Call your
water supplier immediately.

● Have temperatures been exceptionally low recently? If so, your
rising main may have frozen (see previous page).

Make it last IN THE COLD

Beat the freeze by lagging vulnerable pipes—those outdoors
and in exposed areas—using foam insulation.

In cold conditions, run water through outdoor pipes once a day
to prevent ice formation.

When leaving a house unoccupied, set the central heating to come
on for half an hour twice a day. Even leaving a light on in an
unheated room can prevent ice formation in pipes.

Exercise your stopcock by turning it to and fro a few times every
couple of weeks. This will keep it from seizing up. Don't have the
stopcock open all the way—reserve a quarter-turn of movement
to give you some wiggle room if it does get stuck.

FAUCETS AND SINKS

Faucets come in many shapes and sizes, but most work in essentially the same way. Turning the head of the faucet causes a threaded spindle to turn and rise up through the "head" of the faucet. At the base of the spindle is a round rubber washer that presses against the "seat" of the faucet, sealing or opening the hole through which water enters the faucet. Washers will deteriorate and faucets can stiffen and discolor, and sink waste can get blocked and smelly, but most of these problems have a quick and easy solution.

I can't turn the faucet on
Try lubricant and some gentle persuasion

If the faucet handle won't turn, the moving parts within may have corroded and seized.
- Apply some WD-40 or penetrating oil around the spindle—where it rises out of the body. Leave to soak for 2–3 hours. Some faucets have a handle that covers the spindle, so you'll need to remove it to access the spindle (see page 96).
- If you can't turn the faucet by hand, use an adjustable wrench to turn the handle. Wrap a cloth around the handle before tightening the wrench around it, and use as little force as possible.

I can't turn the faucet off
Open up and let the water do the work

If your faucet dribbles or drips when turned off, the washer isn't pressing down firmly enough on the seat of the faucet. A piece of debris, such as a fragment of lime, may be trapped beneath the washer.
- Open the faucet fully—fast-flowing water may dislodge the object. If this doesn't work, you'll need to dismantle the faucet and change the washer (see page 96).

My faucet spits at me
Unclog the aerator

Many modern faucets are fitted with an aerator that gives water a "champagne bubble" effect. The aerator is a fine-mesh screen that screws onto the mouth of the faucet. Try unscrewing the aerator and removing any lime or mineral deposits (see right). Reattach the clear screen—the water flow should now be far more regular.

I can't remove that lime
Treat your faucet to a lemon or vinegar bath

Mineral deposits in hard water can build up on faucet spouts to form a ring of lime. Left alone this can get rock hard and impossible to remove with normal cleaning products. Try the natural way, instead.

● Cut a lemon in half, stick it on the spout and leave it overnight. If the lemon won't stay put, hold it in place with plastic wrap.

● Pour some vinegar (distilled white vinegar is best) into a plastic cup or yogurt container. Secure the container to the faucet with plastic wrap so the vinegar covers the lime ring. Leave overnight and see the difference in the morning.

● Soak a cotton towel in either vinegar or lemon juice and apply overnight to the body of the faucet to remove lime stains here, too.

DESCALE YOUR FAUCET THE NATURAL WAY—IT'S CHEAP, SAFE, AND EFFECTIVE

That dripping faucet is driving me mad
Change the washer or cartridge

Not only is a dripping faucet quite annoying, it can discolor your sink and waste tens of gallons of water every day. The remedy is simple—changing the faucet's washer or cartridge. What you need to do depends on the type of faucet design (see below). In traditional designs, turning the head of the faucet turns a spindle, which presses a rubber washer against the bottom, or seat, of the faucet to control water flow. More modern faucets switch the water from off to on with just a quarter-turn. They use ceramic plates mounted in a cartridge to control the flow.

Time needed **10 minutes**
You will need **Phillips-head and flat-head screwdrivers, adjustable wrench, cloth, replacement washer, or ceramic cartridge**

1 Turn off the water supply to the faucet by shutting off its service valve. If there isn't one, drain the system (see page 89). Open the faucet to drain any remaining water, and put the plug in the sink to catch any small parts that fall from the faucet during the repair.

2 Pry off the top decorative cover of the faucet with a small flat-head screwdriver. Remove the screw that holds the handle onto the spindle. Rising spindle faucets have a metal shroud over the headgear; unscrew this using an adjustable wrench. Wrap a cloth around the metal shroud to prevent scratching its surface.

3 You'll now see an exposed nut. In quarter-turn faucets, this secures the cartridge that holds the ceramic disks. In conventional faucets, this is the headgear nut. Holding the spout of the faucet firmly in one hand, use an adjustable wrench to loosen the nut. It turns counterclockwise.

4 Remove the headgear/cartridge. If you have a quarter-turn faucet, take the whole unit to your local plumber's merchant and buy a replacement. Make sure you specify whether it is for your hot or cold faucet—the cartridges are left- and right- handed. If you have a faucet with a rubber washer, you'll see the washer at the end of the spindle; it usually just pushes on, but is sometimes secured by a small nut. Undo the nut or simply pry off the washer, then fit a new one (take the old one to a plumber's merchant or hardware store if you're unsure of the size to buy). If you don't have a spare handy and the washer looks intact with no cracks, turn it over for an immediate fix.

5 Reassemble the faucet and turn on the water supply. Don't worry if you hear a spluttering as trapped air makes its way through the pipe—it's normal.

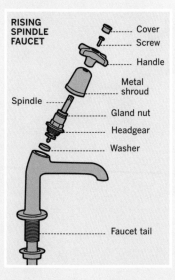

In this older style of faucet, turning the spindle causes the washer to move up and down.

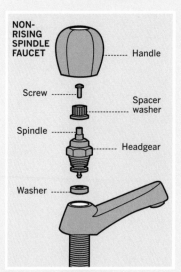

This more compact faucet also uses a rubber washer, though the spindle and handle do not rise when turned.

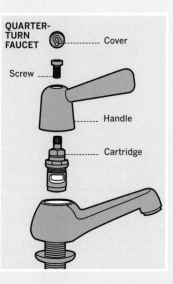

These faucets are increasingly common. They rely on ceramic discs within a cartridge to control water flow.

The drips are keeping me awake
Wick it away for a good night's sleep

You may be staying with friends or at a hotel where you can't silence the dripping faucet with a wrench.
● Wrap a piece of string (or cotton or dental floss) around the faucet so that it trails into the sink or bathtub. Position it so the drips run silently down the string and drain away.
● Turn off the service valve beneath the basin if you can get to it.

Water escapes from the top of the faucet
Block the leak with PTFE tape

Water emerging from the headgear when you run the faucet can be stopped easily. The method depends of the type of faucet (see left).
● Rising spindle faucets are made waterproof by packing around the spindle. This is kept in place by a small nut—the gland nut—at the top of the headgear. Try tightening this nut with an adjustable wrench. If it doesn't work, turn off the water and unscrew the gland nut. Make new packing by wrapping PTFE tape (see page 90) around the spindle and pack it into the gland with a screwdriver. Replace and tighten the nut and turn on the water.
● Non-rising spindle faucets and quarter-turn faucets have no gland packing or gland nut, but use one or more rubber O-rings to stop water leaking from the top of the faucet. You'll need to remove the headgear/cartridge to access the O-rings. Take the worn rings to your plumber's merchant; buy and fit replacements.

Make it last FAUCETS

Turning the faucet off too tightly will quickly wear out the washer and strain other moving parts. Get into the habit of turning it just enough to shut off the flow.

When you visit the plumber's merchant to buy a replacement washer or O-ring, always buy a spare, and store it in an envelope marked with the location of the faucet. Over the years, you'll save lots of trips to the store.

My flow has become a dribble
Clear out the faucet body to get it gushing

Over time, the easy flow of water from a faucet may slow to a frustrating dribble. This happens because sediment, lime fragments, and even worn bits of washer can accumulate inside the body of the faucet. This tends to happen more often in hot than cold faucets.
● Shut off the water supply and remove the faucet headgear or cartridge (see page 96). Tightly roll up an old cloth and ram it into the open body of the faucet, then pull it out, dragging it out along with any sediment. Rinse out the faucet body with a jug of hot water. Repeat a few times; reassemble the faucet and reconnect the water.

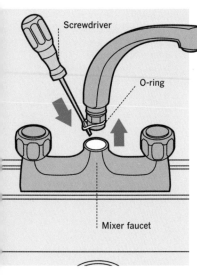

To remove an O-ring, first take off the spout and use a small flat-head screwdriver to lever off the O-ring from the base of the spout.

The spout of my kitchen mixer faucet is leaking
Replace the O-rings in two minutes

The swivelling spout of a mixer faucet contains a rubber O-ring that stops water from leaking out where the spout enters the faucet body. Over time, these rings wear and let water past. Fortunately, you don't need to turn off the water at the water main before making a repair.
● Turn off the hot and cold faucets of the mixer. Remove the spout. It is usually held in place by a small retaining screw, often inconveniently located at the back of the faucet.
● Lift the spout out and pry off the O-rings with a screwdriver (see left). Buy replacement O-rings from your plumbing supplies shop. Before fitting the new rings, coat them with a little petroleum jelly—it will make them easier to slide onto the spout.
● Replace the retaining screw, turn on the faucet, and check for leaks.

There's a rotten smell from the drain
Fizz it clean

It's easy to banish the bad smell with some household basics.
● Pour one cup of white vinegar into the drain, followed by two crumbled effervescent antacid tablets. Leave the mix until it's stopped fizzing, then pour down plenty of hot water.

The sink drains too slowly
Plunge away to bust the blockage

Sink wastes inevitably get clogged with debris, often glued together with soap, fat, or detergent residue.
● First, remove any obvious blockages in the grid on the waste outlet.

Try to "burp" out the air in the plunger cap before you start plunging; if a lot of air is trapped in the cap, you'll be compressing the air rather than removing the blockage as you plunge.

- Shine a flashlight down the waste pipe and use long tweezers, or a hook improvised from a length of wire, to remove debris.
- If this doesn't work, use a plunger—an essential tool to have in your home. It works by forcing air and water down the waste pipe to push the blockage free.
- Run an inch of water into the bottom of the sink—enough to cover the waste outlet.
- Block up the overflow hole at the top of your sink with a damp cloth to keep the waste airtight.
- Put the plunger over the waste outlet, then push it down firmly and quickly several times. You may feel the pressure ease as the blockage shifts.
- Lift off the plunger and the water should drain away—if it doesn't shift, plunge again—the blockage may just have moved down the pipe a little.

I don't have a plunger
Improvise an effective tool from a tennis ball

If all else fails, take an old tennis ball and cut it horizontally one third of the way up. Place the open end of the larger part over the blocked sink-waste pipe. Block the overflow pipe with a damp cloth as above and run a small amount of water into the basin to make a seal with the edge of the ball. Place the ball of your hand over the tennis ball and plunge down hard and fast.

WARNING

Always try to unblock pipes by mechanical means—a plunger, wire, or by taking the waste apart—before trying chemical solutions. Drain cleaning chemicals are not only expensive, but can cause burns. Always wear rubber gloves and guard against splashes when using these compounds.

BATHTUBS AND SHOWERS

Bathrooms are built from tough materials designed to take punishment and repel grime. Making a habit of rinsing the bath or shower immediately after use will slow down the buildup of dirt and soap scum. But leaks, stains, and blockages are a fact of life in this hard-working environment.

My bath is stained
Remove the stains without scratching

Stains in enamel, porcelain, plastic, or ceramic bathtubs can be difficult to remove without harsh abrasives, which risk damaging the surface.
● Remove water stains with a 50:50 solution of water and white vinegar. Soak a paper towel in the solution and lay it on the stain overnight to maximize contact between the two.
● To treat a rust stain, cover it in table salt, then place the cut side of half a lemon on top. Leave overnight while the chemical reaction draws the stain into the salt. Alternatively, wet the rust stain and rub gently with a wet pumice stone. Don't try this latter method on a plastic bath: you'll scratch the surface.

There's a trail of lime on the bathtub
Rub or dissolve it away

Lime—the residue of minerals left behind as water dries—is a common problem in hard-water areas. Rock-hard deposits often form down the side of a bath beneath a dripping faucet. These lime trails can be removed, but be prepared to carry out a few treatments before you solve the problem completely.
● If you have an enameled bathtub, rub the lime with 0000-grade steel wool dipped in denatured alcohol. Be sure to remove all traces of the steel wool afterward, or the steel fibers could cause rust stains.
● Soak a paper towel in white vinegar and place it over the stain; leave it to work overnight.

The bottom of the shower fills up with water
Purge the waste trap

If you find that you're splashing around in the bottom of your shower, it is likely that the plughole, trap, or waste pipe has become blocked. The usual culprit is hair, which catches soap and dirt to form a solid lump. But before you buy a special drain cleaner, try using hair-removing (depilatory) cream to dissolve the blockage.

● Use a plastic cup to bale out any water in the bottom of the shower into a bowl or bucket.

● Lift off the cover of the plughole—it usually pulls straight up—and, wearing a pair of rubber gloves, scoop out any debris that you can reach from the trap. Pour a pan of boiling water down the hole.

● If the water still doesn't flow away, try squirting hair-removing (depilatory) cream or gel into the opening; leave for a few hours and wash through with boiling water. The cream breaks down the structure of hair and will eat through the blockage.

Water leaks around the sides of my bath
Renew the silicone seal

A seal between the sides of your bath and the surrounding tiles is essential to stop water leakage. Silicone sealant is commonly used to make the seal as it's flexible and long-lasting, but over time it will degrade and come away.

Time needed **1 hour**
You will need **craft knife, small towel, silicone sealant and sealant gun, spoon**

1 Use a sharp knife to cut through any old sealant to remove as much as possible. Take care not to scratch the surface of the bath or tiles.

2 Remove any stubborn sealant by rubbing it vigorously with a dry towel or use a proprietary sealant remover, which you can buy from a DIY store.

3 Before you start filling the gap with fresh sealant, run a bath of cold water. If you apply sealant around an empty bath, the weight of the water when you subsequently fill and use the bath will tend to break the seal.

4 Fill any gaps over 8 mm wide with twisted plastic wrap or newspaper before injecting the silicone sealant.

5 Use your knife to cut the nozzle on the sealant tube at a 45-degree angle so that the opening is slightly wider than the gap you're trying to fill. Fit the tube in a sealant gun, and squeeze the trigger until you see sealant at the end of the nozzle.

6 Hold the tube at an angle to the gap and pull it slowly and evenly along the gap, squeezing out just enough sealant to fill the gap without squeezing round the sides (see far left). Try to complete the joint in one smooth movement for best results.

7 If the bead of silicone sealant is uneven, smooth it with a dedicated caulking tool (see left), which is available from DIY stores. If you don't have a caulking tool, the rounded end of a teaspoon will do the job just as well. Don't delay as the silicone starts to set quite quickly. Don't use your finger to smooth the joint—this tends to make the silicone very thin at the edges and so more likely to peel off in use.

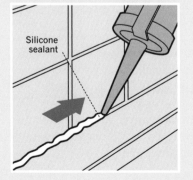

Silicone sealant

Caulking tool

I've scratched my bathtub
Sand and polish to a shining finish

You can polish out light scratches on enamel, plastic, and fiberglass baths, sinks, and shower trays.

● Rub the area with 1500-grit wet-and-dry paper—use it wet. Then gently polish with a cloth that has been dabbed in a little cutting compound. These products (such as T-Cut) are designed primarily to remove scratches from car bodies, but work equally well on bathroom fittings.

● Deeper scratches, cracks, and chips in baths and showers made from plastic, resin, enamel, or porcelain can be repaired, but require special fillers (available from DIY stores) and resins rather than household adhesives.

The grout around my tiles is grimy
Mix your own grout cleaner

The quickest way to brighten up a tired old bathroom is to freshen the grout, which typically becomes discolored long before the tiles themselves start to age.

● In a plastic cup, mix one-quarter thick bleach to three-quarters baking soda into a smooth paste.

● Use an old toothbrush to apply the paste to the stained grout and leave the mixture to work for an hour or so before rinsing it off with a cloth and hot water. Be sure to wear rubber gloves throughout.

The shower door won't close
Repair sagging hinges and tighten up door catches

The hinges of a glass shower door can loosen over time, making the door sag. Water may leak from uneven gaps between the glass panels or—in the worst case—the door may crack when someone tries to force it closed.

● Get a helper to hold the door and support its weight. Use a screwdriver to loosen the screws that secure the hinges to the frame, lift the door slightly to realign it, then tighten the screws again.

● Many shower doors are held shut by spring-loaded nylon roller catches on the door frame. If the catch no longer holds the door, you can extend its length using a flat-head screwdriver. Insert this into the slot on the face of the roller; push down and turn counterclockwise for a longer catch (or clockwise for a shorter one).

IF YOUR SHOWER HEAD IS STUCK TIGHT, BAG IT UP WITH VINEGAR TO RESTORE THE FLOW

My shower is no more than a dribble
Clear the lime to get it flowing

Lime builds up quickly in a shower head, especially in hard-water areas, and it will soon block the small jets in the head, reducing your once-powerful shower to a slow dribble. To compound the problem, shower heads affected by lime buildup can be hard to remove for cleaning without damaging their supports.

● To solve this problem, half-fill a watertight freezer bag with white vinegar. Use electrical tape to secure the bag around the shower head, ensuring the head is completely immersed in the liquid. Leave to soak overnight, then rinse with warm water.

DRAINS AND GUTTERS

When a plunger won't remove a blockage in a drain, there's a pool of dirty water on the patio, or your gutters overflow, you need to brace yourself for an unglamorous job. Clearing drains and gutters may be dirty, but it could also save you lots of money in professionals' service fees.

My sink won't drain
Clear the trap

If you've tried plunging the sink and the blockage won't shift, the waste pipe is probably clogged with soap scum, hair, oil, or kitchen waste. Waste-water outlet pipes are fitted with a U-shaped bend that traps water in the lower part of the "U" and so prevents smelly sewer gas from entering the building. It's here that you're likely to find the source of your blockage.

● Remove the U-bend, or trap. It will most likely be connected to the sink and to the waste outlet pipe with large plastic nuts. Loosen the nuts by hand, or turn them with a pair of locking pliers if they prove stubborn. Place a bowl beneath the trap to catch the water it contains.

● Take care not to lose any rubber seals or washers when removing the trap. Make note of where they go so you can reassemble the trap.

● Once you have removed the trap, clean it thoroughly with a bottle brush, detergent, and hot water. Shine a flashlight down the open end of the waste pipe and remove any further debris using a hook made from a length of coat-hanger wire.

● Smear petroleum jelly on the threads of the trap nuts before reassembly—this will make them easier to remove next time.

It's still not draining away
Remove a blockage further down the pipe

If the drain is only partly blocked, try a chemical unblocking agent. These caustic chemicals are toxic and can cause skin irritation, so always follow the instructions on the bottle and be sure to wear rubber gloves, cover any exposed skin, and ventilate the room adequately. Avoid caustic chemicals if the drain is completely blocked—they can damage plumbing fixtures.

● Buy or borrow a plumber's snake. This is a length of coiled wire that can be wound into the drain—even round corners and bends—to push through a blockage further down the pipe.

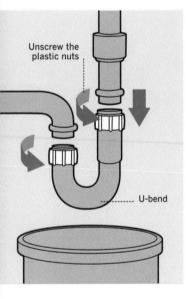

Unscrew the
plastic nuts

U-bend

Unscrew the plastic nuts to free the U-bend. They can often be freed by hand, but if you need to use a pair of locking pliers, wrap masking tape around the nuts to protect them from damage. Catch any water from the U-bend in a bowl or bucket.

Water is rising over the manhole cover
Stop the flooding and clear the drain

Water flooding onto your patio or drive is a sign of a blockage in the pipe between your home and the main sewer or septic tank. You can get to the drain via a manhole or inspection chamber, which is usually situated just outside the house. The chamber, which may be made of plastic, precast concrete, or bricks (especially in older properties), is usually covered with a heavy iron or concrete cover.

• Stop anyone using the toilet or running faucets so that the water levels don't rise any more.

• Scrape away any dirt or corrosion from around the edge of the cover with a screwdriver. The cover has eyes or handles that enable it to be lifted out of position; thread rope through the handles to give you more leverage, and lever the edge of the cover up with a spade or chisel. Lift the cover away from the chamber.

• The chamber will most likely be full of waste water. Poke the bottom of the chamber with a length of wood or a mop handle; you should be able to see or feel the opening of the waste pipe. Prod as deep into the pipe as possible to dislodge any objects that may have got stuck there.

• If you can see the opening of the waste pipe, try a pressure washer. Insert the nozzle of the pressure washer into the pipe and press the trigger—this may shift a blockage that isn't too far along the pipe.

• If the blockage persists, you'll need to reach further down the drain with a set of rods (see page 106).

There's waste water on the patio
Clear up the mess safely

Any pools of water from the main drain are a health hazard and should be dealt with as soon as possible.

• Sweep the water into a flower bed if you can. If the water is deep, use a bucket or dustpan to scoop it up.

• Clean the patio with a pressure washer or broom and detergent, rinsing well afterward. Don't let children or pets onto the patio until it is clean and dry.

<aside>
WARNING

Don't leave an open manhole cover unattended and never climb into a manhole or tank—you could quickly be overcome by toxic fumes.

• Always wear protective clothing when dealing with drains—thick rubber gloves, overalls, goggles, and a face mask are recommended.
</aside>

Water is still backed up
Use a set of drain rods to clear your drain

A set of drain rods bought from a DIY store is an excellent investment. It will pay for itself many times over the first time it is used. It consists of several stiff but flexible plastic or metal rods that can be connected end to end and passed along a drain to remove any blockages. Rod sets come with one or more "heads": some resemble plungers that can push through blockages or scrape the inside surfaces of the pipe; others are corkscrew-shaped and ideal for tearing at tree roots that may have invaded the drain.

Time needed **30 minutes** You will need **set of drain rods, protective clothing, gloves, goggles, hose**

1 Put on your protective clothing before removing the cover from the manhole or inspection hatch. Locate the end of the waste pipe (see page 105).

2 Screw two or three drain rods to the head. Push the rods into the blocked pipe. Rotate the rods clockwise to help them move forward; don't turn them counterclockwise because they may unscrew and get stuck in the drain themselves.

3 If you don't feel any resistance, add more rods until you hit the blockage. Push and twist the rods to shift it; when the blockage moves, the water trapped in the manhole will run away freely.

4 Pull the rods back. Keep turning them clockwise as you withdraw. Clean the rods—and especially their threaded end-connectors—with water from a hose or pressure washer. Allow to dry before storing for the next use.

5 Flush your toilet and run plenty of hot water down sinks to help wash away any debris remaining in the drain.

WARNING

Follow the safety guidelines for working on a ladder (see page 13). Never be tempted to overreach—your belt buckle should always be within the uprights of the ladder and both feet should remain on the same rung as you work.

My gutter is leaking
Stop the spill to protect your home

Leaks in gutters and downspouts will cause stains on walls or paths, or damp spots in the house. Don't wait for this to happen—catch these problems before the bills mount up by taking a good look at your gutters during a downpour and noting the source of the spill.

● Most leaks happen where two lengths of gutter join together. Lengths of plastic guttering are linked by short sections called union brackets, which contain rubber gaskets. These brackets can become dislodged—for example, by a window cleaner's ladder. Dismantle the joint by squeezing the sides of the gutter until it comes away from the union bracket. Clean away any dirt from the end of the gutter section and the union joint using a nail brush and detergent. Before reassembling the joint, wipe the gaskets and joint surfaces with some liquid soap—it'll help everything snap back into place.

● You can make a temporary repair to a metal gutter by cleaning the joint surfaces, then taping over the joint with duct tape, or by painting over the joint with silicone paint formulated for gutter repair.

● Fill holes in corroded metal gutters and downspouts using a fiberglass-based car body filler, available from auto stores. Rub down the corroded area with sandpaper and remove any loose flakes of metal, then follow the instructions provided with the body filler.

Make it last DRAINS AND GUTTERS

When it comes to drains, prevention is always better than cure. Following
a few simple tips will keep your waste pipes flowing freely.

Buy a sink strainer for your kitchen sink and use it when washing the dishes:
it will trap food particles before they reach your drains. Avoid pouring oily liquids
down the drain—they can solidify and cause a blockage. Instead, pour them into
a sealable plastic bag and dispose of them in the household trash.

Use boiling water to melt built-up grease. Once every two weeks, pour a pan of
boiling water down the drain. Once a month, pour half a cup of baking soda down
the drain, then slowly add a cup of white vinegar. Leave for a few minutes, then
flush away with boiling water.

Clear the gutters regularly; don't let leaf litter accumulate. Shape a section
of chicken wire into a ball and push it into the top of a downspout. This will
prevent leaves and other debris from entering and blocking the downspout.

Keep ladders away from gutters because the force of a ladder leaning up against
the plastic can easily crack it or break the seal between adjacent sections of gutter.

TOILETS

Toilets differ in how they deliver water into the toilet bowl from the tank, and how waste is expelled from the bowl. Older toilets use a siphon system to pull water into the bowl and again out into the waste pipe. Modern models use less water per flush; they have a valve unit that lets water flow into the bowl under the influence of gravity and use the flow of the water to carry waste into the soil pipe.

The toilet is completely blocked
Start with some gentle persuasion

WARNING

When dealing with a blocked toilet, gear up with rubber gloves, old clothes, and eye protection to mitigate against splashes. Cover the floor with newspapers to catch any spills.

It's always untimely and sometimes embarrassing, but a blocked toilet needn't mean a call to the plumber. Take these steps to get everything flowing freely again.
- Don't keep flushing. Adding water will most probably just cause an overflow.
- Poke the blockage to break it up; use a toilet brush or straightened coat hanger.
- Add some dishwashing liquid to the bowl and pour in very hot water to help loosen the blockage. Alternatively, add a box of baking soda followed by a bottle of white vinegar. Allow the mixture to fizz for a while. Then add around 5 quarts of hot water to keep the chemicals active—this should help to move the blockage.

It's still backed up
Clear the bowl with a pressure blast

Use a yogurt carton to bail out as much water as possible from the toilet bowl. Put the waste water into a bucket for disposal later.
- Fill a 2-liter plastic bottle with hot water. Keeping your thumb over its opening for as long as possible, push the top of the bottle down hard into the bottom of the toilet to make a tight fit. Hold the bottle firmly in place with both hands and squeeze it hard so the hot water shoots out into the toilet drain to dislodge the clog.
- Try a conventional plunger. Make a tight seal around the hole and pump the plunger to force pressurized water around the bend.
- Connect a hose to your water supply and push its end as far as possible down the toilet. Turn on the hose to blast the blockage out.
- Discard the waste water in the bucket by pouring it down the working toilet; disinfect the bucket and the plunger.

WHAT YOU CAN FIX YOURSELF

Most toilets are "gravity flush" models. The working parts inside the tank vary in design, but they all work the same: When you push the handle, the flapper raises and allows water to gush into the bowl. As the water level in the tank drops, the float lowers. That opens the fill valve, which allows fresh water to fill the tank.

Fill valve
Older fill valves rely on a float ball, while most newer models have a smaller float next to the valve itself. Replacing a fill valve requires some experience, but making adjustments to raise or lower the water level is easy (see page 111).

Toilet seat
Tightening the nuts securing the toilet seat will help it sit squarely on the rim of the bowl (see page 114).

Toilet bowl
This should be connected securely to the floor to prevent movement and possible leakage (see page 110).

Flush valve
This central unit controls the release of water into the bowl. It can be lifted out to clean the large washer at its base if water dribbles into the bowl between flushes (see page 111).

Flapper
When lifted, the flapper opens the flush valve and creates the flush. Flappers often go bad within just a few years but are easy to replace (see pages 111–112).

The toilet bowl overfills with water
Cure a partial blockage

If the water level in the toilet rises high after flushing, but slowly returns to its normal level, the waste pipe is partially blocked.
● Try quickly emptying a full bucket of hot water into the bowl—the sudden additional pressure may push through the obstruction.
● If this doesn't work, try the tips for a blocked toilet (see opposite). A downstairs toilet that you cannot clear may indicate a blockage in the soil pipe or main drain (see page 105).

Water drips from the toilet onto the floor
Find the fault and prevent condensation

It's often hard to pinpoint the source of a leak from a toilet. It may be no more than condensation, which forms on the cold toilet tank in a steamy bathroom and drips onto the floor.

● First, carry out a quick diagnostic check. Lift off the lid of the tank and add a couple of drops of food coloring to the water within. Flush the toilet and then wipe the outside of the tank, bowl, and soil pipe with a paper towel.

● If the paper is clear, the problem may be condensation. Switch off the water to the tank by turning the stop valve on the pipe. Flush the toilet, then line the empty tank with a layer of insulating material, such as an old foam camping mat or even some bubble wrap. The insulation will help prevent condensation.

● Avoid condensation problems by keeping your bathroom warm when in use, and by opening a window or fitting an exhaust fan to clear moist air after you have used the bath or shower.

Water leaks from under the toilet
Tighten the toilet bolts

A toilet is connected to a large waste pipe in the floor. The connection is sealed by a wax ring. Over time, that seal may fail and leaks may appear around the base of the toilet. This is a serious issue and should be dealt with immediately. Left uncorrected, the sewage leak can do major damage to the floor and to the ceiling below.

● Pry off the two plastic caps (one on each side of the toilet's base) that cover the bolts that fasten the toilet to the floor. Tightening the nuts may reseal the connection.

● Also tighten the nuts if your toilet isn't securely fastened to the floor. A toilet that rocks, even slightly, will eventually damage the seal and leaks will appear below the toilet.

● Often, the bolts are corroded and impossible to tighten. In that case, call in a professional plumber before serious damage is done.

Water leaks from the tank
Check the inlet pipe and link between tank and bowl

First check the joint between your domestic water supply and the tank. Wrap a sheet of dry paper towel around the joint (which is usually a compression fitting, see page 90) and leave it for a few hours. If the paper is wet when you return, there is probably a leak in the joint. Try tightening this using a clamp and wrench (see page 90). Apply minimal pressure—a fraction of a turn will often do the job.

• If this doesn't work, the problem may lie in the foam washer (sometimes called a spud washer) between the tank and the bowl. While it is possible to replace this washer yourself, this fix requires the complete removal of the tank from its fittings and so is best left to a plumber.

Water constantly runs into the bowl
Adjust the fill valve

Your toilet's fill valve does a simple job—it allows water into the tank after you flush, and shuts it off when the tank is full. Its action is controlled by a float—either a traditional ball-shaped float or an internal float within the fill valve (more likely in modern toilet units). If too much water enters the tank, it runs over the top of the overflow valve and into the bowl—wasting water and causing a noise nuisance.

• If you have a modern toilet, you can adjust the maximum height of the float by pinching the contacts on either side of the inlet valve and moving the float up or down to the correct level. If you have a traditional toilet with a ball-shaped float on the end of an arm, you'll find a small screw to set the maximum float height on the end of the arm.

Replace the flapper

The flapper is simply a soft rubber disk that opens and closes the flush valve. Flappers have a limited lifespan and are the most common cause of toilet trouble. When a flapper leaks, it allows water to constantly trickle down to the bowl. That in turn causes the fill valve to stay partially open. The result is a toilet that runs constantly.

• To avoid wasting water while you make repairs, turn off the water supply to the tank. If the water supply valve won't close, don't worry; you can still perform the following steps.

• Lift the flapper and run your finger around the opening where the flapper contacts the flush valve. The opening should feel smooth. If the opening feels rough, that's due to mineral buildup which is preventing the flapper from sealing completely. Gently clean the opening with a scouring pad.

• *Don't* scrape off mineral deposits with any type of sharp metal tool. If you damage the opening, the entire flush valve will have to be replaced.

• If the opening feels smooth, the flapper is at fault. Remove it and take it to the store. Choose a flapper that closely matches the old one.

• Install the new flapper, allow the tank to fill and flush the toilet. You may have to adjust and readjust the slack in the chain before the toilet flushes properly (see page 112).

Replace the fill valve

A fill valve allows water to refill the tank after a flush. A malfunctioning fill valve won't close completely, so water constantly flows into the tank. The result is the same as with a failing flapper: constant noise and wasted water.

● Look at the overflow tube. If water has reached the top of the tube and is trickling into the tube, the fill valve is at fault.

● Even if you have an old float-ball style fill valve, you can replace it with newer style.

● Replacing a fill valve isn't difficult, but requires some plumbing know-how. If you don't have experience making plumbing connections, leave this task to a pro.

Remove the old flapper from the ears of the overflow tube and detach the chain from the handle arm.

Attach the new flapper to the overflow tube and hook the chain to the handle arm. Leave 1/2-inch of slack in the chain.

The flush doesn't empty the bowl
Raise the tank's water level

A flush should clear the bowl the first time. If it doesn't, there may be a blockage in the waterway inside the bowl, or the tank mechanism may need a quick tweak.

• First, test for a blockage in the bowl by pouring a full bucket of water into the bowl; if it flows away quickly, your problem most probably lies in the tank. If the bowl empties slowly, try unblocking the toilet (see page 109).

• When you flush the toilet, water enters the bowl through holes under the rim of the pan. If you live in a hard-water area, these may have clogged with lime. Check under the rim with a small mirror; if you can see a buildup of lime around the holes, pick off any large pieces with a bent coat hanger and treat the area liberally with a descaling agent.

• There may not be enough water in the tank to generate an efficient flush. Raise the level of the float on the fill valve to allow more water into the tank for more flushing power (see page 112). Don't raise the level too high, otherwise water will overflow and leak constantly into the bowl.

My toilet is really noisy
Tame the refill to stop the racket

Toilet tanks refill quickly in readiness for the next flush. The rapid inflow of water can cause noise problems if you have a toilet that uses a traditional ball float valve to control the water inlet. Don't let your toilet keep you awake at night—silence the tank with some easy fixes.

• Take the lid off the tank and locate the float valve; it is at the end of the float arm, at the opposite end to the float itself. Flush the toilet and note where the water flows into the tank. It usually enters through a flexible plastic fill tube that prevents the water from splashing; however, it's not uncommon for this tube to slip off. If the tube is loose (and probably lying on the bottom of the tank), simply reattach it to the valve. If the tube is missing, buy and fit a new tube to the fill valve, so that the water doesn't splash into the tank.

• If the tank fills quickly, the float may bounce on the ripples, causing water hammer—a shock wave in the water pipe as the flow is rapidly turned on and off. Fitting a fill tube may prevent this, too.

My toilet uses too much water
Cut your water bills with a plastic bottle

Modern low-flow toilets use 1 1/2 gallons or less per flush—around half the volume used by traditional toilets. This adds up to considerable savings over the year if your water supply is metered. If you have an older toilet and want to save water, simply fill a plastic soda bottle with water and place it in the tank. Make sure the container doesn't interfere with the flush mechanism; don't be tempted to put a brick in the tank—it may crumble and damage the toilet's valves.

When I flush the toilet, my shower runs hot
Reduce the water flow

The speed at which a toilet tank refills means that it draws a lot of cold water. If your home has an old plumbing system, you may find that faucets and showers will run hot as the toilet refills.
● Try turning the service valve on the incoming water pipe to a partly closed position to reduce the rate at which the tank refills.
● Reduce the volume of water that your tank draws by placing a water-filled plastic bottle into the tank.

I can smell sewage when I flush
Keep your toilet airtight

Water will evaporate from the toilet bowl, and if you don't use your toilet for a while, the water level may drop enough to let air from the drains past the trap. Simply flush the toilet once a week to prevent this from occurring.
● Check the vent pipe, or soil stack, outside your building. A nesting bird or debris may be blocking the exit at the top, causing foul air to back up.
● Pour a cup of bleach into the tank's overflow tube (the one that pokes above the water surface in the tank) and flush the toilet.

My toilet seat is loose
Tighten up to stop the wobbles

Check that the wing nuts securing the seat to the toilet unit are tight. They may be corroded; if so, soak them with penetrating oil before tightening them. Replace any corroded metal washers on the seat fittings with new stainless-steel washers and retighten the nuts.

My toilet is very stained
Make it sparkle like new with some chemical warfare

Ceramic toilets are highly resilient and even bad stains on neglected toilets can be removed with household chemicals. The cleaning methods outlined below need time to work, so make a sign saying: "Do not flush" and leave it on the bathroom door or toilet seat as a reminder. Put on some rubber gloves, then use a paper cup or yogurt carton to bale out the water in the toilet bowl. Soak up what remains with an old cloth. Now you're ready to try one of the following treatments.

● Pour in cheap cola up to the toilet's waterline. Leave overnight, then flush it away to leave a clean ceramic surface.

● Pour in three cups of white vinegar, then add half a cup of baking soda. Leave to fizz overnight, then flush and scrub with a toilet brush to loosen any remaining limescale.

● Try a mixture of a quarter of a cup of salt and one cup of baking soda, followed by one-and-a-half cups of white vinegar. Leave to fizz for 10 minutes, then scrub with a brush or plastic scourer—the abrasive salt will shift stubborn lime.

● For really stubborn stains and tough lime, pour a bottle (16 oz.) of hydrochloric acid into the bowl (see box, right). Close the lid of the toilet and leave for 4 hours before flushing.

WARNING

Hydrochloric acid is a strong acid and highly corrosive. Always wear rubber gloves when handling it and keep your skin covered. Open windows, keep ventilation fans running, and avoid breathing in chemical fumes.

NOISY PIPES

Water rushing through the pipes in your home will always make some noise, but loud bangs, knocks, shrieks, and whistles are usually a symptom of a problem that may have a simple solution—as long as you can get access. Unfortunately, the pipe work to blame is often hidden under floorboards or buried in walls.

Creaking noises are coming from the floor
Clip down or wrap the pipes

Bangs and creaks under the floorboards are usually caused by the expansion and contraction of hot water and central heating pipes. The noise means that the pipes are rubbing on joists or floorboards and have no packing around them to allow them to slide quietly. Stopping the noise isn't hard, but tracking down its source requires floorboards to be lifted—not an easy job and one for which you may need professional help.

● Pipes usually run across joists in notches under the floorboards. They should ideally be clipped down on every joist with a special plastic joist clip that holds the pipe securely but allows for silent expansion and contraction. If the pipe isn't clipped, wrap it with felt, strips of old towel or foam pipe insulation where it crosses the joists—this will allow the pipe to expand quietly.

There's a knocking when I turn off the faucet
Reduce the flow to silence the hammer

A banging sound that reverberates through the pipes when a faucet is turned off or a washing machine stops filling is caused by water hammer (see page 113). Sharp knocking noises also result from unsupported pipes that move when under pressure, banging against adjacent walls or floors.

● Partly close the service valves on water pipes supplying the sink or appliance near the source of the sound. This will ease the pressure of water when the tap or valve is closed, so reducing the noisy shock waves at the cost of increasing the appliance's fill time a little.

● An unsupported pipe will move as water flows within. Make sure all the pipes in your home are clipped securely to the wall or floor at least every 6 feet or so. Plastic pipe clips are inexpensive and available from all home improvement stores.

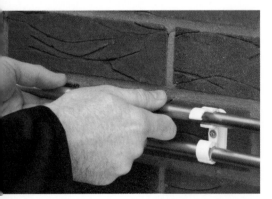

Movement of pipes can be reduced by using inexpensive clips to secure exposed pipes to walls and floors.

The faucet plays a tune
Add a new washer

A washer loses flexibility as it ages, and water rushing past makes it flutter like a reed in a clarinet, creating a tuneful noise. To silence a singing faucet, simply replace the washer (see page 96).

My hot faucet makes a spluttering noise
Replace the washer and purge the airlock

If your hot-water splutters and delivers water as a series of gushes rather than an even flow, you probably have an airlock in your system.
● Turn on all the faucets in the house to see if the additional flow moves the air bubble.
● If you have separate faucets in the kitchen, attach a length of hose between the cold and hot ones and secure it tightly into position using hose clamps. Fully open both faucets—the pressure from the cold will push water back up the hot pipe into the overflow tank, hopefully shifting the airlock in the process.
● Alternatively, if you have a mixer faucet in the kitchen, put on a rubber glove and hold your hand tightly over the spout. Open the hot and cold levers.

You can sometimes shift a stubborn air pocket in your plumbing system simply by running all the faucets in your home at once.

HEATING, COOLING, AND VENTILATION

Systems for controlling the temperature in your home range from the decidedly low-tech—such as using blinds on south-facing windows in summer and ensuring good ventilation—to sophisticated, electronically regulated heating and air conditioning units. Most common problems don't need a professional fix—a little effort and good maintenance will help you stay comfortable year-round.

HEATING

Problems with heating often come to light in the autumn when you turn on your system, or light your wood-burning stove, after a summer break. Most can be avoided by running the heating for an hour or two every few weeks through the summer. And many, such as cold radiators or stuck pumps, can be addressed in minutes.

My radiators are stone cold
Check your central heating boiler and pump

If all of your radiators are cold, read on. If only some are cold, see page 120.

● First, check that the heating programmer and thermostat are set correctly. Make sure that both Hot Water and Central Heating are enabled on the programmer—you can usually override its timer to activate both instantly; the button that does this is often labeled "Continuous." Set the thermostat to a higher temperature.

● Confirm that the boiler is working. Does it feel warm? Most boilers have a dial that allows you to control the temperature of the water as it leaves the boiler for the hot-water tank and heating system. Make sure this is turned up. If the boiler won't fire up, call a technician.

● The problem may lie in the electric pump that circulates hot water through the radiators; this can get clogged with particles, especially if inactive over the summer. Can you hear it working or feel it vibrating? If not, remove the screw on the face of the pump with a large flat-head screwdriver. Beneath, there is a smaller slot that connects directly to the pump's movement; insert a screwdriver into the slot and turn it gently each way—this is often enough to get the pump moving.

The top of the radiator is cold

Bleed air from the radiator

A radiator that is hot at the bottom and cold at the top needs bleeding to remove any trapped air. You'll need a bleed key, which can be bought from any hardware store (though some valves can be opened with a screwdriver).

- Switch the heating off at the control panel and locate the radiator's bleed valve; it is usually at one end of the top of the radiator.
- Insert the key and turn the valve counterclockwise until you hear air hissing out; as the air is released, the radiator fills with water.
- Be ready with an old cloth to soak up any water that spurts out of the valve once the radiator is full. Close the valve the moment this happens; don't overtighten it, or you'll have trouble opening it next time you need to bleed the radiator.
- If your radiator is cool at the bottom and hot at the top, it is probably clogged up with sludge. It will need to be removed and flushed clean—a job for a plumber.

BLEED YOUR RADIATORS REGULARLY FOR AN EFFICIENT HEATING SYSTEM

Some radiators are still cold
Adjust the radiator valves

Hot water from your boiler is pumped to the radiators via a flow pipe; cooler water is fed back from the radiator to the boiler through a return pipe. Each radiator has two valves: a handwheel valve, or thermostatic radiator valve (TRV), allows you to control the flow of hot water into the radiator, while at the other end, a lockshield valve controls the flow of water out of the radiator.

● Open the handwheel valve fully by turning it counterclockwise, or if you have a TRV, turn it to its highest (warmest) setting. Open the lockshield valve fully. To do this, remove its protective cap and turn it counterclockwise with an adjustable wrench.

Balance the system

Do the radiators closest to your boiler get much hotter than those farthest away? If so, you need to balance the system to even out flow differences. This requires a little time but is not difficult and will make your house feel much more comfortable. Start with the heating system cold and switched off, and make sure you have bled all the radiators (see page 119).

● Fully open the handwheels, or TRVs, on all the radiators.
● Turn on the heating system and make a note of which radiator starts to warm up first, which is the last to heat up, and the approximate order of those in-between. Recruiting a few people to help with this task makes it a lot easier.
● Fully open the lockshield valve on the radiator that warms up last (see left).
● Next, work on the radiator that warms up first. Fully close its lockshield valve, then open it up by just a quarter turn.
● Adjust the lockshield valves of the radiators in-between proportionally—wider open for the cooler radiators.
● Open or close the lockshield valves of the radiators until they are all around the same temperature. It helps to use an inexpensive radiator thermometer to do this (you can buy one from your plumbing supply store), but you can get reasonable results by judging relative temperatures with your hand. Remember to take the temperature of each unit in the same place—at the top right of each radiator, for example. This adjustment is a process of trial and error, so be patient!
● When the temperatures of the radiators are as consistent as possible, adjust the TRVs to set the desired temperature in each room. Your system is now balanced.

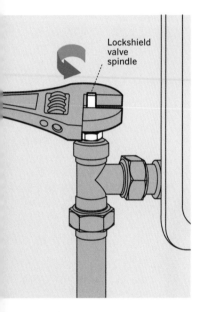

Lockshield valve spindle

To balance your heating system, you'll need to adjust the lockshield valves on your radiators. To do this, first remove the protective cap from the lockshield valve. Then use an adjustable wrench to grip and turn its spindle. Turn clockwise to close the valve, counterclockwise to open it.

My radiator has sprung a leak
Tighten up the joints

Over time, steel radiators will rust from the inside. You can make your system last longer by adding corrosion inhibitor (see page 124), but a leak doesn't necessarily call for a replacement radiator.
● If the leak is coming from a joint around a TRV, or lockshield valve, grip the valve itself with a pair of pliers, then use an adjustable wrench to tighten the nuts connecting the valve to the radiator or the pipe.
● If small amounts of water are seeping from the body of a radiator or from joints in the heating system, try adding proprietary leak-repair fluid to the system, just as you would add corrosion inhibitor (see page 124). The fluid will coagulate in the hole, sealing it; this will not work with larger holes, when a call to the plumber is the only option.

The thermostatic valve won't turn
Bust the lime to get it moving

Thermostatic radiator valves (TRVs) are prone to sticking closed, so avoid turning them off completely (to 0) during regular use—set them to 1 or 2 to reduce the heat output.
● If the valve sticks, remove its plastic head from the brass body by unscrewing the ridged ring or nut. This will reveal a small pin that controls the valve. Normally, this can be pressed down against a spring and will spring back up when released. If the valve is stuck, try freeing it with a gentle tap from a hammer; don't pull the pin out as it can be hard to refit.

Go gently when you tighten up the nuts on the radiator's valves. It may only require a fraction of a turn to make everything watertight again.

The boiler doesn't fire up
Ensure that the power is on and the settings are correct

Run through this checklist of fixes before calling the emergency heating engineer.

● Are the boiler and its controls receiving power? The boiler is often on a separate electrical circuit, so check its circuit breaker or fuse if it won't fire up but the power is on elsewhere in the house.

● Is the programmer working? Can you see the digital display, if it has one, or any on/off lights?

● Turn up your room thermostat(s)—the boiler won't fire up if heat is not needed.

● Does the boiler have fuel? If your home runs on oil or bottled or bulk gas, check that you haven't run out.

● Is the pilot light still lit? If it has blown out, follow the boiler instructions to relight it.

● If you have a condensing boiler, check that the condensate pipe hasn't frozen as this will cause the boiler to shut down (see below).

● If your home has multiple room thermostats, each controlling a zone of the house, your system is probably fitted with zone valves. These valves—square boxes attached to pipes near your boiler— regulate the flow of hot water to the various zones in your home and can sometimes get stuck in a closed position—if they won't operate, the boiler may not fire up. They usually have a lever for manual operation so try moving it and seeing if the boiler starts. Call a professional to check and replace the faulty valve.

My condensing boiler won't come on
Thaw the condensate pipe

Condensing boilers are a highly efficient way of heating your home and producing hot water. That's because they extract energy directly from burning fuel, but also by condensing the steam created during combustion. As this steam condenses, water must be removed via a drain tube—the condensate pipe—to the outdoors. Unfortunately, the design of the boiler makes this tube vulnerable to the cold: if it freezes, the boiler will shut down.

● If the boiler has a digital display, it may be showing a fault code, or a warning light might be illuminated. Double-check the instruction manual to see if this indicates a freeze.

● Is there a gurgling sound coming from the boiler or the condensate pipe? That's a good indication that the pipe is frozen up.

● The pipe is most likely to be frozen at the end where it runs into

the drain, or perhaps where it turns a corner—you should be able to feel the frozen section with your hand.
● To defrost the pipe, pour hot, but not boiling, water over it until the ice blockage has thawed.
● To stop the pipe from freezing in the future, wrap the pipe with burlap, old towels, Bubble Wrap, or foam pipe insulation.

My boiler is noisy
Check the temperature control and fill the system

Boilers can emit loud and worrying rattles and bangs—but they don't mean it's about to explode. There are a few things you can do before you call in the professionals.
● The water in the boiler may be getting too hot and turning to steam. Try turning the temperature control on the boiler down a bit and see if the noises stop.
● If you have an open-vented heating system (see box, opposite), check that there's water in the expansion tank in the attic—if there's no water in the tank, turn off the boiler immediately. Has the float valve on the expansion tank corroded and stuck in the closed position? If you cannot free it, call a professional to install a new valve. If you have a sealed heating system (see box, opposite), check that its pressure gauge shows the desired reading (consult the user's manual for your model); if not, refill the system to the correct pressure following the manufacturer's instructions. If the problem persists, call a professional to check for leaks in the system.
● Loud bangs are often caused by lime in the boiler. With time, lime can get baked onto the sides of the boiler causing localized hot spots where steam bubbles form and make knocking or "kettling" sounds as they rise. This can be reduced by adding specialist descaling fluid to the system; you can buy this from a home improvement store or plumbing supply store. Be sure to follow the manufacturer's instructions. You will need to add the fluid, run the system to allow the fluid to work, then drain, flush, and refill the system. This is a job best left to a professional unless you are very confident with plumbing projects.

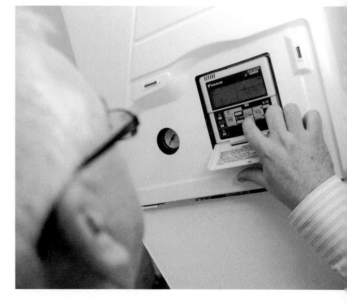

The control unit on the boiler regulates the temperature at which water leaves the boiler. Set it to around 176° in the winter and down to around 149° in the summer.

Make it last
CENTRAL HEATING

Add liquid inhibitor to your heating system every 4–5 years. The steel components of a system will corrode over time, depositing particles of rust inside your boiler, pipes, and radiators. Adding inhibitor will slow this reaction, making your heating more efficient and extending its life. The type and amount of inhibitor needed, and how it is applied, will depend on the type and age of your system; consult a professional for advice.

Be sure to have your boiler serviced annually (right)—you'll prolong its working life and save money on fuel.

My wood-burning stove is hard to light
Build an effective fire

Cast-iron or steel wood-burning stoves are an efficient way to heat your home and help create a cozy atmosphere. However, they can be tricky to light, especially if you're used to the push-button convenience of central heating.

● To light your wood-burning stove, empty and clean the ashpan and grate. Fully open the bottom air vent and the flue damper at the top (if present). The flue damper's job is to restrict the flow of the hot gases leaving the burner.

● Scrunch 5–10 sheets of dry newspaper into loose balls and place these at the bottom of the grate. Top these with pieces of dry kindling, no more than 1 cm in diameter—enough to form a small tepee, which will allow the logs to fall inward as they burn and feed the fire—and then lay a couple of larger pieces of wood on top.

● Light the newspaper and close the door almost fully—a small opening will help the fire burn hotter. Don't leave the fire unattended while the door is open. Add larger logs only when the fire is burning very strongly. Don't overfill the firebox—the flames and air should be able to reach every piece of wood. Fully close the door and refer to your owner's manual for the best way to control air flow in the burner using the main air vent and damper controls.

● Only burn well-seasoned wood that has been air-dried for at least one year. Burning damp wood is not only inefficient, but can release large amounts of soot and tar, which can lead to chimney fires. Buy your wood from a reputable retailer.

There's a burning smell coming from my electric heater
Give it a winter clean

Over the summer, dust will accumulate on electric elements. When the heater is switched on during cool weather, the dust will burn.

● To clean it, unplug the heater and use the brush attachment of your vacuum cleaner on low power, a soft lint-free cloth, or a small paintbrush to dust any visible heater elements and clean the grille. If possible, open the casing of the heater and do the same on the exposed elements. Lift the fan (if present) off its spindle and brush its surfaces clear of dust before reassembling the heater.

● If you have a radiant heater (one with a silica-glass element, which resembles a glass tube), lightly dust the glass frequently with a clean lint-free cloth. Avoid touching the glass with your fingers because the oils present on human skin will burn onto the tube.

My storage heater is cold
Get the best from its settings

Electrical thermal storage heaters use cheaper "low-rate" electricity available at night to heat up bricks or ceramic blocks. This stored heat is then released when needed during the day. Most have two controls, usually on the top right-hand side of the heater.

● The input or charge control regulates how much heat is stored. In very cold weather, set this dial to maximum. When it's milder, choose a lower setting. The output, room temperature, or boost control, regulates how much "stored" heat is released by opening and closing the flap behind the front grille. The higher the number you choose, the more the flap opens, giving more heat.

● For the most economical heating, leave the output control on a low setting during the day (when you are out). Turn it up in the evening or when you come home if you need more heat. Turn it back to the lowest setting before you go to bed.

COOLING AND VENTILATION

Air conditioning allows you to control your environment at the click of a button. However, there are also many other ways to keep cool at lower cost. Insulation, energy-efficient windows and doors, shading, and good ventilation can help regulate interior conditions with a minimum of energy input.

The air conditioner doesn't cool the room
Unblock the drain and clean the filters

If the air conditioner shows no signs of life, check that its thermostat is set to "Cool" and that it hasn't blown its fuse or tripped its circuit breaker. You'll need to call a repair service if this doesn't work—one of the fans may have blown.

● If the air conditioner is functioning poorly and is dripping water onto the floor, its drain pan may be overflowing due to a blockage in the drain pipe. This pipe usually protrudes outside the building or into a nearby floor drain. Try unblocking the pipe by prodding a length of stiff wire into its opening or attach a garden hose to the open end of the pipe and blast a pulse of water into the pipe to clear any buildup.

● Clogged filters block airflow through the air conditioner and will significantly reduce its efficiency. Disconnect the machine from its

Remove the filters from the front of the air conditioner—they are usually held in place by plastic tabs.

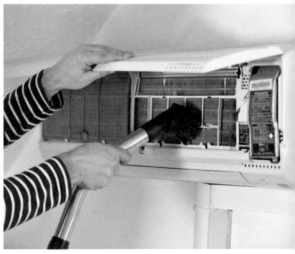

Gently pass a vacuum cleaner with brush attachment over the evaporator coils beneath the filters to remove any dust.

power supply, unscrew the grill facing into the room and take out the filters. Some models require filters to be replaced (consult your user's manual), but others can be cleaned in warm soapy water. Allow them to dry completely before replacing them. You should clean or renew filters every two months in the summer.

● With the filters removed, use your vacuum cleaner's brush attachment to clear any dust off the evaporator coils.

● Check the outdoor side of the air conditioner. Using a soft brush, clean leaves or other debris from the fins on the condenser coils and trim back any foliage to improve airflow around the machine.

● When your air conditioner is on, be sure to close your home's windows and outside doors.

● If your air conditioner is still not cooling the room, the system probably needs to be recharged with refrigerant—you'll need a professional to carry out this work and to check the unit for refrigerant leaks.

My air conditioner smells musty
Disinfect the drain tray

A bad smell from an air conditioner suggests that water is collecting within and becoming stagnant. This can become a breeding ground for bacteria so it is more than just an inconvenience.

● Unplug the air conditioner and, following the instructions in your user's manual, remove the cover. Inside, you'll see a metal drip tray—its job is to catch any condensation that forms within the machine. Thoroughly sponge over the surface of this tray with household disinfectant.

● Clean or replace the filters (see opposite).

My desk fan is making a racket
Bend the blades back into shape

An upright desk-type fan that rattles as it spins probably has misaligned blades.

● Unplug the fan, then unclip the front section of the grille—you may need to undo some small screws around the edge. The hub where the fan blades are mounted will normally just pull or twist off, or it may be held in place with a clip.

● Remove the hub and blade assembly and lay it down on a table: each blade should touch the surface at the same point along its length. Use your hands, or a pair of pliers if the metal is too stiff, to bend any misaligned blades back into position, then reassemble the fan.

Take the cover off your fan from time to time and give the blades a good dusting to help keep them balanced.

My ceiling fan wobbles
Clean and tighten the blades

Ceiling fans help cool your home at little cost. However, they become inefficient when their blades are not completely balanced; even a coating of dust is enough to throw them off-kilter.

● Set up a ladder securely so that you can comfortably reach all of the fan blades. Give each blade a good clean with warm soapy water; protect the carpet or furniture beneath the fan with a plastic sheet before you start.

● Let the blades dry, then rub car wax on the upper side of each one to help prevent the dust from building up again.

● While you're on the ladder, check that all the screws holding the blades into their central mount are tight. It's important that there's no play in these screws, because once they become a little loose, the rotation of the fan will shake them out even faster. Running your fan with a wobble will put strain on the bearings inside.

● If your fan still wobbles, try juggling the positions of the blades. One pair at a time, swap adjacent blades and then try the fan at all available speeds. Be systematic, so you can be sure you have tried all the possible options. Number each blade and write down a plan: 1 to 2, 1 to 3, 1 to 4, 2 to 3, and so on.

● If the fan remains out of balance, try taping washers or small coins to the upper sides of the blades, near the tip. Experiment with different blades, different positions and more than one coin or washer until your fan runs smoothly at every speed.

My home is too hot in the summer
Cool your home passively

It pays to insulate your home. Not only does good insulation (such as fiberglass blanketing in the attic and weather strips on doors and windows) keep your home warm in winter, it will help keep it cool in the summer, too.

● On the hottest days, keep your doors and windows shut to exclude heat and humidity. Use your air conditioner, ceiling fans, and shading to keep your home cool during the warmest times of day. Avoid running heat-generating appliances, such as the dishwasher, washing machine, and dryer, until the evening.

● Ventilate your home naturally in the evening by opening windows on the side of the house facing the wind, and on the opposite side, too. Open connecting doors to create a cross-draft.

● Keep your air conditioner in the shade—it'll work more efficiently.

The sun turns my house into an oven
Block the heat

Passive shading is remarkably effective at keeping interior temperatures down in sunny climates or during heat waves.

- Close the curtains on south- and west-facing windows during the day; keep the windows closed, too.
- Consider installing white sunshades (or dense bamboo blinds) on south-facing windows, or fitting awnings that shade the windows from the outside. Alternatively, cover the window panes with energy saving-window films that reflect sunlight away.
- Plant bushes and trees to cast shadows on south-facing aspects of the house. You can achieve the same effect with trellises and rambling plants.

USING BLINDS, CURTAINS, AND AWNINGS TO BLOCK OUT THE SUN WILL HELP KEEP YOUR INTERIORS COOL

POWER AND LIGHTING

Repairs to your home's wiring and electrical systems should always be left to qualified professionals. However, there are still many steps you can take to restore power in the event of a outage, to increase energy efficiency, and to improve the safety and reliability of your home appliances.

HOME APPLIANCES

JARGON BUSTER

Panel box
The electrical panel is a box wired between your electricity meter and the electrical outlets in your home. Its job is to distribute power to subsidiary circuits, and protect these circuits from dangerous overloads. Older boxes contain fuses for this purpose, while modern ones have miniature circuit breakers (MCBs) that switch off the power if it exceeds a set value. The panel box may also contain a ground fault circuit interrupter (GFCI). This detects the leakage of electrical current that may occur if your wiring is faulty, or if someone receives an electric shock, and cuts the power immediately. A main on/off switch in the box cuts power to all circuits in the home.

Over the last 20 years, home appliances have become much more sophisticated, incorporating systems such as low-voltage lighting, underfloor heating, outdoor lighting, and powering sensitive electronics. It is not a good idea to attempt a repair yourself—find a reliable electrician to address any faults and install new fixtures. Meanwhile, get to know your system so that you can spot emerging problems before they become crises, and so that you know what to do in case of an interrupted power supply.

The power's gone off
Check your breaker panel or fuse box

Keep a small flashlight next to your electric panel for use in emergencies—it'll save you from hunting for a light in the darkness.
● When the power goes off unexpectedly, check if the whole house is affected, or just one circuit (one group of power outlets or lights). If the whole house is dark, call your neighbors to check if their supply is working—the power outage may be affecting the neighborhood, in which case you should report the problem to your electricity supplier.
● If the power went off when you turned on an appliance (a kettle or toaster, for example) or a light, turn off its switch.
● Go to the panel box. Make sure your hands are dry and that there's no water leaking on or near the box. If there is, don't touch any appliances; shut off the water supply (see page 88) and call an electrician immediately.
● It is likely that one or more of the MCB or GFCI switches is in the "Off" position; simply move them to the "On" position and check if

power is restored. If the power continues to trip off, unplug any appliances connected to the circuit and try again. Identify the appliance that is causing the power to trip by a process of elimination. Have it repaired if it is broken, or take it for recycling.

• Some high-wattage appliances, such as microwave ovens and hair dryers can cause an MCB to trip after they have been on for a while. Ideally, the circuit should be upgraded by an electrician, but in the meantime, limit the number of appliances used on that circuit or turn the appliance down to a lower power setting.

• Call an electrician if the problem isn't resolved—your wiring could be in a dangerous state.

• Fuse boxes in older homes may contain wire fuses rather than modern circuit breakers. Here, you'll need to check each fuse to see if the wire within has melted, or if the glass window of the fuse has darkened. Remove the blown fuse and replace it with a new fuse of exactly the same size and rating: if you're unsure, take the broken fuse to a hardware store or electrical supplier.

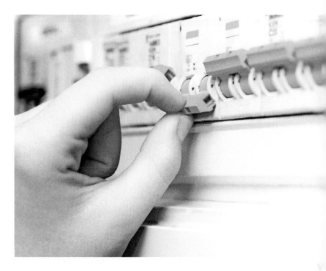

To restore power to a circuit within your home, reset the miniature circuit breaker in your breaker panel.

The plug feels hot
Sand the contacts

A hot plug on an appliance is unsafe, so don't ignore the problem. If the appliance is plugged in via a power strip (a block that turns one wall outlet into several sockets), try plugging directly into the wall socket. If the problem persists, try lightly rubbing the prongs on the plug with fine sandpaper to remove any oxidation on their metal surfaces. Next, try replacing the plug or (if possible) the entire cable that connects to the appliance. A continued problem indicates a fault within the appliance or in the wall socket—don't use either until they have been checked out by an electrician.

The socket is dead
Reset the trip switch or call an electrician

Check if the other nearby sockets are working. If not, you may have tripped a MCB or GFCI in the electrical panel (see opposite), so try switching this back on. Modern sockets may be fitted with their own, individual GFCIs on their faceplates—try pressing the "Reset" button. If your problem persists, call in a professional.

WARNING !

Even though some electrical repairs may appear simple, they may not be easy to carry out safely. Attempting to do it yourself may lead to death, injury, or fire, and leave you in breach of building laws and regulations. You should always contact a qualified electrician if in doubt.

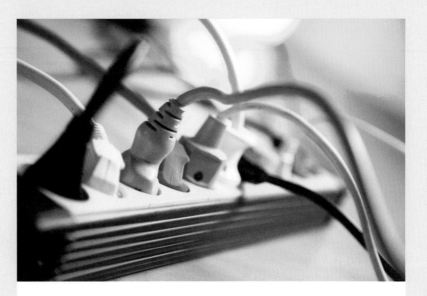

Eight ways to improve electrical safety

Faulty or aging wiring is a major cause of fires and accidents in the home, but you can take some easy steps to keep your family safe.

1 Remove plugs from sockets carefully by pulling straight back on the plug; never tug the cable.

2 Switch off electrical appliances at night unless they are designed to be left on (like refrigerators).

3 Never use power strips with appliances that have a high-power (wattage) rating, such as electric heaters, irons, and toasters. Don't plug adaptors into other adaptors. If you don't have enough sockets in your home, have more installed by a qualified electrician.

4 Dry your hands before touching electrical equipment. Never dry clothing over an electric heater.

5 Avoid running cables under carpets; run them around the edge of the room instead, securing them to the walls or baseboards with cable clips or within plastic casing.

6 Don't wrap electrical cable around any appliance (such as an iron) until it has completely cooled down.

7 Examine the cables of appliances for signs of wear, cracking or darkening of their plastic sleeves. Open the plug from time to time; make sure there are no loose strands of wire or blackening visible. Make sure the flex is gripped tightly at the base of the plug and that the correct fuse has been fitted (check the manual of the appliance for guidance). If you don't feel confident rewiring the plug or cable, get professional help.

8 Renew old wiring that may no longer be safe. Call in an electrician for advice if your home has wall-mounted switches in the bathroom; sockets mounted on baseboards; an old fuse box with a wooden back or cast-iron switches; cables coated with fabric, lead, or black rubber.

DON'T OVERLOAD A SOCKET BY PLUGGING IN TOO MANY APPLIANCES— AVOID USING POWER STRIPS IF AT ALL POSSIBLE

LIGHTING

Lighting technology has changed dramatically in the last decade with the widespread introduction of low-energy bulbs, but some common problems still have simple fixes. For example, dusting your light bulbs and fixtures with a lint-free cloth when they are turned off can boost light output by one fifth, saving your eyes and conserving energy, too.

The bulb keeps blowing

Fit a quality replacement

The lifetime of a light bulb will be shortened by poor connections, overheating, and rough handling. CFL and LED lights are replacing traditional incandescent and halogen bulbs (see box, right) because they have longer lives and use less power, so it's worth switching to these designs if you haven't done so already.

● The main reason that bulbs blow is poor manufacture—paying more for bulbs of reputable brand will save you money in the long run.

● Check that the bulbs you are using don't exceed the maximum wattage rating of the fixture. If this isn't stamped on to the fixture, use bulbs rated at 60 watt or less.

● Make sure the bulb sits tight in its fitting—a loose bulb may cause electricity to arc across the contact, causing a blowout.

● Clean the electrical contacts in the fixture. First, make absolutely sure that the power is off: turn off both the wall switch and the MCB that controls the lighting circuit within your breaker panel. Remove the bulb and rub the metal contacts on the light fixture with some sandpaper. The fixture may have a flexible metal contact at its base. Bend this up by 1/4 inch using your fingers or a flat-head screwdriver, so that it makes better contact with the bulb when it is inserted.

● If the bulb won't sit tight in the fitting, the spring loading in the fitting may have failed: call an electrician to install a new one.

● Use a clean tissue to handle halogen bulbs—grease deposits from your fingers on the glass can cause these bulbs to blow.

● Avoid switching CFL bulbs on and off too frequently—this shortens their life. For the same reason, don't use CFL bulbs in light fixtures controlled by a motion sensor.

● If you have a dimmer switch, check the packaging of the new bulb to ensure it is compatible—some CFL and LED bulbs are not.

● A fixture in which bulbs blow repeatedly could indicate a more serious wiring problem—call an electrician to investigate.

JARGON BUSTER

Incandescent bulbs These "classic" bulbs produce light when a wire filament is heated by an electric current.

Halogen bulbs These are a type of incandescent bulb that contains a small quantity of a halogen gas within the glass. They are longer-lasting and produce a brighter light than a classic bulb of the same size.

CFL bulbs Compact fluorescent light bulbs are basically fluorescent tubes that have been made in the shape of a classic bulb. They last about five times as long as classic bulbs and use around one quarter of their power.

LED bulbs These use an array of light-emitting diodes to produce light. They have very long life spans (up to 100,000 hours) and use around 80 percent less energy than classic bulbs, but are expensive to buy.

My fluorescent tube won't light
Replace and dispose of it safely

If a light doesn't come on when you throw the switch, the tube's contacts may need cleaning, or the tube may need to be replaced. Safely set up a stepladder so that you can reach the tube without overstretching (see page 13). Switch off the electrical circuit supplying the light at your panel box. Then climb the ladder and remove the cover over the fixture and pass it down carefully to a waiting helper.

● Remove the tube. Most have two prongs at each end and need a quarter-turn to line up the prongs with the slots in the sockets. Lower the tube and lightly rub the prongs at both ends with some fine sandpaper; straighten them with a pair of pliers if they appear bent. Dust the tube with a lint-free cloth and replace it in the fitting.

● If the tube still fails to light, you may need to replace it, or the problem may be with the starter—a small cylindrical component usually found beneath the tube or on the side of the fixture. It's simple to remove—just turn its body counterclockwise. Take both tube and starter to your electrical store and buy and fit exact replacements. If this doesn't restore the light, call an electrician to replace the fixture.

My lights flicker
Install a new switch or transformer

Try checking and cleaning the bulb's connections or replacing the bulb. If this doesn't work, there may be a problem with the switch, especially if you can hear a buzzing or fizzing noise when the switch is on. You'll need to call an electrician to install a new switch mechanism.

● If you use low-voltage bulbs in your ceiling fixtures, and you have replaced halogen bulbs with energy-efficient LEDs, you may observe flickering, or the new bulbs may not work at all. If so, call an electrician to replace your old transformer with an LED driver.

My chandelier is dusty
Clean it with cotton gloves

As dust settles on a chandelier, it dulls its light output and robs it of sparkle. Using a cloth to clean your chandelier can be an arduous job, so make life easier by buying a pair of white cotton gloves (available from home improvement stores). Switch off the light and remove the bulbs. Put on both gloves and moisten one with some window cleaning liquid; wipe each crystal with this glove first, then dry with your other gloved hand.

A bulb has broken in the socket

Remove it safely with a potato

Bulbs can shatter when hit accidentally, or if exposed to moisture; when this happens, it can be hard to remove their sharp broken ends from the socket.

● First ensure that the affected circuit is switched off at the breaker panel.

● Cut a medium-size potato in half. Push the cut side firmly into the remains of the bulb and turn the potato to unscrew and free the bulb. Clean the inside of the socket by rubbing it with fine-grade steel wool before inserting a new bulb.

DOORS AND WINDOWS

Doors and windows have a tough job keeping your home warm, dry, and secure through the seasonal extremes of temperature and moisture. Wear and tear, the elements, and slight movement in the walls of your house conspire to put windows and frames out of alignment, making them stiff to open and close, and opening up drafty gaps.

DOORS

Problems with doors often develop gradually as hinges age, paint finishes break down, and houses settle. A wooden door that rubs on the frame one day may soon stick shut as moisture in the air causes the wood to swell. Old hinges will wear and cause the door to sag or drop, while badly installed hinges might make the door hard to close.

The door sticks

Whack the frame to get some clearance

First, check if the door is warped (see box, right) and ensure that the hinges have been correctly installed (see page 139). If the door is straight and hung correctly, you'll need to find the high spot where the door catches the frame.

- Rub a stick of colored chalk on the edges of the door, then repeatedly open and close the door. Chalk marks on the frame will indicate the high spot.
- Find a piece of scrap wood and a hammer. Place the wood against the frame at the point where the door is sticking and give it a couple of sharp whacks with the hammer—this may be enough to shift the frame back sufficiently to accommodate the door.

Sand down the high spots

- If the door still sticks, you'll need to sand down the high point on the edge of the door. Keep the door still as you work by pushing two wooden wedges under the bottom edge, one facing in each direction. Use a power sander, or sandpaper wrapped around a wooden block, to make sure that you keep the surface flat. Sand a little deeper than is necessary to free the door to allow for a layer of paint. If you need to remove more than 1/4 inch of wood, use a plane to level out the high point.
- Paint the bare wood exposed by sanding—it'll help prevent moisture getting in and causing the wood to swell.
- If the door is sticking on the floor—for example, if you've recently laid a new, thicker carpet—you'll need to take it off its hinges to reach the bottom edge. Recruit a helper to support the weight of the door while you tap out the pins from all the hinges (see page 138). Take care to control the door's movement as you work. With the hinges removed, lift the door away, sand and paint the bottom edge as described above, then rehang the door.
- For a quick fix, try rubbing a bar of soap along the top and side edges of the door—it may help to fix sticking.

The door slams loudly

Make a cushion with a blob of silicone sealant

A door that always slams shut is simple to silence. Apply a few blobs of clear silicone sealant onto the edge of the door stop—four evenly spaced dabs will do. Allow the sealant to dry thoroughly before closing the door. The sealant remains springy after it has set, providing a cushion for the slamming door.

CHUCK IT?

A warped door is likely to stick. There's little you can do to straighten it, so you'll need to consider a replacement. Warping may be obvious from looking at the door sideways, but if in doubt, open the door and hang a plumb line from the top of the open edge. If the edge of the door deviates from the line further down, the door is probably warped.

Colored chalk rubbed on the edges of the door will quickly show the point at which the door is sticking.

Draft-proof a door over a carpeted or tiled floor by screwing on a length of brush strip.

The door's hinges are stiff

Apply some lubricant

Hinges—especially those on external doors—may rust or corrode over time.

● First, try applying some WD-40 or penetrating oil to the hinge pin—squirt it onto the top of the pin so that it runs down the shaft.

● Some hinges have removable pins. You can drive them out by aligning a nail with the bottom of the pin, then tapping gently upward with a hammer. Take the pin out of one hinge: rub it with steel wool to remove any corrosion, coat it with some light machine oil, then replace it. Now remove the next pin and repeat. Don't remove all the pins at once unless you want to take the door off.

There's a draft from my door

Stop the winter chills

It's easy to banish drafts around the sides and top of a door with some inexpensive DIY products. Rubber, foam, and plastic strips are quick to fit on doors and windows (see page 146).

● A draft from the bottom of a door requires a different approach. If the floor is even and covered with smooth vinyl or laminate, screw a flexible plastic or rubber strip to the front face of the door. This forms a seal between the door and floor. On an uneven or carpeted floor, fit a brush strip instead—it's made up of lots of nylon bristles that can pass over lumps and bumps more easily.

● Don't forget to fit a mailbox flap and a cover plate over any keyholes that run through the door.

The door won't close
Make it fit by adjusting the hinges

Badly fitted hinges are a common cause of door problems. A door that springs open and is hard to close is termed "hinge-bound." Its hinges are recessed too deeply into the door or frame; the door and frame make contact before the door is fully closed so the two parts of the hinge can't come together properly. This puts strain on the hinge and can loosen the fixing screws.

- To remedy this problem, remove the hinge screws from the top hinge, then insert one or more layers of cardboard (cut to the same size as the hinge plate) into the recess cut for the hinge plate. After you have packed out the space, screw the hinge back on; you may need to use a slightly longer screw to bite into the wood. Do this for each hinge in turn to fix the door's action. You should not need to completely remove the door.
- If the top corner of the door farthest from the hinges rubs on top of the frame as it closes, try packing out the top hinge only—this will lower the corner.
- Check that the screws used to secure the hinges sit flush with the surface of the hinge plates—if screws with too large heads have been used, the hinge won't be able to close fully.

The door sags
Tighten up the hinges

Loose hinges may make a door rub on the floor. Check to see if the screws securing the hinges are loose.

- If the screws have lost their grip on the wood, first remove them. Push one or two matchsticks, dipped in PVA glue (white school glue), into the screw holes and trim the matchsticks flush to the wood with a craft knife. Allow the glue to set before driving the screws back in— they'll now have some fresh wood to secure their grip.
- You can use the same technique to pack out screw holes on loose door handles too (see right).

The door keeps swinging open
Bend the hinge pin to keep it in place

If your door won't stay shut, but mysteriously swings open, simply remove one of the hinge pins (see opposite), lay it across a nail or screw, and tap the pin with a hammer to give it a tiny kink. Reinsert the pin, and the extra friction should prevent the door from opening.

Packing out an old screw hole with matchsticks dipped in PVA glue will give a new screw more purchase.

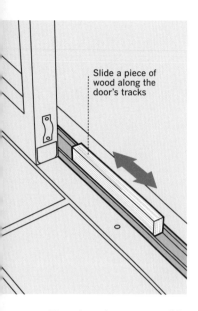

Slide a piece of wood along the door's tracks

To make a door run smoothly in its tracks, use a length of wood just wide enough to slot into the track. Slide it forcefully down the track to even out its metal sides.

The sliding door sticks
Clear the tracks and adjust the rollers

Sliding doors move on rollers that run within tracks. Heavier patio doors tend to have their rollers and track beneath the door, while lightweight internal doors or room dividers may hang from the ceiling. Try these troubleshooting tips if your doors get stuck.

● Pebbles, coins and children's toys can get wedged in the track, so first make sure it is clear.

● Look along the metal track to check if it is bent. Localized bends can be reshaped with a pair of pliers, but a larger kink in the track needs a different treatment. Find or buy a piece of wood, about 1 foot long, that just fits inside the track. Run this to and fro along the inside of the track to force the gap open just enough to let the door slide without hindrance.

● Check that the door hasn't jumped off the track. With the help of a friend, lift the door up and lower it gently back onto the track. Take care—the door may be heavier than it looks.

● Is the door scraping on the track? If so, try raising it up on its rollers. Many patio doors have adjustment screws along the edge of the door's bottom rail, sometimes hidden behind button-sized covers. Remove the covers and turn the adjustment screws beneath—usually clockwise—to raise the door.

● Clean the track with a cloth dipped in denatured alcohol. Over time it can get dirty, which will cause the rollers to slide, rather than roll, along the track. Don't lubricate the track—this can make matters worse.

Make it last DOORS

A door that won't open or close without applying force is likely to get worse—manhandling may warp its structure, bend its hinges, or break its joints.
Lubricate hinges regularly to prevent stiffness. Use a light mineral oil for interior hinges, and thicker grease for exterior doors. Don't use lubricant on doors that slide on tracks. Use powdered graphite, not oil, to keep locks working smoothly.
Tighten rattling doorknobs by loosening the grub screws that hold the doorknobs in place, then center the spindle on which they turn so that it extends equally on both sides of the door. Reposition the doorknobs and adjust the grub screws for a snug, but not binding, fit.

The garage door is jammed
Cure a stuck up-and-over door

When an up-and-over, or canopy, garage door doesn't open, it may have dropped out of its vertical guide track. This can happen when you open or close the door from one side, rather than in the middle, or try to open or close it too quickly.

● To put it back, lift the side that's in the track as high as possible while keeping the loose side low. With a bit of pushing, you should be able to pop the loose roller back into the track.

● Check that the rollers aren't worn or missing. Replacements are available from garage door specialists.

● Dirty tracks may cause the door to stick and make you pull it unevenly. Clean out the tracks with a rag soaked in denatured alcohol—take care as the metal edges can be sharp.

The garage doors drag
My side-hinged garage doors drag on the ground

Hinged garage doors are heavy and can sag over time. If the lower edge of the door drags on the ground, it will sustain damage and make a grating noise whenever it is opened and closed.

● Open the door, and push a wooden wedge beneath the edge farthest from the hinge so that the door is level. Loosen—don't remove—the screws or bolts holding the hinges to the frame and door. Tighten the screws holding the hinges in place. If the screws are loose, replace them with longer screws with the same head size, or pack out the screw holes with matchsticks (see page 139).

● For a long-term solution, buy and fit a caster to each door. These large wheels, available from DIY stores, fix to the bottom of the door and support it against the ground. Installing the casters will involve taking the doors off. Casters are usually spring-loaded to cope with uneven surfaces.

(see page 139)

WARNING

Many canopy, or up-and-over, garage doors have a large spring to provide the lifting power. The spring stores a huge amount of energy and can cause serious injury if released or removed incorrectly. Don't attempt a garage-door repair unless you know exactly what you are doing. If in any doubt, call in a professional.

WINDOWS

Modern sealed-unit vinyl windows require little maintenance, and if they crack, break, or fall out of their tracks, you'll need to call a specialist. Wooden windows, however, can be repaired and maintained with ease—you can sort out everyday problems such as cracks, poor insulation, and sticking and sagging frames to help keep your home secure, dry, and warm.

The window is stuck shut
Get it open without cracking the glass

Windows get stuck for a variety of reasons—condensation can swell the wooden elements, building settlement can skew the frame, and a rushed paint job can effectively glue the window shut. To free a stuck window, work slowly, without applying excessive force.

● For a wooden casement or sash window, run a kitchen spatula or putty knife all the way around the gap between the window and the frame. Tap the spatula or knife gently with a hammer to push it into the gap. If possible, go round the window in this way from the inside and also from the outside.

● For a casement window, wrap a cloth around a block of wood; place the block along the "opening" side of the wooden inner-frame and tap it gently with a hammer. For a sash window, insert a broad chisel beneath the window from the outside and lever gently upward.

● Don't attempt these solutions if you have a stuck vinyl window as it is likely that the locking pins have jammed; call a specialist.

CHUCK IT?

If rot has eaten through joints in a window frame, repair is rarely worthwhile, although it may be viable for expensive, period sash windows. Old single-glazed steel windows rust and are very poor insulators—replace them if possible.

I can open the window, but it's very stiff
Get it open without cracking the glass

A drop of 3-in-One oil will get window hinges moving and glazed panels sliding easily in their metal tracks. If your windows have plastic tracks, try some talcum power or a little soap instead of oil. For wooden windows, rub a candle on moving surfaces for quick lubrication. Clean out the window tracks with an old toothbrush and wipe the edges of the window to remove any old cobwebs and other debris that may interfere with the window's movement.

My window is cracked
Deal with minor damage and scratches without replacing the pane

Temporarily seal the crack and prevent it from spreading further with a strip of waterproof tape on the outside of the window.
● For a more durable and almost invisible repair, brush a thin layer of clear nail polish onto the crack; allow it to dry and repeat the process until the polish is level with the window glass.
● Surface scratches in a window can be buffed away using a bit of non-gel toothpaste, a lint-free cloth, and a little elbow grease. "Whitening" toothpastes that include baking soda in their formula are the most effective.

The window is broken
Make a temporary fix

If any glass is missing, remove the whole pane to make it safe.
● Lay newspaper on the ground on both sides of the window to catch the pieces of old glass. Put on gloves and safety glasses, and wear thick shoes to protect your feet.
● Pull out any loose pieces of glass by hand. For glass that can't be easily removed, cover the edge with a sheet of newspaper and then gently but firmly grab the fragment with a pair of pliers, wiggling the glass back and forth until it comes away from the frame.
● Remove the putty and any small pieces of glass around the inside of the frame with a hammer and an old chisel. Use long-nose pliers to pull out any holding pins or spring clips.
● Dispose of the large glass pieces carefully, then vacuum the inside of the frame and the floor to pick up any stray fragments.
● When the frame is clean, measure the space and cut a piece of plywood to size. Insert the plywood in the hole and tape it in place with weatherproof tape all the way round the inner frame.

Fill a small hole or crack in a window with clear nail polish; clean the window first with a damp paper towel.

The glass needs to be replaced
Do a professional job of installing a new pane

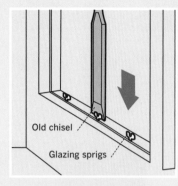

Old chisel

Glazing sprigs

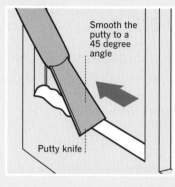

Smooth the putty to a 45 degree angle

Putty knife

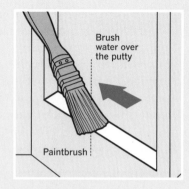

Brush water over the putty

Paintbrush

You don't need a glazier to replace a pane of glass; save yourself the service fee by taking on the job yourself. First, you'll need to remove the old glass, putty, and pins (see page 143). Make a cardboard template that fits snugly into the inner frame and take it to a glass supplier. Tell them the location of the window so they can provide the correct weight of glass.

Time needed **1 hour**
You will need **old chisel, paintbrush, tape measure, glazing push points, putty, putty knife**

1 Work a lump of putty in your hands until it's pliable. Lay it about 3 mm thick around the inner frame to form a bed. Press the new glass gently onto it, working from the edges, not the middle, to avoid cracking.

2 Measure regular intervals around the glass, and use the back of an old chisel to tap in glazing push points, with their heads just projecting enough to hold the glass firmly (see above, left). Resecure any spring clips on metal windows.

3 Press more putty around the front of the glass, then use the flat edge of a putty knife to form a neat bevel. Smooth the putty to

a 45 degree angle and remove surplus putty from both sides of the window (see above, center). Dab a paintbrush in water and brush over the putty to get rid of any irregularities (see above, right) and ensure that the putty is in close contact with both glass and frame.

4 Don't paint the putty for at least two weeks to allow it to harden. When painting, overlap the glass by 1–2 mm—this will help prevent water from penetrating behind the putty and into the wooden frame.

A chunk of putty has fallen off
Replace the putty without cracking the glass

Linseed oil–based putty will harden and crack and eventually fall out. Act fast to renew it or the wooden frame will soon begin to rot. Wear gloves and eye protection when you are removing the old putty.
- Remove loose putty with a screwdriver or paint scraper; lever the sections out against the wood of the frame, not against the glass.
- Use a heat gun on a low setting to help soften stubborn putty, but be careful not to heat the glass too much.
- Press the new putty into place following steps 3 and 4 above.

There's condensation on my windows
Warm up and dry out

Condensation running down your windows is not only unsightly, but will stain curtains and carpets, cause wooden window frames to rot and encourage the growth of mildew. Unfortunately, there's no simple way to eliminate condensation, but you can make a difference by following two main strategies—reducing the amount of water vapor in the air of your house and raising the temperature of the inner surfaces of the windows.

● If you have exhaust fans in your kitchen and bathroom, use them. Running ceiling fans will also help by mixing moist and dry air.

● Open windows very slightly to balance the amount of water vapor inside with that outside; don't open the windows fully if it is cool outside. Don't keep house plants or stacks of firewood in rooms that are prone to condensation.

● Try rearranging the furniture. An armchair in front of the window may be stopping heat from reaching the glass and so encouraging condensation on its surface.

● If possible, run a dehumidifier in the affected room(s) to extract moisture from the air, or buy a window-film kit from a DIY store to add temporary "double glazing" through the cold winter months.

Avoid drying clothes on radiators in a room that is prone to condensation; keep a window very slightly open to allow moist air to balance with that outdoors.

WARNING

If you have installed window locks, make sure there is a key close to every window in case of fire. Keep it out of sight of burglars—a small hook next to the window does the job perfectly.

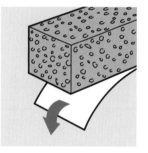

Draft-proofing products include (from top): "P" profile rubber strips, polypropylene V-strips, silicone brush strips and strips of foam.

My windows are cold and rattly
Buy inexpensive draft-proofing strips to suit your window

Installing inexpensive draft excluders will save you an average of 15 percent on heating bills as well as silencing any annoying window rattles. Self-adhesive draft excluders are made from a variety of materials and are available in different depths and colors:
● Squashy adhesive rubber strips, available in "P" or "E" profiles, compress so that the rubber forms a tight seal.
● "V" profile weatherstrip, made of polypropylene, has a fold down its length; it is ideal for filling thinner gaps between the frame and the window.
● Strips of siliconized nylon brushes make a seal between the bristles and the window edge.
● Strips of foam about 1/3 inch wide make a seal when compressed.

Install the strips

● Clean the surfaces where you intend to stick the strips with a damp rag; allow them to dry fully. Stick the draft-proofing strip to the inside of the window frame, as near as possible to the inside of the house.
● Stick on a short test strip, then close the window. Insert a credit card between the strip and window; if it is loose and falls out, you'll need a deeper strip to block the drafts effectively.
● Sash windows are notoriously drafty. Fit brush strip onto the inside of the bottom sash and the outside of the top one and stick a compressible foam strip onto the top and bottom edges of the sashes.
● Seal casement windows with self-adhesive foam or rubber strip around the inner edge so it compresses when the window is shut. If there's not enough of a gap to fit foam or rubber, fit V-strip instead.

My windows leak heat
Install some temporary double glazing

Single-glazed windows are very poor insulators, but a temporary fix will help you keep warmer in the winter months.
● Clean the inside of your window frames thoroughly with a cloth and mild detergent; allow to dry.
● Stick double-sided tape along the window frames.
● Stretch plastic wrap tightly across the window frame and secure it to the tape. It should not touch the glass, but form a second layer, about 1/2 inch from the pane.
● More robust secondary glazing kits, using tougher glazing film, are available from home improvement stores.

HOME SECURITY

Effective home security gives you peace of mind and could help reduce your insurance premiums, too. But it's no good securing windows, doors, garages, and sheds if locks don't work properly and alarms fail to sound at the right time.

LOCKS AND KEYS

Problems with locks should never be ignored; if a lock is stiff or a key is bent out of shape, then it may just fail next time you use it, leaving you inconvenienced at best and in danger at worst. Lubricating your locks every few months will keep them in good shape, and replacing damaged keys before they snap will save you frustration and expense.

I'm locked out
Use a plastic card to open the lock

It pays to keep spare keys with friends or neighbors, or in a key safe in your garden, but what if you've locked yourself out without any backup? If the door is locked with a surface mount lock, you can try a card trick you may have seen in the movies. If you have a dead bolt, you will need to call a locksmith; this is because dead bolts require you to turn the key in the lock to move the bolt and open the door, whereas surface mount locks employ a spring to keep the bolt in place, and the bolt can be pushed back externally.
- Insert a plastic card into the gap between the door and the frame where the latch is located, bending it back toward the doorknob while pushing it in as far as it will go.
- When you've pushed it in as far as it will go, straighten the card while opening the handle and leaning against the door. With some luck, the door will come open.

WARNING

Don't use a credit card or other important plastic in your attempt to unlock your door—it may well get damaged in the process.

My key is bent
Flatten it in a vice

If you don't have a spare key, squash the damaged key flat in a vice. Alternatively, hold it at either end with a pair of pliers and bend it straight. Replace the key as soon as possible—once bent, it is far more likely to shear off in use, leaving you out in the cold.

A FEW STROKES WITH A SOFT PENCIL CAN HELP EASE A KEY INTO A LOCK

The key is stiff in the lock
Overcome friction with some pencil power

Locksmiths use powdered graphite to lubricate the workings of locks, and if your key refuses to slide fully into the lock, you can do the same. Simply rub the key with a pencil until its surface is covered with the graphite "lead"; try again and the key should glide home.

I can't turn the key
Clean and lubricate to free the movement

Is the key new? If so, it might not be a perfect fit in the lock. Take it back to the key cutter to get it ground down slightly. Don't try to force the key to turn. Locks exposed to the elements may have corroded or the grease within may have dried up—apply too much pressure and you could have a broken or bent key.

● Spray WD-40 into the keyhole, catching the lubricant that runs off in a cloth. At first, the runoff may be black because it contains oil and grime that has built up in the lock. After a while, the liquid will be clear—the lock is then clean. Never put heavier oils, such as 3-in-One, into a lock; they will trap grime in the lock and may make your problems worse.

● Wipe the key with some WD-40 or lemon juice until it's bright.

● The bolt of the lock may be catching on the striker plate—the metal plate on the door frame that "receives" the bolt. This makes the key difficult to turn, but it can be fixed by adjusting the position of the door or the strike plate (see page 150).

My key has snapped off in the lock
Get the key out and yourself in

A snapped key presents a double challenge—how to get back into the house and how to remove the broken key from the lock. Before you start, spray a little WD-40 into the lock.

● If the key snapped when fully inserted into the lock and part of it is protruding, you're in luck. Use a pair of long-nose pliers to pull out the broken key (if you have a spare key handy) or to turn the broken key in the lock to open the door (if you don't).

● If the key snapped within the mechanism and is not protruding, push a straight-bladed screwdriver into the lock and try turning it to open the door.

● Straighten a couple of paper clips. Push one paper clip along the serrated edge of the key within the lock. Move it in and out to get it as far in as possible. Push the second paper clip over the top (non-serrated) side of the key. Using the two paper clips as "chopsticks," try pulling the broken key out far enough so you can grab it with a pair of pliers.

● Snap a small hacksaw blade in two—these blades are usually sold very cheaply in hardware stores; select the half in which the teeth point backward at the broken end. Insert this end into the lock against the serrated edge of the key and use the teeth of the saw to hook onto the body of the key and pull it out.

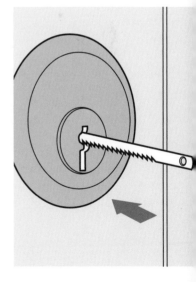

Wiggle the broken end of a hacksaw blade into the lock to try to grab the toothed side of a stuck key fragment.

The door lock has frozen me out
Thaw your way back inside

Subzero weather combined with moisture in the air can cause locks to freeze shut. With a little ingenuity you can heat your way indoors.
● Try breathing on the frozen lock to free its movement.
● Heat the key on the hood of your car if you've just driven home, dip it into a cup of hot coffee, or even heat it gently with a lighter. Wear a pair of gloves and be careful not to burn your fingers.

Dip your key into some hot coffee—this may heat the lock sufficiently to melt any ice within and free the mechanism.

My mortise lock won't catch
Realign the hardware

Mortise locks have a stout rectangular bolt that fits in a recess in the door frame. The edges of the recess are usually reinforced with a metal plate, called a strike plate. If the bolt won't go into the recess or if your key is hard to turn when locking and unlocking the door, the likelihood is that something is out of alignment.
● Examine the gap between the edge of the door and the frame—it should be consistent all the way along. If the gap gets wider toward the bottom, the door has probably slumped on its hinges making the lock catch on the bottom of the recess. As a remedy, unscrew the bottom hinge of the door from the frame and pack it with card until the gap is even (see page 139).
● Lift the door by its handle and see if the lock now engages. If it does, your hinges are worn and due for replacement. If you don't want to take on this job, you can enlarge the lock recess instead; use a metal file to file away at the lower lip of the hole in the strike plate until the bolt fits into the hole.

The door rattles when it is locked
Tighten up the fit of your lock

If your door rattles when it is locked, the lock itself may be loose or the recess for your mortise lock may be oversize, allowing the door to move in the wind.
● Fit draft-proofing strip on the inner edge of the door frame so that it pushes the door back slightly and makes the lock contact the striker plate.
● Tighten the screws that secure the lock on the edge of the door. If they won't tighten, replace them with longer screws, or put matchsticks in the holes to give the existing screws more to bite on (see page 139).

I can't see the keyhole at night
Light it up with luminous paint

Paint a ring around your door lock using some luminous paint—this can be bought from hardware shops and is often used commercially to identify doors and fire exits.

My sliding door won't lock
Secure your home quickly

Some sliding patio doors and sliding windows have complex locking mechanisms. If yours fails, there's an easy way to secure your home while you sort out the problem. Measure the distance between the inner edge of the sliding door and the frame, and cut a piece of wood or an old broom handle to this length. Fit the wood into the track in which the doors slide; it will prevent anyone from opening the door.

● Check there's no debris on the track that might be stopping the door from closing; squirt a little WD-40 along the track and wipe it clean with a cloth. Check that the door hasn't slipped off its rollers; if it has, you'll need to lift it back into position.

● Some doors and windows can be adjusted up or down on their rollers—look for a hole on the edge of the door near the bottom, which may be covered by a plastic cap. There'll be one on both edges. Turn the adjusters with a screwdriver—usually clockwise for up and counterclockwise for down—until the door lock aligns properly.

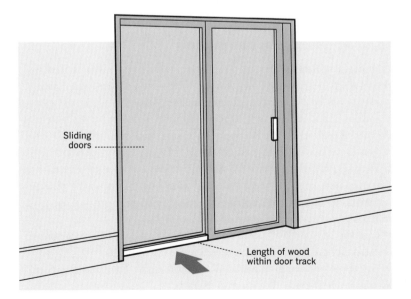

Sliding doors

Length of wood within door track

A length of wood or broom handle will restore temporary security if the lock fails on your sliding doors.

ALARMS AND SECURITY LIGHTS

Alarms safeguard your property and can save lives, but you'll aggravate your family and your neighbors if they are not set up correctly. Most problems with alarms come down to issues of power supply or poor installation and are usually simple to fix.

My smoke alarm goes off for no reason
Reposition the alarm for optimum safety

Smoke alarms are sensitive devices. If you have positioned them carefully, they'll need only minimal attention to keep them working reliably.
● Don't place smoke alarms in kitchens, bathrooms, garages, or next to fireplaces. Fresh paint may sometimes trigger alarms, too, so be sure to air a newly painted room before considering that the alarm may be defective.
● A regular chirping sound indicates the battery needs replacing—get and install a new one immediately. Don't remove the old battery until you are ready to install the new one—chances are that you'll forget to replace it once the alarm is silent.
● Some alarms can be triggered by dust in the air and may sound when you do your spring cleaning. Open the alarm casing and vacuum the inside using the brush attachment to remove dust particles.

The security light is faulty
Adjust the sensor to stop false positives

Automatic security lights are usually triggered by infrared radiation (heat) from an intruder. They are also fitted with a light sensor that prevents the light operating during the day. Security lights need careful positioning and setting up if they are to work effectively. If the light is switching on and off for no apparent reason, ask yourself:
● Is it being activated by people or cars moving past the house? If so, angle the unit downward more to restrict its field of vision. Alternatively, you can select the area "seen" by the sensor by masking off parts of the lens with insulating tape. Masking the top of the lens will restrict long-range detection, for example.
● Can the sensor "see" other heat sources, such as air vents or other security lights? If so, reposition the sensor accordingly.
● Are there overhanging branches near the unit? They could trigger an alarm on a windy day, so trim them back.

Eight ways to prevent false alarms

Modern burglar alarm systems contain sophisticated electronics to prevent false alarms, but there are still a few steps you can take to keep your alarm from tripping when it's not needed.

1 Your alarm comes with a battery within the main control panel. With a life expectancy of around five years, the battery keeps the system working even if the power fails. A dead battery means false alarms. Turn off the main power supply, remove the cover from the control panel (you'll need to undo a couple of screws), and remove the battery; buy and install a replacement.

2 Remove the covers of the Passive Infrared (PIR) detectors in the rooms of your home and clean out insects or webs before replacing them.

3 Ensure that the covers of the control panel and of the PIR detectors are secure or you may trigger the system's "tamper" alarm.

4 Position PIR detectors away from heat sources, such as dishwashers, clothes dryers, or security lights.

5 Close windows before setting the alarm; the movement of curtains, plants, or decorations in the breeze may be enough to trigger the alarm.

6 Check that the two parts of a door or window sensor are correctly aligned—it's easy to knock one out of position when cleaning or moving furniture.

7 Some wireless alarm systems can be affected by remote controls and other wireless devices. If the alarm goes off every time you change channels, you may need to select a different transmission channel for your alarm through its control panel.

8 Monitored alarm systems—those connected to the alarm company via the telephone—may sound if the telephone line fails. Check that the phone is working and that it is still connected to the alarm box.

WHEN LEAVING THE HOUSE, MAKE SURE THAT ALL WINDOWS AND DOORS ARE SECURE AND THAT PETS CAN'T GET INTO ALARMED AREAS

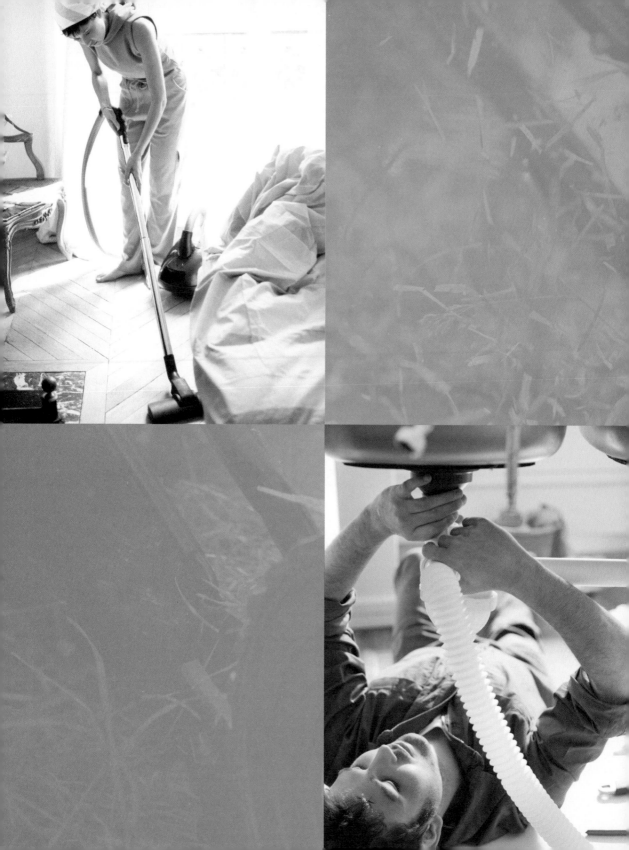

3

Household
and More

IN THE KITCHEN

LIVING SPACES

BEDROOMS AND BATHROOMS

CLOTHES AND
PERSONAL ITEMS

IN THE KITCHEN

Household appliances and kitchen equipment make life easier—until the dishwasher leaks onto the floor and the toaster burns your bread to charcoal. But don't rush to replace your faulty appliances without trying some simple remedies first.

COOKING AND CLEANING

Clean and well-maintained kitchen equipment, sharp blades, and keen cutting edges on your blender make cooking so much easier, safer, and more pleasurable.

The riveted handle of my knife is loose
Firm up your grip

The metal rivets that secure the handle onto a knife (or other cutlery) can work loose over time, but are easy to tighten. Place the handle on a solid surface and position the tip of a center punch—a hardened steel spike—on the center of the rivet. Use a hammer to strike the center punch just hard enough to leave a small dimple; this will slightly expand the rivet and hold the handle firmly.

My kitchen knife is blunt
Sharpen your blade with a whetstone

A dull blade will bruise soft foods, and is far more likely to slip in use than a sharp knife because you need to apply more pressure when cutting, making it less safe. Sharpen your knife when it seems blunt—you shouldn't need to do this more than a few times per year. You'll get the best results using a sharpening or whetstone—an abrasive, usually rectangular stone that you can by from any good cookware shop (see box, left). Some whetstone makers recommend wetting the stone with water or oil (confusingly the term "whet" means "to sharpen" rather than to get wet), while others are designed to be used dry—check the instructions supplied with your stone.
● Place the whetstone on a flat surface; lay a cloth beneath the stone to prevent it moving around. Angle the knife at about 20 degrees to the surface of the stone or match the existing angle of the sharp edge if it is clearly visible. Wipe the blade—cutting edge first—across the stone, as if trying to cut a fine slice from the top of the stone.

JARGON BUSTER

Sharpening and honing There are two distinct processes involved in keeping a knife in top condition—sharpening and honing. Sharpening abrades tiny pieces of metal from the knife, so bringing the cutting edge to a point. There are many dedicated knife-sharpening devices on the market, but an old-fashioned whetstone is hard to beat for the keenest edge. The fine edge of a knife gets bent out of shape in use: honing gets the cutting edge straight, and is done using a honing steel.

- Make sure you run the whole length of the blade across the stone in one fluid motion. Turn the knife over and repeat on the other side of the blade. Give each side around 20 strokes, alternating sides as you go. Keep the angle of contact consistent throughout.
- Wash the knife thoroughly before use as sharpening leaves tiny fragments of metal on the blade.
- If you don't have a whetstone, try using the unglazed bottom of an old ceramic bowl or coffee mug. Run the blade across its abrasive surface in the same way as described above.
- After sharpening, hone your knife.

Hone your knife with a steel

You should hone your knife regularly—ideally before every use—with a honing steel. This is a purpose-built metal rod, which can be purchased from any good cookware shop.

- Hold the honing steel vertically, with the handle at the top. Rest the base of the steel on a folded paper towel (for stability) on a chopping board. Angle the knife at about 20 degrees to the surface of the steel and wipe the blade—cutting edge first—downward across the steel. Repeat at least 20 times on each side, keeping the pressure light and the angle consistent as you go.
- Note that expensive Japanese knives and ceramic knives have extremely hard blades that need specialist sharpening and honing; consult your owner's manual for advice.

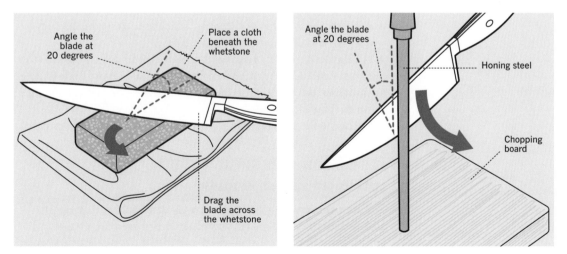

Sharpen the blade using gentle strokes across the surface of the whetstone.

Hone the knife by wiping it down the surface of a honing steel, maintaining a consistent angle.

My kitchen knife is bent
Warm the metal to work it more easily

If you suspect your knife is bent, lay the blade on a flat tabletop; if the blade doesn't make contact with the table consistently along its length, it will need straightening to ensure a clean, safe cut.

● Most knives are made from stainless steel, which is tough to bend if it gets out of shape. To make the job easier, stand the bent knife in a jug of boiling water for a few minutes.

● Establish where the bend occurs by looking carefully down the length of the blade. Lay the blade on the edge of a solid table with the bowed side facing downward. Position the knife so that the bent area is directly over the edge of the table, which will act as the fulcrum when you bend the knife back into shape.

● Place a cloth over the blade and press it down hard on the tabletop with one hand. Use the other hand to push down on the knife handle to straighten the blade. Work gently and slowly—one large bend may cause the blade to fracture.

● Check the blade, then repeat the process until the blade is straight.

My can opener seems blunt
Clean the cutting wheel with paper

The cutting edge of a can opener can get gummed up, making it almost unusable. The easiest way to clean it is to insert a waxed baking sheet into the cutting wheel and turn the can opener to "open" the paper. This will clean and sharpen the can opener's mechanism in one quick step.

My blender has lost its bite
Remove obstructions and sharpen the blades

If your blender takes an age to whiz your veggies into soup, the blades may be running slowly or may need sharpening. With use, gunk builds up at the bottom of your blender. This can be difficult to remove with routine cleaning and can interfere with the movement of the blades.
- Mix half a cup of baking soda with an equal amount of warm water and pour into your blender. Let the solution stand overnight, then run the blender at full speed in the morning—this should dislodge any stubborn matter.
- Remove the blade assembly from the blender and sharpen the cutting edges on a whetstone (see page 156). Try to follow the existing angle of the sharp edges of the blades.

My kettle has lime buildup
Dissolve the sediment buildup

A kettle with lime buildup is a hazard because it may fail to turn off when it boils. Descaling your kettle will not only prevent possible damage but will also save you energy and time.
- Fill the kettle with a 50:50 mixture of water and white vinegar. Boil the kettle and let the mixture sit overnight. Scrub any visible areas of scale with a clean toothbrush. Empty and rinse the kettle, and repeat the process if you can still see lime within.

The toaster won't stay down
Clean the safety switch

The mechanism that lowers the bread into your toaster is held down by an electromagnet: crumbs between the magnet and toast holder may interfere with its operation, so your toast won't stay down.
- Unplug the toaster, remove and empty the crumb tray. Take it outdoors, turn it upside down, and shake. This will dislodge any loose particles.
- If this doesn't solve the problem, you may be able to take off the cover of the toaster; if so, remove the securing screws, usually found in the base of the unit.
- With the cover off, you should see the electromagnet—a large block at the bottom of the toaster. Push down the lever to see where the electromagnet meets the toast holder; clean both surfaces at this junction using a cloth dabbed in isopropyl alcohol (rubbing alcohol), then reassemble the toaster.

TOOLS OF THE TRADE
Steel wool for metal surfaces

Aging chrome kettles or stainless-steel surfaces can be made to gleam again. First, clean the metal with a household cleaner. Wipe it dry and then scrub with 0000 steel wool. For stainless steel, be sure to rub in the same direction as the existing polish lines. Clean the surface again with warm water to remove any remnants of steel wool.

My coffee tastes sour
Purge your coffeemaker with a vinegar wash

A clean coffeemaker will keep your brew from tasting sour or bitter. Fill the coffeemaker to capacity with a 50:50 mix of white vinegar and water. Place an empty filter in the machine to catch any dislodged scaly chunks and run the coffeemaker as normal. Run through another three or four batches of clean water to remove any traces of vinegar before brewing a fresh batch of coffee.

My ice cream maker is squeaking
Use some Teflon spray for a quiet life

Kitchen appliances such as bread makers, juicers, ice cream makers, and food processors may squeak or grind as they get older. The safest way to silence them is with a squirt of Teflon lubricant—be sure to ask for this rather than an oil-based lubricant at the hardware store.
● Unplug the appliance and take off its bottom panel by removing the assembly screws found on the base. Lubricate all the moving parts in the appliance with the Teflon lubricant (but avoid getting it onto any rubber belts) then reassemble the device.

My pans are ruined
Give your old cookware a makeover

Clean a rusty or encrusted cast-iron pan by heating it in an oven at 475° for 30 minutes. Allow it to cool and scrape off any debris with a metal spatula, then scrub the surface with a scouring pad in warm, soapy water. Reseason the pan before use by coating the dry pan with vegetable oil, then heating it upside down in an oven at 475°. Place a sheet of foil on the rack under the pan to catch and dripping oil.

Before replacing a crusty, stained, or burnt pan, try some of these cook's favorite remedies.
● Remove burn marks from a stainless-steel pan by sprinkling baking soda onto the surface and rubbing vigorously with a kitchen sponge. For ingrained burns, pour 1/2 inch of water into the pan and bring it to a boil. Add two tablespoons of table salt, remove the pan from the heat, and leave it overnight before scrubbing the area with a nonmetallic scouring pad.
● Clean an enamelled pan by squeezing the juice of a lemon over any stains. Sprinkle on a tablespoon of salt, and scrub with a nonmetallic scouring pad before rinsing.
● To loosen encrusted food on cast-iron pots and pans, bake them at a high temperature in the oven (see left). For other types of cookware, bring a little water to boil in the pan, then add a tablespoon of liquid laundry detergent. Simmer for 5 minutes and use a clean toothbrush to lift the caked-on material. Rinse thoroughly.
● Avoid using abrasive scrubbers on nonstick pans—their nonstick surface may be removed by harsh cleaning.

FRIDGES AND FREEZERS

Maintaining food at a low temperature keeps it safe to eat for longer. A problem with your refrigerator will show up in your electricity bill, but, more seriously, it could put your health at risk. There's no need to take a chance—refrigerators can be restored to good working order with just a little effort.

The food in my refrigerator isn't cold
Check the temperature and diagnose the problem

Even small deviations from recommended storage temperatures can cause food to spoil. Unfortunately, many fridges have control units with an arbitrarily numbered scale (with 1–6 representing warmest to coolest, for example). So if you suspect that your refrigerator or freezer is too warm—or too cool—your first job is to accurately measure its temperature with a refrigerator thermometer (see right). If your fridge or freezer proves to be too warm, try the following steps:

● Turn the control dial on the unit to a higher setting. Make a small adjustment, then leave the door closed overnight. Check the temperature with a thermometer. Repeat until you achieve the desired temperature. Use a waterproof pen to mark the optimum setting on the dial so that you can set it again if the dial gets knocked out of position.

● Pull the refrigerator away from the wall and use a vacuum cleaner fitted with a brush attachment to clear dust and cobwebs from the metal coils on the back.

● Leaky door seals can put a strain on the refrigerator. Check the seals by inserting a sheet of paper between the door and the fridge as you close the door. The paper should stay put; if not, clean your seals and doors thoroughly using household detergent. The door may have sagged over time, moving out of line with the refrigerator and creating a gap around the door. To realign the door, simply loosen the screws of the door hinge with a screwdriver: hold the door so it is "square" and retighten the hinge screws.

Check the fridge light

The tiny fridge light can warm the contents of your fridge significantly if it fails to switch off when you close the door. Use a blunt knife to pull the door seal back from the frame when the door is closed. If you can see light, the switch is probably stuck or misaligned and will need to be fixed.

TOOLS OF THE TRADE

Fridge thermometer

This simple and inexpensive gadget, which is available from kitchen-equipment suppliers and online shops, will help save energy and ensure that your food is kept fresh and safe. Use it to set and monitor the working temperature of your refrigerator and freezer. The inside of your fridge should be at 35–40°; any higher may be dangerous. The inside of your freezer should be close to 0°. Always monitor temperatures on your thermometer in the morning, when the door has been closed overnight.

Why is my refrigerator icing up?
Control the humidity for an ice-free interior

Ice buildup reduces the space inside your refrigerator and also makes it inefficient. It can be avoided by regularly cleaning the coils on the back and checking the door seals (see page 161).

● Don't put warm food into the fridge—not only will it heat up the fridge contents, but any water vapor that it gives out will condense within, forming ice.

● Adjust your refrigerator's humidity setting (if it has one). A lower setting will reduce the amount of ice buildup.

The bottom of the fridge is wet
Clear the drainage hole

Most refrigerator are self-defrosting, which means that the cooling element in the fridge is periodically heated to melt any frost that has formed on its surface. The melted water runs away through a small drainage hole at the back of the fridge. This hole can get blocked by food or dirt, and water will then collect at the bottom of the unit.

● The solution is simple—use a toothpick or cotton swab to clean out any debris from the hole, then pour a small amount of warm water through the drain to ensure it is clear and dry the bottom of the refrigerator thoroughly with a paper towel.

The refrigerator light doesn't come on
Check the bulb and switch

A blown bulb is the most likely cause of a dark refrigerator. Remove its translucent cover, unscrew the bulb and install a replacement. It this doesn't do the job, focus attention on the door switch.

● Clean the switch by spraying compressed air, or a specialized electrical contact cleaner, around its edges. Test the light again.

● The door may have sunk on its hinges so that it no longer makes contact with the light switch. Try realigning the door with the body of the fridge (see page 161).

The fridge door keeps falling open
Tip it back on its legs

If the door won't stay shut, extend the front legs by two turns so that the fridge tips very slightly backward, making the door close with the lightest push. Don't overdo it—it should be as close to level as possible.

My freezer takes a long time to defrost
Thaw it out quickly and safely

Defrosting a freezer can take hours, especially if the room is chilly.
● Unplug the freezer, then fill a pan with hot, but not boiling, water. Place it inside the freezer on a heatproof dish and close the door. Leave the pan for 5 minutes before taking it out, reheating the water, and putting the pan back in the freezer. Repeat until all the ice has melted.

The freezer section is too warm
Clear the airways in your fridge freezer

Most refrigerator freezers have one cooling mechanism for both the fridge and freezer compartment. So, if your refrigerator is working, but your freezer is not, there is likely to be a blockage in the airway between the two—possibly a bag of frozen peas or a box of fish.
● Look inside your freezer and you'll see a hole about 1 1/2 inches across, often covered with a plastic grate; this is the cold-air inlet. Keep the opening and the area around it clear to allow the air to flow through the freezer.
● Some high-end refrigerator freezers have separate cooling systems for the fridge and for the freezer; for such models, persistent problems will need a professional repair.

Defrost your freezer using a pan of hot water. Place it in the freezer and reheat the water every 5 minutes.

WARNING

It's tempting to use a hair dryer to help thaw your freezer, but take care. Hot spots can damage the inner walls of the fridge, and any stray water on the hair dryer presents a danger of electrocution.

My vegetables keep spoiling
Zone your refrigerator to extend the life of foods

Vegetables need to breathe, so don't keep them tightly wrapped in plastic—a loose or perforated bag is best. Keep vegetables away from the back wall of the fridge where the coldest air will pass over them. Most vegetables will live longer in the fridge, but potatoes and onions should be stored in a cool, dark cupboard to delay sprouting.

My fridge is making an annoying noise
Balance the refrigerator and secure the compressor

Years of service will take their toll on a refrigerator; parts can shake loose and make an irritating and persistent noise.
● First, make sure the fridge is level. Adjust the height of the legs at the corners of the fridge by turning them clockwise (to raise the leg) or counterclockwise (to lower it). Check that it is level with a spirit level.
● If the noise persists, unplug the fridge and pull it away from the wall. Identify the compressor—this is a large, typically dome-shaped unit at the base and back of the fridge. It is sometimes behind a panel that can be easily removed by undoing a couple of screws. The compressor is attached to the body of the refrigerator by bolts or—often—by simple clips. Tighten the connections so that the compressor doesn't vibrate when it runs; while you have access, vacuum the area around the compressor and the cooling fan underneath the refrigerator—this will help the refrigerator run more efficiently.

Compressor unit

Tightening the bolts that secure the compressor unit may silence annoying rattles and humming noises from your refrigerator.

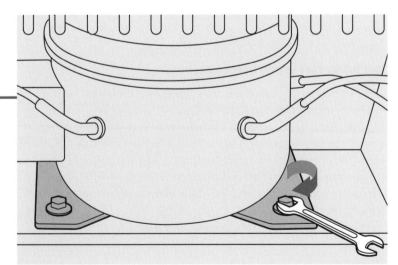

Ten ways to store your food more safely

Stacking your refrigerator sensibly will preserve food for longer and save you money on power. It'll also help to reduce the risks of cross contamination between different food types.

1 Put items that you use often toward the front of the fridge. This cuts the time the door is held open and so helps keep the fridge cool.

2 Cold air sinks to the bottom of the fridge, so keep the most perishable items, such as raw meat, poultry, and fish, on the bottom shelf. Store them in sealable plastic containers to prevent any juices from leaking into the refrigerator.

3 Place newly purchased items behind older ones, so that you use the older foods first.

4 If you wash fruits and vegetables before refrigerating, dry the items with some paper towels first.

5 Use your door to store less perishable goods that you want to keep cool—condiments, wine, beer, and sodas, for example.

6 Store milk, eggs, and dairy products on a middle shelf—don't keep them in the door because the temperature here can fluctuate greatly as the door is opened and closed.

7 Cover glass refrigerator shelves with a layer of plastic wrap—in case of a spill, just remove and replace the plastic wrap.

8 Keep cooked items on higher shelves than raw ingredients.

9 If you don't have a frost-free fridge, defrost regularly following the manufacturer's guidelines.

10 Observe the "best before" dates on food, but don't rely on them completely. If food looks or smells unusual, throw it away—it's not worth taking any chances with potentially harmful microbes.

DON'T OVERFILL YOUR FRIDGE—LEAVE ENOUGH SPACE BETWEEN ITEMS FOR THE COLD AIR TO CIRCULATE

FRESHEN UP YOUR FRIDGE WITH A SIMPLE SOLUTION— BALLS OF NEWSPAPER

My refrigerator smells terrible
Eliminate the odor with vinegar and newspaper

Over time, the walls of a fridge absorb food smells. These odors can taint your food, but they can be neutralized effectively.

● Switch off your refrigerator and clear out its contents. Make a mixture of equal parts of water and white vinegar and use this to wipe all the inner surfaces of the fridge.

● If your refrigerator hasn't been used for a long time and the smell is more stubborn, remove any food from the fridge. Ball up sheets of newspaper and lightly moisten them with water, then run the fridge as normal for a few days. Remove the paper, and clean the fridge with vinegar as above before restocking with food.

How do I prevent "freezer burn"
Fill your freezer to create a thermal buffer

If your frozen food looks gray and leathery, it has suffered freezer
burn, which discolors and dries the food (though it is still edible).
● Keep your freezer full. As you use up frozen food, replace it with
nonperishable items, such as rice and flour, to use up the free space, or
partially fill some open plastic containers with water and place them
in the freezer.
● Make sure the food is in sealed packages.

There's no ice coming from the ice maker
Check the ice tray arm

Most domestic ice makers have a thin metal shutoff arm that hovers
over the ice tray. Its job is to tell the freezer whether to make more ice;
when the tray is full, the arm is up, and no ice is made. It's easy to
accidentally bump this arm up—simply pull it down gently and
you'll see ice in about an hour.

Make it last FRIDGES AND FREEZERS

Dust and ice are the enemies of fridges and freezers. Be sure to defrost your freezer whenever
the ice within gets more than 1/4 inch thick, and vacuum the heat exchange coils on the
back of the machine every six months or so.

To prevent ice buildup in your freezer, wet a paper towel with vegetable oil, and rub it
lightly over the inner walls of the freezer. Rub a little on the rubber door seals, too—this
will make the door close more tightly.

Keep your fridge smelling fresh by leaving a bowl of oats in the back of the fridge
to absorb odors. Renew it every few days if the smells persist.

Store food in airtight containers in the refrigerator or freezer to help keep it—and your fridge—
from becoming tainted with odors.

If you need to switch the refrigerator off for a long period, first clean the fridge and remove all
the food, then leave it with the door slightly ajar so that air can circulate. Be sure to block the
door so that children can't get trapped inside.

When moving your fridge or freezer from one place to another, switch it off for at least 12
hours before the move to give the gases within time to condense. This will minimize the
chance of damage in transit.

WASHING MACHINES

All washing machines have the same basic parts: a watertight container (the tub) encloses a drum that holds the clothes; electrically operated valves allow water into the tub and a heating element raises the water temperature; an electric motor turns the drum; and a pump drains the water. These systems are coordinated by an electronic or mechanical controller. Most common problems involve a blockage in the machine's internal plumbing and can usually be cleared in minutes.

My machine won't start
Check your power and the door lock

Make sure that the machine is plugged in. Test the wall socket with another appliance—for example, a lamp—that you know is working. If the socket is dead, check the circuit breaker or fuse that protects the outlet.
● Push the door firmly shut. Your washing machine is fitted with an interlock that prevents operation unless it is closed.
● Make sure that your home water supply is on—turn a nearby tap to check.

Why won't my washing machine fill up?
Check the water inlets

If water is coming out of your kitchen faucet, but not filling the washing machine, you'll need to check the inlet hoses. To do so, you'll need to move the machine away from the wall.
● Washing machines are awkward to move safely. Begin by tilting the machine backward; slide a piece of fiberboard under its front feet. This will allow you to slide your machine across the floor without causing damage. Then, open the door of the machine and put your hand at the top of the opening. Gripping the inside edge of the door frame, pull the machine away from the wall until you have enough room to get access to the inlet hoses at the rear.
● Make sure the water hose is connected to the washing machine and ensure the inlet valves are open. Check that the service valves between the water supply and your machine are open, too.
● Straighten out any kinks in the water hose and restart the machine.
● If it still doesn't fill with water, or fills only slowly, try cleaning the filters in the inlet hoses (see page 170).

WHAT YOU CAN FIX YOURSELF

A washing machine can quickly get clogged up with undissolved detergent, lime and lint, and parts will wear out causing leaks or other faults. Many components, such as valves, hoses, the filter, the detergent tray, and the door seal, are relatively simple and quick to fix, but for problems with the pump, motor, or controller call for professional repair.

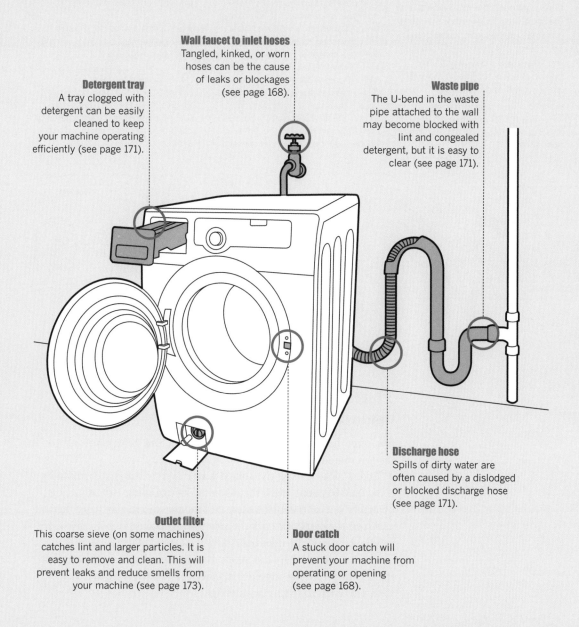

Wall faucet to inlet hoses
Tangled, kinked, or worn hoses can be the cause of leaks or blockages (see page 168).

Detergent tray
A tray clogged with detergent can be easily cleaned to keep your machine operating efficiently (see page 171).

Waste pipe
The U-bend in the waste pipe attached to the wall may become blocked with lint and congealed detergent, but it is easy to clear (see page 171).

Discharge hose
Spills of dirty water are often caused by a dislodged or blocked discharge hose (see page 171).

Outlet filter
This coarse sieve (on some machines) catches lint and larger particles. It is easy to remove and clean. This will prevent leaks and reduce smells from your machine (see page 173).

Door catch
A stuck door catch will prevent your machine from operating or opening (see page 168).

The machine fills really slowly
Clean the water inlet hose filters

Washing machines may draw hot and cold, or only cold, water from your plumbing system. Incoming water passes through small mesh filters between the inlet hoses and the machine. These trap any small particles in the water supply and so protect the machine. If blocked, the filters will slow or stop the inflow of water, but they can easily be removed and cleaned.

Time needed **30 minutes**
You will need **pipe wrench, pin, long-nose pliers**

1 Unplug the machine and turn off the water supply by turning the stop faucet(s) on the water pipes supplying the machine. Remove the inlet hose(s) from the back of the machine; use a wrench if you cannot unscrew them by hand (see below, left). Take care to keep the washer and the hose connected.

2 In some machines, the filter is located in the end of the inlet hose. Use a pair of long-nose pliers to pull the filter out from the hose (see below, center). Remove the rubber seating on the filter and put

it somewhere safe. In other models, the filter may be located in the washing machine, at the hose inlet. Again, use long-nose pliers to pull the filter out (see below, right).

3 Wash the mesh filter under running water, picking out any bits of grit with a pin.

4 Replace the rubber seal and push the filter back into place. Screw the hose back onto the machine—don't overtighten the plastic connector. Repeat with the second inlet hose, if present.

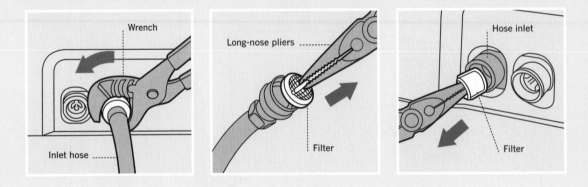

Wrench

Inlet hose

Long-nose pliers

Filter

Hose inlet

Filter

There's a puddle on the floor
Tighten your hose connections

It is often hard to tell where a washing machine is leaking—all you'll see is a telltale puddle on the floor.

● Take a close look at the spilled water. If it's clear—and especially if the leak happens when the machine isn't running—the source is probably one of the inlet hoses. Pull the machine away from the wall and turn the stopcock on its supply pipe to isolate it from the water supply. Unscrew the inlet hoses and look inside the connectors to check that the washers are intact; if they are split, buy replacements from your plumbing supplier. Replace the hose and tighten gently with a wrench to ensure a watertight fit.

• If the water on your floor is soapy or dirty, the door seal or pump could be leaking. But before calling a repairman, check the plumbing at the outflow of the machine—this is very often the site of a "dirty water" leak. You'll see that the flexible, corrugated discharge hose of your washing machine feeds into a long, hard, plastic waste pipe attached to the wall. This channels waste water to the external drain via a U-bend trap, which is highly susceptible to blockage. Unscrew the plastic fittings holding the U-bend in place and clean it thoroughly with hot water and detergent; use a lime remover if necessary. Refit the U-bend and push the discharge hose securely back into the waste pipe before running the machine.

My washing machine won't spin
Spread the load

Washing machines contain sensors that disable the spin cycle if the load is unbalanced. They may be triggered if the machine is overloaded (try removing some items) or if you are washing just one heavy item, such as a towel (try adding more items to balance the load). If the problem persists, try the following fixes.
• Clean the door mechanism. Vacuum around the door catch and open and close the machine a few times to dislodge any debris that may be caught in the switch. Blast compressed air from a can through the switch mechanism.
• Reset the machine's circuits by unplugging it and waiting 24 hours. Plug it back in and try a normal wash cycle.
• If these solutions don't work, you'll need a professional repair.

My wash comes out dirty
Clean the detergent tray

If your machine consistently fails to get your clothes clean, first check that you are not overloading the drum. Don't exceed the maximum weight of wash recommended by the machine's manufacturer because this will affect its ability to wash and may strain the motor.
• Try cleaning the detergent tray. Congealed powder or washing liquid can build up in the reservoir, choking the supply of detergent to your wash. Pull the tray out completely and scrub it in hot water, paying attention to the channel that passes from the tray into the drum.
• While the tray is out, use a long-handled brush to scrub the water outlets above the tray. Push the bristles of the brush into the water jets to clear any blockages.

A dishwashing brush is the perfect tool to reach and clean the water outlets above the detergent tray.

My clothes smell bad
Run a maintenance wash

Today's liquid detergents are formulated to work well at low temperatures. However, low-temperature washes don't kill the bacteria that thrive in the drum of your machine. This can lead to a smelly machine and clothing, and even to black marks on your laundry when lumps of microbial growth wash out of the drum.

• Run an empty wash cycle at the highest possible temperature (about 200°) using a bleach-containing powder detergent, not liquid soap. Carry out such a maintenance wash at least once a month.

The washer shakes noisily
Get it level for a quieter spin

An unbalanced load will cause your washing machine to vibrate violently in its spin cycle, but if your machine habitually wobbles across the laundry room floor it probably needs leveling.

• Carefully pull the machine away from the wall (see page 168). Place a level on the top of the machine, aligned from left to right. Adjust the machine's feet by turning them with a wrench or pliers; clockwise movement will raise the corner.

Use a level to ensure that the machine is level from front to back, as well as from side to side.

My machine won't empty
Drain out the water and clear your outlet filter

A partly blocked outlet filter will make your machine smell stagnant and will eventually stop it from draining, trapping your wash in soapy water. The filter is usually located behind a hinged panel at the bottom of the machine.

● Run the machine's drain cycle a couple of times to remove as much water as possible from the drum.

● Lay an old towel on the floor and tuck it under the front of the machine to catch any splashes.

● Place a shallow but wide container—a baking tray is ideal—under the filter, then release the filter by twisting its handle or grip-point. Allow the water to flow out gradually; you may need to empty the container a few times.

● Switch off your washing machine and unplug it. Remove the filter from the machine and clean it with a stiff brush under running water. While the filter is out, feel carefully within the filter chamber and remove any stray objects, such as coins, buttons or small toys, trapped inside.

● Replace the filter and check that it's tightly in place. Close the filter cover and try the machine again.

Make it last WASHING MACHINES

Air out your machine between washes. Keep the door open and its detergent tray extended to ventilate the machine and so prevent the growth of mildew. Wipe down the door seal to remove any trapped water.

Wash at the temperature indicated on the garments—not lower—and use the precise amount of detergent recommended by the machine's manufacturer for different loads. Too much liquid detergent can encourage the growth of bacteria in the tank.

Cut lime if you live in a hard-water area. Use a water-softening powder in your machine to reduce lime buildup on the heating element. Alternatively, descale your machine every three months using a dedicated descaler product or a cup of white vinegar added to an empty wash at 140°.

Check pockets before washing for coins, pens, and—especially—children's toys. These end up in the wash all too often and can cause damage or blockages.

CLOTHES DRYERS

There are two main designs of domestic clothes dryers—those that vent moist air to the outside of your house and those that condense the moisture in a reservoir. Many problems that affect dryers are concerned with the buildup of lint in the machine. This is easy to clear. Failures in the motor, heater, or the machine's electronic controls will need professional repair.

My dryer won't start
Check the power, switch, and drum

First, check that the dryer is receiving power. Plug a working appliance, such as a table lamp, into its socket: if this doesn't illuminate, replace the fuses, or reset the circuit breaker. If the dryer repeatedly blows its fuse or trips its circuit breaker, call for a repair—it may indicate an electrical problem within the machine.
- If you have just dried a load, wait for 30 minutes before restarting—the dryer's thermal overload protector may have been triggered.
- Inspect the door catch. This usually has a plastic peg that pushes an electrical switch in the door casing. If the plastic appears cracked, or the door doesn't close easily, you'll need to call for a repair, but if the mechanism appears intact, try spraying a little switch cleaner (available from electronics stores) into the switch. This solvent may dislodge any grease or debris that is blocking the switch's contacts.

The clothes get warm but don't dry

Sort your loads

Don't exceed the maximum recommended load for your dryer—check the user's manual to find out the weight of laundry it can handle. Clothes that tumble freely will dry faster and with less creasing.
● Always spin dry your clothes in the washing machine before putting them into the dryer, and if possible, separate heavy items (such as towels and jeans) from lighter ones and dry them in separate loads.
● Try saving up two or three loads of laundry and dry them one after another in the machine. The dryer will remain warm and get through your laundry more quickly and efficiently.

Clean out the lint and clear the vent

Your dryer has one or two mesh filters that catch the lint released from clothing. Simply slide out the plastic tray that holds the mesh and pick off the layer of lint; if the mesh is dirty, clean it with some warm, soapy water and allow to dry before replacing it.
● If your dryer vents hot, moist air to the outdoors, lint can accumulate within the duct between the dryer and the vent flap. This can block the flow of air and prevent your laundry from drying.
● Check the vent flap or hood on the outside of your house. Can you feel a flow of air when the dryer is running? If not, use a length of stiff wire to clear away any dust buildup around the vent.
● Switch off the dryer and unplug it. Pull the dryer away from the wall and disconnect the vent duct from both the dryer and the wall—you may need to unscrew a couple of clamps.
● Remove any obvious clumps of lint, then use the nozzle of your vacuum cleaner to suck out particles deeper within the pipe. Vacuum inside the opening of the dryer, too, before replacing the duct.
● If the duct is too long, it may kink and impede the flow of air within. Try compressing the hose and securing it with duct tape.

Clean the condenser

Condensation dryers work in a similar way to vented dryers, except that the water extracted from your clothing is not vented to the outside, but condenses on a cooled plate within the body of the dryer before running into a plastic reservoir.
● Empty the water reservoir after every drying cycle.
● Every few weeks, remove the condenser unit—it usually slides out easily from the dryer. Take it outside and wash it with cold water from a hose, removing any lint trapped on its plates. Allow it to dry before you put it back into the machine.

Pull the lint off your dryer's filters after every load to ensure good results.

> **WARNING** ⚠
>
> A build-up of lint in your clothes dryer is dangerous because it can start a fire. Clean your lint filters after every load and inspect the dryer's vent or condenser unit every few weeks.

DISHWASHERS

Washing dishes is a job that few people enjoy. Dishwashers not only do away with the chore, they cut down on hot water bills, too. Most problems with dishwashers can be avoided by regular cleaning and using the correct amounts of cleaning agents.

The dishwasher won't start
Reset the programmer

The electronic control panels on modern dishwashers allow you to select from a multitude of wash programs. Faults in their circuits are a common cause of appliance failure.

● If your dishwasher won't start, first check that it is plugged in. Then try resetting the controller—you'll usually need to press a combination of buttons and wait for a given period before restarting. Consult your user's manual for details.

The dishwasher leaks
Identify the source and stop the flow

If the leak is a one-off, check that you have loaded your machine correctly (see page 179); if the dishwasher's spray arms are stopped from spinning by a protruding pan or knife handle, water may be jetting directly at the door seals and leaking out of the machine. If the leak is persistent, you'll need to locate its source. To do this, first empty the dishwasher, pull it away from the wall and run a normal cycle. Watch the machine to pinpoint whether the leak is coming from the front or from the inlet or outlet hoses at the rear.

Check the door seals

If water is dripping from the front of the machine, check the filter and waste hose; blockages will cause the water level to rise within the dishwasher and breach the rubber door seals.
● Open the machine and check the rubber door seals—if they are dirty or covered in lime, wipe them down with a cloth soaked in white vinegar.
● Worn or cracked seals will need to be replaced. The seals at the top and sides are easy to replace; lower seals are harder to replace because the door needs to be removed first—leave this job to a professional. Pull out the old seals, making sure to remove any fragments of rubber trapped around the edges. Clean the metal frame beneath the seals with household detergent, and press in the replacement rubber. You can buy this direct from the manufacturer or from online parts stores: make sure you buy a seal suited to the make and model of your machine.

Tighten the plumbing

If water is leaking from the inlet or outlet hoses at the rear of the machine, try tightening any plastic compression joints between the machine and your plumbing and waste systems.
● Check the hoses for cracks; depending on the model, damaged hoses may be simple to replace with new ones, or may require partial disassembly of the machine.
● Call a repairman if the leak is from the body of the dishwasher—it is likely to need a professional repair.

Lime and food debris can build up on the rubber door seals of a dishwasher, causing water to leak. Wipe them down with a cloth dipped in white vinegar to make them watertight.

The plate rack is chipped
Touch it up with epoxy paint

When the coating on the tines of your dishwasher's racks chips off, heat and moisture soon cause corrosion in the metal beneath. This is not only unsightly, but can scratch your dishes and stain them with rust. You can cover the holes with a little paint as a short-term fix, but you should replace the rack as soon as you can.
● Use a tough, waterproof, epoxy-based paint (available from most hardware stores) to paint over the chipped areas. Allow it to dry for at least 24 hours before running a wash cycle. If the problem returns, you may have no option but to buy a new rack.

The dishwasher won't drain
Clean the filter and check the waste hose

Most drainage problems stem from a blocked filter. You should clean the filter weekly to prevent problems (see opposite).

● Switch off the machine at the main power source, then empty it of plates, pans, and cutlery and remove the lower rack. Beneath, you'll see the filter assembly. Turn the lever on top of the assembly to remove the mesh filter. Clean it under a running hot water, using a scrub brush to shift any trapped particles. Replace the filter and make sure it is securely tightened in place—if it is loose, dirty water will circulate around the dishwasher.

● Carefully pull the dishwasher away from the wall and locate the waste hose—a corrugated plastic pipe that runs from the rear of the machine (usually at the bottom left) into a hard plastic drain pipe. Make sure that the waste hose has not become squashed behind the dishwasher and straighten out any kinks.

● If the machine still won't drain, you may have a faulty pump or drain valve—call for repair.

My glassware looks cloudy
Make it shine with a vinegar rinse

Glasses that emerge from your dishwasher with a bluish haze can often be cleared by dipping them in white vinegar. However, sometimes the cloudiness will persist because the glass itself has become irreversibly etched by the strongly alkaline dishwasher detergent, which can eat into the surface of glass. To minimize such damage, try washing at a lower temperature and regularly top up the level of dishwasher salt in your machine. Changing your dishwasher detergent can help, too. Delicate or expensive glassware should always be washed by hand, never in the dishwasher.

Try treating a cloudy glass with pure white vinegar: if this doesn't clear the glass, it may have been permanently discolored.

The dishwasher makes an alarming noise
Remove obstructions and balance the machine

Open the door of the dishwasher and check that no utensils have fallen loose or become lodged between the racks and sprayers. Make sure that the wheeled racks are sitting within their tracks.

● Use a level to ensure that the machine is level from front to back and side to side. Turn the dishwasher's adjustable feet until it is balanced.

● If the noises persist, call for repair—the bearing on the motor may be worn.

My dishwasher smells foul
Refresh it with lemon juice

Begin by cleaning the filter and wiping the rubber door seals with vinegar. Wash the interior of the dishwasher by running the machine empty on its most intensive program; listen out for the end of the first draining cycle—a gush of water being emptied into the drain. Open the door and place a cup of white vinegar onto the top shelf of the dishwasher; close the door and allow the program to finish. Next, rid yourself of the vinegary odor by putting half a cup of lemon juice into the dishwasher and running a short program. Never use bleach in your dishwasher.

● Don't let dirty dishes sit in the machine for too long—run a rinse and hold cycle if they are unlikely to be washed within a day.

● Avoid stopping a program until it has finished; if the cycle is not complete, dirty water will remain in the bottom of the machine.

Remove and clean the dishwasher's filter weekly. If possible, use your fingers to scoop out any food debris that has accumulated in the recess beneath the filter.

There is still food stuck to my plates
Load the dishwasher for best results

If your tableware comes out dirty from your dishwasher, it is most likely because the machine has been badly loaded. Every surface of your plates, pots, and pans must be exposed to your dishwasher's hot jets of water; and you need to be sure that nothing will obstruct the rotation of the spinning arms.

● Scrape the plates thoroughly before putting them into the machine, but don't bother to rinse them.

● Place heavy casserole dishes on the bottom rack at a slight incline, rather than flat, so they don't obstruct the flow of water. Slot baking trays and cutting boards along the outer sides of the lower rack.

● Slot plates into the bottom rack; they should face inward. Keep their surfaces well separated.

● Make sure breakables, such as glasses, don't touch one another—vibration can cause them to shatter.

● Don't overfill the cutlery basket, but don't worry about the orientation of knives, forks, and spoons. Avoid placing kitchen knives in the machine—wash them by hand.

My dishes are still dirty
Clean the spray arms

There are several possible causes of a loss of cleaning power. Before you start suspecting a faulty heater or pump, take a few easy steps that may solve your problem.

● Make sure your machine is correctly filled with dishwasher salt (needed to soften the water) and rinse-aid (needed to avoid smears on tableware and reduce drying times). Don't use table salt in place of dishwasher salt—you are likely to damage the machine.

● Clean the dishwasher's filter regularly and load the machine carefully to ensure that water and detergent can reach all its contents.

● Unblock the jets on the spray arms. Over time, the small holes on the rotating spray arms can become blocked with food particles or lime. Remove the spray arms from the machine—they are usually secured by a simple plastic clip around the collar or attached on a bayonet mount. Use a darning needle to gently clear any debris from the holes—don't use a wooden toothpick, the tip of which can snap and get stuck within the jet. Run some water from the faucet into the center of the spray arm and check that it flows easily through each jet before reassembly.

● Try selecting a different program or another formulation of dishwasher detergent.

CLEAR THE NOZZLES ON THE DISHWASHER'S SPRAY ARMS WITH A NEEDLE, THEN RUN WATER THROUGH THEM TO ENSURE THEY'RE CLEAR

OVENS, STOVES, AND HOODS

Cooking is a messy business, and appliances will inevitably suffer from spills, knocks, and the effects of heat. Stoves and ovens rely on high-power electrical circuits, flammable gas, or dangerous microwaves, and you should avoid getting out of your depth with repairs—call for service if in doubt. But there's plenty you can do to keep your oven looking good and working well.

My oven cooks unevenly
Clean the oven and elements

A dirty oven will distribute heat less evenly, so begin by giving it a thorough clean (see page 182). Don't use oven cleaning products on the heating elements, fan, or gas pilot light.

• Clean the heating elements of an electric oven by running it at its highest temperature with the door open for 30 minutes. This will burn off any grease stuck to their surfaces. The process will generate a lot of smoke, so switch off nearby smoke alarms and ensure the kitchen is well ventilated. Don't leave the oven unattended with its door open, and be careful not to trip over the open door. Keep all children and pets away from the kitchen until the oven has cooled.

• Remove any cooking stones, foil, or other cooking aids that may be blocking the flow of air through the oven or touching the thermostat sensor (which looks like a long tube inside the oven).

• If you have a self-cleaning oven, run a cleaning cycle once a month.

The gas rings burn orange
Identify the source and stop the flow

A gas flame should always burn blue. An orange flame indicates incomplete burning of the gas and is potentially dangerous because it results in the release of poisonous carbon monoxide gas.

• Switch off the gas burner and allow it to cool. Lift off the burner assembly and place it in a bowl of warm, soapy water for 10 minutes. Wipe off any visible grime, and then use a pin to clear any debris from the inside of the holes of the burner, where the gas flames are emitted. Allow the burner to dry; replace it and try again. If the problem persists, call for repair immediately—do not use the stove until the fault is resolved.

• If the flame is blue but uneven, clean the burner as described above and make sure it is correctly seated when replaced.

TOOLS OF THE TRADE

Oven thermometer

When you set your oven to 400°F, it's unlikely that it heats up evenly to this temperature. Most ovens have hot and cool spots and getting to know where they are will make you a better chef. Use an inexpensive oven thermometer (which can be bought from cooking stores) to compare the actual temperature of different parts of the oven with that set on the dial. Draw a simple map of the oven for future reference.

The oven's control dials are melting
Check and replace the door seal

An oven's control dials may be located just above the oven door and so may get warm in normal use—especially if you have an older model. If they become hot to the touch or even start melting, it's probably a sign that heat is leaking out of the oven because its rubber seals have worn out.

● Allow the oven to cool and switch it off at the main power source. Open the door and inspect the silicone rubber door seal; if it's intact but hanging away from the metal, try pressing it back into position. If it has become brittle and parts have fallen away, it's easy to install a replacement.

● Depending on your model, the rubber seal may be pressed into a groove, or retained behind metal clamps. Pull away the seal or loosen the screws to remove it. Pry away any stubborn pieces of rubber with a plastic scraper, then wash the area behind the old seal with strong detergent. Rinse and allow to dry.

● Buy a new seal—make sure it is compatible with the make and model of your oven—and press it into position, ensuring that it is free from kinks.

The oven doesn't heat up
Let it cool before a restart

Ovens are fitted with thermal cutoff switches that kill the power to the elements if the oven overheats. Try switching the oven off at the main power source and wait until it has cooled completely before attempting a restart. If this doesn't work, call for repair.

The oven is dirty
Reduce the pain of cleaning

Cleaning an oven is a daunting task, but it is possible to reduce the amount of effort needed to do a good job.

● Fill a heatproof dish or metal tray with water and place it in the oven; set the temperature to its highest setting and leave for an hour or so—the steam will help loosen accumulated grease and grime.

● Allow the oven to cool down, then remove the door—it's easier than it sounds and it'll make it far easier to reach the oven interior. To do this, fully open the oven door to expose the hinges; each hinge is fitted with a locking lever that keeps the door in place. Flip the levers up and grip the door firmly with both hands. Close the door until you feel some resistance—you should now be able to lift the whole door away from the oven. Place the door unit on an old towel on top of the kitchen counter. Use a glass scraper to remove any grease baked onto the window glass.

● Before cleaning the inside of the oven, lay down a few layers of newspaper on the floor to catch the inevitable drips, and protect your hands and arms with rubber gloves and long sleeves.

● You can use caustic cleaner (available from all supermarkets) to clean the oven, but be aware that these chemicals are extremely strong and can damage rubber door seals and the glue that secures the oven's glass window. Keep the liquid or gel away from these areas, and carefully follow the instructions.

● A more traditional and gentler method is to use a combination of baking soda and vinegar. First, wet the cold oven with water and use an old cloth to rub a thick layer of baking soda over all the surfaces except the heating elements. Leave this for 4 hours, then fill a spray bottle with white vinegar. Spray the vinegar over the baking soda paste and leave it to fizz away and penetrate the grease for another few hours, before scrubbing the interior with a plastic (not metal) scouring pad and rinsing with warm water to finish. Now clean the door in the same way. Give the window some sparkle by spraying it with pure white vinegar before wiping it away with a damp sponge.

● Metal oven shelves can be cleaned in the dishwasher—run an intensive program with your usual dishwasher detergent. Alternatively, cover the shelves with a commercial oven cleaning gel or paste and place them in a large plastic bag, such as a garbage bag, for a few hours to keep the gel moist and active. Scrub clean with hot water. If you don't have a commercial cleaner, use a strong solution of biological clothes-washing liquid instead.

Removing the door makes it much easier to clean the inside of the oven. Locate the hinges (see below, left) and fully open their locking levers (see below, center); if you don't, the hinges could snap shut with great force. Grip both sides of the door, then close the door until you feel some resistance. Close it just a little further, then pull the door away from the oven (see below, right).

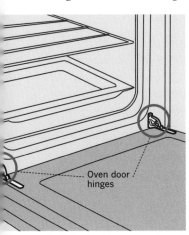

Oven door hinges

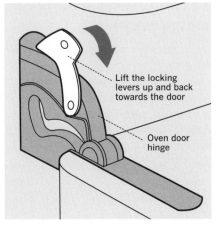

Lift the locking levers up and back towards the door

Oven door hinge

Lift the door away from the oven

When the igniter clicks, but doesn't make a spark to light the gas, scrub the head of the igniter with an old toothbrush to clean any food or grease from its surface.

The gas flame won't light
Clean the spark igniter

Lighting a gas flame on your cooktop should just be a matter of pushing the ignition button. This triggers a spark between the metal of the burner and an electrode (which resembles a small ceramic spark plug) next to the burner assembly.

● If your stove doesn't spark, first turn off the power to your stove. Lift off the burner head to get full access to the igniter, then scrub its surface with an old toothbrush. If it's covered with grease, wash it with a damp cloth and allow to dry before turning on the flame.

My microwave's carousel is stuck
Get it back on track

If your microwave's carousel isn't rotating, a good cleaning will often free it up.

● Lift the glass platter and wheeled turntable out of the microwave. Beneath, you'll see the track in which the wheeled ring turns, as well as a notched wheel in the center.

● Close the door and, very briefly, turn the microwave on; look through the window to see if the notched wheel is spinning. If not, you will need to have the microwave serviced by a professional. If it is, clean the carousel track and turntable well with a household degreaser. Before you put it back in, apply a drop of cooking oil to each of the wheels.

My microwave oven is dirty
Steam it clean

Mix a cup of vinegar with a cup of water in a large, microwave-safe bowl. Microwave the mixture on high to a full, rolling boil. Let it boil for around a minute, then remove the container and wipe the microwave clean with kitchen towels while it is still warm and damp.

I can see sparks inside my microwave oven
Check for stray metal

Stray scraps of foil or metal become charged when bombarded by microwaves. The air around the scrap also becomes charged, creating electric sparks and potentially causing the microwave to overheat. To cure the problem, start by giving the oven a thorough cleaning (see above).
● Unplug the microwave and clean the waveguide cover—a plate with a metallic sheen, which is usually secured to the back or side wall of the oven interior with a screw or clips. The plate protects the workings of the microwave from splashes, but if food gets stuck to it, it can burn and send out sparks. Carefully unscrew or unclip the cover and clean it with a household detergent. Allow it to dry completely before replacing.
● If you find any burn spots—brown marks on the inside walls of the microwave—sand them smooth with sandpaper then paint over with a specialist microwave touch-up paint (available online). If there are any holes in the walls, unplug the microwave immediately. Do not use it until it has been checked by a technician.

The exhaust fan doesn't clear the kitchen
Change or clean the filters

Clearing blocked filters will extend your exhaust fan's life and reduce the risk of fire caused by a buildup of grease. Before starting, switch off the power to the fan. There are two types of exhaust fan: those that are flat, and chimney-style designs.
● Flat fans usually can have paper filters, which should be replaced around every six months, or whenever they become saturated with grease. Chimney-style fans have mesh filters, which you can clean in a dishwasher set to its intensive cycle or by usinging the baking soda and vinegar combination used to clean ovens (see page 183).
● With the filters removed, clean the fan. Wipe its surfaces with household detergent to remove grease that may unbalance the fan.
● Check the fan's exhaust vent on the exterior of your house, making sure it is not obstructed by leaves or by a bird's nest.

WARNING

Microwave ovens operate at very high voltages, and charge remains stored when the microwave is switched off. Never remove the casing.
● Avoid running the microwave when it is empty—you risk damaging it.

LIVING SPACES

Your choice of interior fixtures and furnishings is a statement of your individuality and helps turn your house into a home. These big-ticket items are subject to heavy everyday wear and occasional spills, knocks, and tears; most can be restored or maintained in good condition at minimal cost.

CURTAINS, BLINDS, CARPETS, AND FLOORS

A scratch on your new wooden floor, a glass of red wine spilled on a cream carpet, or a collapsed curtain needn't ruin your day. Quick and inexpensive fixes using everyday household items can restore your pride in your home.

My curtain rod has fallen down
Strengthen the fixtures and reattach the rod

A fallen curtain rod can mean that the original hardware fittings were too weak or that the plaster that they were screwed had "blown" or crumbled with age.

● Tap the wall above the window: if the plaster sounds hollow, it has probably blown—meaning that it has become detached from the wall. If there is an adjacent area of sound plaster, simply reposition the brackets. If not, screw a long batten to the top edge of the window and fix the rod brackets to the batten to spread the load.

● If the plaster is sound, you can reuse the existing holes. Drill the holes deeper with a power drill so that they can accommodate a heavier-duty wall plug. Use a vacuum cleaner to suck any plaster dust from the enlarged holes. Squirt some quick-drying, strong adhesive into the hole, then push in the new plug and allow it to set overnight. Reinstall the curtain rod with new, longer screws.

My curtains don't hang straight
Train your curtains or weight the seams with coins

If your curtains just won't hang in neat pleats, it's time for a little training—"teaching" the fabric how to move.

● Hang your curtains on the rod or track and open them fully. Push the fabric into the desired wave shapes until you are happy with the depth and interval of the folds. Then, use a strip of plastic wrap to make a loop

Secure plastic wrap around the pleats in your curtains and leave for a few days to train them how to hang.

around the bunched curtain, holding it in position. Secure a band of plastic wrap every 24 inches or so down the length of the curtain, and leave the curtains tied in this way for three days. When you release the fabric, it should have "learned" its new shape.

● If you have a steam cleaner, close the curtains and direct steam from the nozzle, working evenly from the header to the hemline. Open the curtains before they have cooled, and tie them with plastic wrap as above; leave for three days.

● If your curtains are lined, try sliding a coin or fishing weight into the hem, where the lining and panel hem meet. The extra weight will encourage the curtains to hang straight down.

The curtains stick
Clean and straighten the curtain track

Curtains that run on tracks should open and close smoothly; if they stick, the track itself could be bent or the rollers and pulleys that carry the curtains could be jammed.

● Close your curtains to the point at which they stick. Using a stepladder, climb up and inspect the track at this point. If it is visibly bent, use some pliers to gently work it back into shape.

● Move the pulleys and roller with your fingers—if any of them is stuck, give it a squirt of WD-40 and manipulate it until it is free.

● Make sure there are no knots in the cords used to open and close the curtains, and use the brush attachment of a vacuum cleaner to clean any dust or debris from the curtain tracks.

My blinds won't open or close
Unjam the locking mechanism

If your venetian blinds sag at one side or won't move up or down at all, the gear that grips the control cord has probably seized.
● Try exaggerating the action you use to operate the blinds, pulling the cord high up to the left and then to the right to free it from the gear.
● If this doesn't work, erect a stepladder and climb up so that you are at eye level with the top bar of the blinds. Peer into the hole where the control cord enters the bar; you should be able to see a small metal lever or gear. Use a small flat-head screwdriver to lift this mechanism and free the cord.

My window shade has lost tension
Adjust the tension by hand

Sprung roller shades are made of an aluminum tube that encloses a coiled spring. When you pull down on the shade, the tension on the spring increases; when you stop pulling, a ratchet engages with a pin to keep it extended until the tension is released and the shade rolls back up. If your shade won't roll up, there's a simple solution.
● Unroll the shade a further 24 inches, then lift it off its mounting brackets. Roll up the shade evenly by hand and replace it in the bracket. Repeat the process until it rolls up freely.
● Conversely, if the shade won't stay down, the tension is too tight. Take down the shade, unroll it by about 24 inches, then replace it and test the tension by opening and closing it. Repeat if necessary until the blind operates perfectly.

Someone's treaded gum into my carpet
Cool the gum to remove the problem

Lay a freezer block, a handful of ice cubes wrapped in a plastic bag, or a packet of frozen peas over the chewing gum to chill it. Then just peel off the gum.

I've singed my carpet
Snip away the damage

If the burn isn't too deep, try cutting off the burnt tips of the carpet's pile with a sharp pair of scissors, leaving the good fibers underneath. You can try the same approach with a stain if it doesn't go deep into the pile.

Using an ice pack to cool gum makes it lose its grip on carpet fibers, allowing you to pick it off with ease.

There's a deep burn on my carpet
Match it and patch it

If the damage is too deep for a quick fix (see left), you can make and fit a patch to improve the carpet's appearance. You'll be glad if you've kept some offcuts of carpet, but don't fret if not—you can cut a patch from an out-of-the-way place, such as under the sofa. If your carpet is patterned, cut a patch that duplicates the pattern of the damaged piece.

Time needed **1 hour**
You will need **trimming knife, metal ruler, hammer, carpet adhesive, double-sided sticky tape**

1 Using the trimming knife, cut a square patch slightly larger than the damaged area. Use the ruler to keep the edges neat. Lay the patch over the burnt area, making sure that the pile of both runs in the same direction. Run your hand over the carpet—the smoothest direction is the run of the pile. Hold the patch down firmly with the ruler and cut in a straight line through both the patch and the carpet beneath with the knife.

2 Lift out and remove the damaged piece of carpet, revealing the floor underneath. Squeeze carpet adhesive around the edges of the hole, no more than halfway up the

pile of the carpet (see below, left). Do the same along the edges of the patch for maximum adhesion.

3 Lay down a rectangle of double-sided tape under the edges of the hole so that half of the tape width is under the carpet and half protrudes into the hole (see below, center). Peel the backing off the tape and press the carpet down firmly.

4 Place the patch in position and press down firmly to stick the patch to the protruding tape. Finally, tap lightly round the join with the hammer to secure the patch (see below, right).

Furniture has left dents in my carpet
Iron out the problem and make the room look great

The pressure of heavy furniture will leave long-lasting dents in carpets that become glaringly obvious when you rearrange the room. For a quick fix, try putting an ice cube on the indentation. Allow it to melt and dry. If the dent is more stubborn, try the following:

● Plug in your steam iron near the dent, setting it to a medium heat. Dampen a clean cotton rag with water and place it over the dent.
● Lightly run the iron over the dent; the fibers should spring back up.
● Allow the carpet to dry fully, then run over the edges of the dent with the side of a coin to fluff up the final reluctant fibers.

ALWAYS TEST YOUR CLEANING SOLUTION ON AN INCONSPICUOUS AREA OF CARPET BEFORE USING IT ON THE STAIN

Seven ways to save a stained carpet

Whatever you've spilled on your carpet, start by blotting up as much of the liquid as possible with an absorbent white paper towel before dabbing with your solution of choice (see below). Never scrub the carpet—you'll end up pushing the stain deeper into the fibers.

1 Ink stains: spray the area with WD-40. Leave for 15 minutes before dabbing the stain with a cloth soaked in warm water and detergent. If this doesn't work, try dabbing the stain with a cloth dipped in isopropyl (rubbing) alcohol.

2 Grease and oil: sprinkle the mark with salt, baking soda, or cornstarch; don't rub it in—allow it to work for at least a couple of hours before vacuuming the area.

3 Fruit juice: gently work a little shaving cream into the stain, then wipe it away with a damp sponge.

4 Coffee or tea: sponge on a 50:50 mixture of warm water and white vinegar, then blot the stain clean with an absorbent paper towel.

5 Red wine: deal with red wine stains as soon as you can after the spill—if left, the stain turns purple and becomes near-impossible to remove. Pour some white wine directly onto the stain; dampen a cloth with cold water and dab the stain to lift out the wine. Alternatively, cover the stain generously with table salt; allow to dry before vacuuming.

6 Pet urine: you'll smell this but may not see it! Buy or borrow an ultraviolet light—it makes urine stains glow in the dark. Mark the outline of the stain in chalk, blot thoroughly and treat with a specialist enzyme cleaner from a pet store or a "biological" washing agent.

7 Mud: allow the mud to dry completely and vacuum thoroughly using a machine with a beater brush. If marks remain, saturate the stain with soda water, then blot with a clean cloth. Repeat until the stain has vanished.

My rug slips on the wooden floor
Make it safe with an old inner tube

A sliding rug can be a real hazard. A quick and temporary way to stop it moving across the floor is to spray the underside of the rug with hair spray. For a more permanent fix, try the following:
● Cut an old bicycle inner tube lengthways and flatten it out. Use a rubber-based adhesive to glue the rubber strips to the edges of the rug.
● For the best, if not the cheapest, solution, buy a roll of rubber mesh from a carpet store, cut this to the size of your rug and place it between the rug and the hard floor. The mesh provides a little space between the floor and the rug, allowing it to "breathe."

The rug looks faded and lifeless
Restore it with salt treatment

If your rug has started to look past its best, you can refresh it with a salt wash.
● First, thoroughly vacuum the rug.
● Test the process on a corner of the rug to ensure color fastness.
● Stir around 1 cup of table salt into a gallon of warm water.
● Wet a microfiber cloth in the concentrated salt solution. Wring out the cloth—it should be damp, not dripping.
● Rub the rug vigorously with the damp cloth; allow it to dry thoroughly and vacuum it once more to remove any salt crystals.

Make it last CARPETS

Clean your carpet regularly—don't wait for it to look dirty. Grit and dust work their way down into the carpet pile and act as abrasives as you walk on them, destroying the carpet fibers.

Change the layout by moving furniture around in a room every six months or so. Changing the direction of traffic in the room will even out wear and tear and extend the life of your carpets.

Close blinds when you're out because strong sunlight will bleach exposed areas of carpet, leaving behind darker patches beneath objects that become all too obvious when the objects are moved.

The floorboards squeak
Get some peace with powder and a brush

Noisy boards are easy to silence—when you can get at them. If they are covered by carpet or other flooring materials, don't risk putting a nail or screw through "blindly" as you could hit a water pipe or an electrical cable. Once the carpet is out of the way:

● Walk slowly over the floor to locate the source of the squeak. Sprinkle talcum powder between the floorboards in the squeaky area; this will help boards move past one another silently.

● Boards will squeak if they are not fixed firmly to the supporting joists. Find the loose board and try hammering the nail back into the joist. Use a nail punch to help you to drive the nail below the surface of the board. If it will not hold, drive a new nail into an adjacent area of wood.

I've scratched my wooden floor
Disguise the damage

Wooden floors are usually protected by layers of wax or a coat of tough polyurethane varnish. Waxed floors are especially vulnerable to scuffs, scratches, and staining.

● Polish out light scuff marks with a damp cloth, then apply a little shoe polish in a matching shade to disguise them even further.

● Rub over a deeper scratch with the edge of a penny—this will soften the hard sides of the gouge enough to make it less noticeable.

● Choose a marker or felt-tipped pen in a color that matches your floor, and color in the exposed wood left by a deep scratch.

● Wood floors can be dented by stiletto heels or by dropped objects. If your floor is untreated or waxed, try dampening a microfiber cloth and leave it over the dent for a few hours—this may plump up the wood fibers and level the surface.

There's a stain on the wooden floor
Use some abrasive to remove the marks

Most stains and heat marks on waxed wooden floors can be removed by rubbing the surface with fine steel wool or sandpaper (for deeper stains) and then feathering in wax to finish.

● If the stains are dark, use a clean cotton cloth to apply some pure white vinegar to the spots after rubbing them with steel. Hold it in place for 5 minutes before sanding again. Allow to dry and reapply wax to finish.

Moving the furniture scratches my floor

Put a sock on it to protect those boards

Wooden floors look great and are warm underfoot, but they are easily damaged. When shifting heavy furniture over a wooden floor, slip a thick sock onto each leg of the table or cabinet. Not only will this prevent you from damaging the floor, but you may also be able to slide the furniture instead of lifting it. Try moving it a small distance first, checking as you go that you are not leaving a mark.

TAKE THE STRAIN OUT OF MOVING FURNITURE BY SLIPPING SOME SOCKS ON ITS LEGS

There's a bubble in my vinyl floor
Burst and flatten it to a level finish

Changes in temperature or humidity can make bubbles appear under your vinyl or other layered flooring—this can also happen to flooring that was laid hastily or using an inappropriate adhesive. You can deal with the bubbles and save yourself the expense of a new floor.
- Use a craft knife or scalpel to make a small cut through the middle of each bubble.
- Squirt vinyl adhesive from the bottle into the cut.
- Use a rolling pin or a bottle to flatten the bubble and spread out the adhesive within, and wipe away any glue that has been forced out onto the surface of the floor.
- Place a heavy, flat object (such as a pile of books) on the bubble and leave overnight. Allow the adhesive to dry.

I've gouged my vinyl floor
Make your own floor filler

If possible, find a leftover piece of vinyl or cut a small fragment from an unseen part of the floor—under an appliance or within a cupboard, for example. Grate your scrap of vinyl on the finest side of a cheese grater and mix the vinyl shavings with clear nail polish in a jar. Use an old flat-bladed knife or putty knife to apply your homemade filler to the damaged area; build up the repair in a few layers for a perfect color match.

Make it last FLOORS

Protect vulnerable floors by gluing felt pads to the underside of chair legs. Place rugs in areas where people are likely to drop heavy objects—for example, on the floor in front of a cabinet.

Clean up quickly after a spill of liquid—even water. Don't place old bottles on the floor—traces of liquid they contained may run down the outside of the bottle, making stubborn rings on the floor.

Keep your leftovers in a designated box in the garage or a cupboard. Pieces of flooring, carpet, curtain, or upholstery material can be invaluable when it comes to patching up damage.

VACUUMS AND FLOOR CLEANERS

A vacuum cleaner might cover thousands of miles over a decade of heavy use, so it's bound to suffer a few problems in its life span. If your cleaner's motor has blown, it's rarely worth the cost of a repair, but many everyday vacuum problems have quick fixes.

My vacuum has lost its suction
Check for blockages and air leaks

A vacuum cleaner is basically an electric fan that sucks air and dust up a tube into a bag or chamber. The air is then filtered and expelled. Upright cleaners have revolving, belt-driven brushes to beat dust out of carpets, while cylinder cleaners rely on suction alone, and some designs have bags to collect dust while others don't.

● If suction drops when using a cylinder cleaner, check that you haven't sucked up something that has blocked the hose. Turn off the machine and take off each section of the hose in turn, starting with the one farthest from the motor. Switch the cleaner on after each stage and check the suction; if it comes back, the obstruction must be in the hose section you just removed. Now you can focus on unblocking the hose (see 196).

● If the hose is clear, check the dust bag and filters. Replace a full or ripped bag right away, or, on a bagless model, empty a full dust canister. Wash or replace clogged filters. Don't be tempted to repair a burst dust bag with tape—they're not reusable.

● Check the revolving brush on your upright cleaner—it can get stopped up with tangles of hair or string, which reduces cleaning power. Cut the strands with scissors and unravel them.

The cleaner's hose is blocked
Push out the obstruction

Is something wedged in your vacuum cleaner's hose? If shaking, blowing, and jiggling have failed, try pushing it out, but not with a stick—a damaged hose is just another problem to fix.

• A length of garden hose is the perfect tool: flexible, long enough to push all the way through (most vacuum cleaner hoses extend at least 6 feet) and the rubbery plastic won't tear the hose.

• Disconnect the blocked pipe and feed the garden hose in from the vacuum cleaner end until you reach the obstruction. It's usually easiest to push the blockage back out the way it came in. Gently prod to try to shift it.

• If you can't make the blockage move, remove the hose and try again from the other end, alternating ends until the blockage comes free.

The suction is still poor
Patch any splits in the hose

• Check the vacuum's hose for splits. Bandage damaged areas with duct tape, pushing it firmly between the ridges of the corrugated hose.

Make it last VACUUMS AND FLOOR CLEANERS

Always empty dust bags before they get full. A loaded bag puts extra strain on the vacuum's motor and makes it likely to burn out before its time.

Check that the "bag full" indicator on your cleaner is working. Cover the end of the hose with your hand to simulate a loss of suction and watch or listen for the warning to activate. If there's no alert, you need help.

Listen to your vacuum—if its sound suddenly changes to a higher pitch, turn off the power, unplug the vacuum and check the bag, hose, and filters for any sign of an obstruction.

Don't wait for a problem to occur: check hoses regularly for splits or obstructions and change or wash all filters every three months.

Look where you're going because vacuuming up objects such as paper clips or toys can damage the internal parts of your machine. Pick them up before they clutter up the hose. Try fixing a magnetic strip to the front edge of the vacuum's cleaning head—it will trap small metal objects before they can do any damage.

TABLES AND CHAIRS

The white stain on your best table where someone forgot to use a coaster, the dent in the kitchen table where you dropped that can of beans, and the sagging cane seat can all be fixed with ease.

My wicker seat is saggy
Give it a lift with a vinegar bath

Over time, a woven wicker or rattan seat will begin to sag, but it's easy to get it as tight as a drum again.
- Mix hot water with an equal amount of distilled vinegar: you'll need about one quart per chair.
- Take the chair outdoors, soak an old towel in the liquid and swab it generously onto the top of the wicker seat. Then turn the chair upside down and drape the wet towel over the bottom of the wicker seat.
- Allow to soak for 2–3 hours, then let the chair dry fully; the seat should now be taut.

The dining table is wobbly
Get it back on the level

Start by making sure that the legs are secure: tighten any loose brackets or screws and pull apart and re-glue any loose joints (see page 199). If that doesn't fix the wobbles, try these temporary solutions:
- Place the table on a completely level floor and identify which of the table's legs is shorter than the others.
- Use a sharp knife to cut several thin slices from a wine cork. Clean the bottom of the short leg and glue a slice of cork in place using wood glue, wiping away any glue that squeezes out of the joint.
- Allow the glue to dry and check the level of the table. If it still rocks, add another slice of cork. Repeat this process until you have completely banished the wobbles.
- For an even quicker fix, upend the table and squirt a little silicone bathroom sealant onto the "short" leg. Smooth it to the required depth with a flat knife; allow the sealant to set. Turn the table over and test its level. You can add another layer of sealant if the leg is still too low, or pare the sealant back with a craft knife if it is too high.

Slice and glue thin sections of cork to the short leg of a wobbly table to build up its height.

Seven ways to make that scratch disappear

A gouge or scratch will spoil the look of a tabletop. Dust the affected area and clean it with a microfiber cloth, then try one of these remedies to match the color and texture of your table.

TREAT CRACKED WOOD WITH A LITTLE MAYONNAISE FOR TWO TO THREE DAYS. OILS IN THE MAYO WILL HELP SWELL THE WOOD AND FILL THE CRACK

1 Make a small cup of very strong coffee and apply it to the scratch with a soft cloth. This should stain the exposed wood to the darker color of the finished wood.

2 Hide the scratch by rubbing it over with a little shoe polish of a matching color. Alternatively, try an eyebrow pencil—this is soft, oil-based, and brown colored—ideal for camouflaging anything from small surface scratches to deeper ones.

3 If the scratch is deeper, raid your children's wax crayon set. Grate part of a crayon into a small bowl; rest the bowl in a pan of boiling water to melt the wax, then drip the wax into the gouge, smoothing it with a flat knife. You can mix a color to match your wood by adding shavings from crayons of several colors.

4 Nut oils are perfect for repairing damaged wood. Rub a walnut kernel over a scratch to diminish it, or apply a little walnut oil with a soft cloth.

5 Peanut butter makes a good beauty treatment for damaged wood. Rub a little on, leave it for an hour or so, then clean and buff.

6 Smear petroleum jelly over a scratch and leave it overnight. It might help the surrounding wood to plump up and fill in the scratch. Wipe away in the morning and polish the surface.

7 On a French-polished tabletop, try removing the scratch with car polish. Take care to polish lightly so that you don't rub away the rest of the finish.

My favorite chair is falling apart
Belt up and get it back into shape

Loose or wobbly legs are a common problem in older chairs. Take action by re-gluing the horizontal bars, or stretchers, that hold the legs together.

- First, pull out each stretcher where it meets the leg and use a little sandpaper to remove the old glue.
- Apply some new wood glue and refix the joint. Work your way round the chair until you have re-glued all the joints.
- Now you need to hold the joints firm while the glue dries. The easiest way to do this is to take a couple of belts (or an old suitcase strap) and buckle them together. Wrap the belts round the legs, tighten them as much as you can, fasten them together and leave to set for 24 hours.

A drink has left a white ring on my table
Rub it out with a homemade paste

Moisture on the outside of a glass or bottle can drip down to its base and penetrate beneath some wood finishes to leave an ugly white ring. The first remedy to try is drying; blast the ring with a stream of cool (not hot) air from a hair dryer. If the ring persists, you'll need some very light abrasive to remove the stain.

- Mix a dryish paste from a tablespoon of salt or baking soda and a little water. Apply to a cloth and rub the white ring gently in a circular motion. You could use white (not gel) toothpaste instead.
- If your table is valuable or antique, don't try to fix it yourself—leave it to a professional.

A pair of belts buckled together into a loop will hold wooden joints together while a glued repair sets.

I've dented the tabletop
Plump it up with a steam iron

Dropping a hard object onto a table may leave behind a shallow dent. Try plumping up the wood fibers again to repair the damage.

- Lay a damp dish towel or microfiber cloth over the damage and gently iron over it with a warm iron to encourage the squashed wood to swell up. Work slowly, checking your progress as you go, so that you avoid scorching the wood.

BEDROOMS AND BATHROOMS

The bedroom and bathroom are the most personal areas of the home—where we rest and prepare for the day ahead, where we store and care for our clothes and groom ourselves. Keeping control of this environment will boost your sense of well-being and make your daily routines far more pleasant.

THE BEDROOM

We spend about a third of our lives in bed, so there's every reason to make our nocturnal environment as comfortable as possible. A sagging mattress, limp comforter, or creaking bed can ruin your sleep, while a broken hair dryer will get your day off to a bad start, but there's no need to put up with these problems.

My mattress is sagging
Give it a little more support

First, lift up your mattress and take a look at the frame beneath. You may find that some of the supporting wooden slats are cracked or broken. If so, try the following remedy:
- Measure the slats and buy exact replacements—most DIY stores will cut wood to size for you if you don't want to trim it yourself. Make sure the new slats are the same depth as the old ones so you don't create dips or bumps beneath the mattress. Remove the broken slats, and screw the new ones into place using screws slightly longer than the original ones.
- If the bed slats are intact, but the mattress is still saggy, lay a couple of sheets of Peg-Board across the whole area of the frame to spread the load when you are lying in bed. Don't use solid board: the holes in the Peg-Board will let your mattress breathe.
- A mattress that dips in just one area can easily be fixed to give you a good night's sleep until you buy a replacement. Take one or two spare blankets and fold them in half, and then in half again. Place the folded blanket(s) beneath the sagging area, and adjust its position until the mattress is level.

Fitting replacement bed slats is a simple job that will give you a smoother and more comfortable night's sleep.

Make it last MATTRESSES

Turn your mattress regularly to prolong its life. Make a habit of turning the mattress every time you change the sheets: alternate rotating it from top to bottom with flipping it over to ensure that it wears evenly. Tuck a note under the mattress to remind you which way to turn it next time around. "No turn" mattresses (which have one sleeping surface) should not be flipped but should still be rotated.

My mattress doesn't smell too fresh
Deodorize and freshen with baking soda

Deal with a musty mattress by making up a dry mixture of 50:50 baking soda and dried lavender (an herb that aids sleep and restfulness). Sprinkle the mixture evenly onto the surface of the mattress and leave it for a couple of hours before vacuuming off. Flip the mattress over and repeat on the other side.

My creaking bed is keeping me up at night
Check the frame, the mattress, and the floor

Loose joints are usually to blame for a squeaky bed, especially if the bed has a wooden frame, the components of which can swell and contract with the changing seasons.
● Tighten all the bolts and screws holding the frame and headboard together, and squirt a little WD-40 around each joint—even on a wooden frame—to subdue the sounds.
● Check that the mattress is centered on the frame.
● An uneven floor can make the bed frame twist and creak. Shift the bed slightly to ensure all the legs make good contact with the floor, or build up a short leg with slices of cork (see page 197).

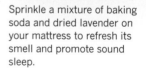

Sprinkle a mixture of baking soda and dried lavender on your mattress to refresh its smell and promote sound sleep.

The plump has gone from my comforter
Fluff it back up in your clothes dryer

When a good shake is no longer enough to plump up the fibers in your comforter, pop it in the dryer on a cool setting. Add a couple of new tennis balls and run the dryer for 30 minutes. The action of the balls as the comforter tumbles will bring the bounce back to your bedding.

My sliding closet doors shake
Clean the tracks

Debris in the tracks can obstruct the rollers on the underside of your closet doors. Use a vacuum cleaner with a brush attachment to pick up any dirt or larger objects in the tracks, then spray a little WD-40 onto the tracks and rollers, and spread it evenly with a dry cloth.

● Reattach any loose sections of track—these can often be clicked back into place or secured by tightening the retaining screws.

● Straighten any bent or dented sections of track with a pair of pliers wrapped in insulating tape to prevent scratching.

My drawers keep getting stuck
Get rid of the clutter and wax the runners

Old wooden chests of drawers can get sticky, especially if you tend—as many do—to overstuff them with clothes. Start by rationalizing your storage and bundling up unwanted clothes for the secondhand store. Make your drawers move more smoothly by rubbing candle wax or soap onto the runners in the frame and on the underside of the drawers. If this doesn't help, remove the drawers and lightly sand the runners with fine-grade sandpaper.

Rub a candle on the runners, frame, and underside of a sticking drawer to smooth its movement.

The rod in my closet is sagging
Reinforce it from within

An overburdened closet rod will begin to sag over time, causing your clothes to bunch up in the middle. This will wrinkle your clothes and make retrieving a particular garment from the crush a real struggle. The best remedy is to replace the rod, but the following fix provides an inexpensive solution.

● Most closet rods are no more than hollow metal tubes. Take the rod out of the closet by undoing its retaining screws at both ends. Buy a length of wooden dowel—the thickest that will fit within the rod—and cut it to the length of the rod. Insert the dowel into the rod and reinstall the strengthened assembly.

Seven ways to keep moths at bay

The central heating that keeps our homes warm year round also makes them into perfect breeding grounds for clothes moths. Female moths—small, silvery brown insects—lay their eggs, which resemble rice grains, in dark, warm places and the larvae that emerge feed on natural fibers in your clothing and carpets. So how can you keep your house moth-free?

1 Switch off your heating as early in the year as possible and keep windows open whenever you can to allow air to circulate.

2 Keep any secondhand clothes purchases in sealed plastic bags until you've had a chance to wash or dry clean them thoroughly.

3 Shake out your clothing in the daylight once a month to dislodge larvae, which have a life cycle of three weeks. Beat rugs and soft furnishings in the daylight, too—brushing destroys eggs, and larvae will release their hold in daylight.

4 Vacuum clothes and fabrics to remove eggs from the fibers: be sure to dispose of your vacuum bag afterward. Vacuum carpets, under beds, and behind radiators regularly.

5 Moths love dirty fabrics, so always wash your clothes thoroughly (ideally at a temperature of 100°F or more, which destroys the larvae) or take them to the dry cleaners before storing them; once clean, keep your prized items in sealed plastic storage bags.

6 Try chemical repellant products. Mothballs will work, but only if used in a space where the fumes can build up to high concentrations—most will also transfer their strong smell to your clothes. Try more natural solutions, such as cedar. You can purchase blocks or shavings of this wood, or hangers made from cedar, from most department stores or online.

7 If all else fails, call in the professional pest controllers.

MOTHS LOVE SKIN AND HAIR PARTICLES, SO DON'T PUT DIRTY CLOTHES BACK INTO THE CLOSET

My hair dryer blows weakly
Free the fan from tangled hair

Every time you use your dryer, its fan pulls dirt, dust, and loose hair into the machine. These will eventually accumulate and slow the fan mechanism—your dryer may then overheat and blow its element. Prevent problems by cleaning the fan from time to time.

● Switch off and unplug the hair dryer. If it's hot, let it cool down, then use a flat-bladed screwdriver to pry open the casing or remove the screws holding the casing together.

● Use tweezers to pull out any hairs wrapped around the fan or motor (especially its spindle) and to pick off any hair or debris trapped elsewhere within the casing. If there is a removable filter, take it out and rinse it in warm water then leave to dry completely.

● Dust inside the casing with a soft paintbrush and vacuum the grille of the air intake vent, scrubbing it gently with an old toothbrush. Reassemble the hair dryer, test it, and you're ready to go.

My flat iron is too cool
Use a towel to remove baked-on hair products

The ceramic plates of your flat iron will pick up the residue of hair-care products every time it is used. The products can fuse to the plates, and over time build up into a thick film that stops heat from reaching (and straightening) your hair.

● To clean the plates, switch on the flat iron and use it on a damp towel, gripping and sliding along the towel as if it were your hair. This should shift most of built-up residue, but if some remains, allow the plates to cool and rub their surfaces with a rag dipped in ceramic-oven cleaner. Wipe the cleaner off with a damp cloth before using the iron on your hair.

My hair clippers are sluggish
Clean and oil the blades

Electric hair-clipper blades are self-sharpening, so if your blades are dull, it is probably because the clippers are dirty.

● Remove the blades unit from the clippers; dip an old toothbrush in isopropyl (rubbing) alcohol and gently scrub the blades. Place a couple of drops of blade oil (or light machine oil) onto the blades and run the clippers for 10 minutes—they'll sharpen themselves. Be sure to brush any debris from the blades after every use to keep them in good working order.

SHOWER AND BATHROOM

Bathrooms suffer from the combined effects of humidity, which can cause mildew, and lime, which clings to shower doors. These and other bathroom problems can be addressed with common household materials and a little know-how.

There's mildew on my walls
Clear it with bleach

Mildew is a mold, or fungus, that grows wherever it is damp and warm. It can indicate a water leak from a pipe or gutter, but is most often caused by condensation of warm, wet air on cooler walls and surfaces—conditions that prevail in the bathroom. If your wall is stained by mildew, try the following remedy:

• Wearing rubber gloves, mix three parts water with one part household bleach in a bucket. Soak a sponge in the solution, then thoroughly wet the affected area of the wall. Leave for 20 minutes, then repeat, whether the stain has disappeared or not. After another 20 minutes, rinse the wall with water. Allow to dry completely and then spray the wall with an antimicrobial agent. This can be bought from hardware shops.

• When you buy a new shower curtain, soak it overnight in salt water before you hang it to keep mildew at bay. Get into the habit of closing the curtain after use, so that it dries quickly and isn't left bunched up. If you do notice mildew developing on your shower curtain, pop it in the washing machine with a couple of towels to help cushion the curtain from impacts with the machine's beaters, and wash it on a gentle cycle with detergent and half a cup of baking soda.

My shower curtain has torn from its hangings
Reinforce the top strip

It's easy to accidentally rip a shower curtain if you slip and grab it for support; damage usually occurs to the holes at the top of the curtain.

• For a temporary fix, cut a strip of self-adhesive shelf liner 5 inches deep and as long as the curtain is wide. Stick this along the entire top edge of the curtain, with half the depth of the strip on the front side of the curtain. Fold the strip over the top and press it against the back of the curtain, too. Use a hole punch to reinstate the holes in the reinforced curtain top. Choose the color of the shelf liner to match or complement the color of your shower curtain, or go with clear liner.

Attach a strip of self-adhesive shelf liner (top) to a torn shower curtain and make a new hole with a hole punch (bottom).

The exhaust fan isn't clearing the bathroom
Free any blocked ducts

A sluggish exhaust fan will fail to clear your bathroom of steam after you've taken a bath or shower. Surface dampness will cause mildew and condensation stains unless you take action.

● Check the point on your outside wall where the fan duct meets fresh air. Clear any obstructions, such as climbing plants or birds' nests, away from the vent.

● If the moist air is carried out via ducts in the attic of the house, climb up into the roof space with a flashlight. Check that a box or suitcase hasn't fallen onto the ducting, kinking it or flattening it altogether. Look along the whole length of the duct pipe, searching for cracks or tears that might reduce the fan's efficiency. Bandage any splits with duct tape.

My bathroom scales are flattering me
Clean and recalibrate for an accurate reading

If you suspect that your bathroom scales are inaccurate, weigh yourself on some reliable scales at your doctor's office or health club. A difference between the two readings indicates that your scales may need some attention.

● Dirt or dust can interfere with the mechanism within your bathroom scales, giving a false reading. Open the casing of the scales. You'll probably need to remove two screws or springs holding the top and bottom together; then use your vacuum cleaner with its brush attachment to remove any dust and debris. Squeeze a drop of light machine oil onto all the moving parts, such as the levers and springs within the mechanism.

● Next, calibrate your scales; start by placing them on a level, hard surface (not a carpet). If you have analog scales (with a moving needle display), find the adjustment wheel or lever (usually on the side or back of the unit). Place an object of known weight (a dumbbell is ideal) in the center of the scales, then turn the adjustment lever until it shows the correct weight (20 lbs., for example). The scales are now calibrated.

● If your scales have a digital readout, make sure that you have inserted fresh batteries and then follow the manufacturer's guidelines for calibration.

CLOTHES AND PERSONAL ITEMS

Accidental damage can shorten the lives of our clothes and shoes, and put essential accessories, such as eyeglasses and hearing aids, out of action. And a stone lost from a brooch or a snapped necklace can be heartbreaking because such objects often carry sentimental as well as financial value. There are plenty of steps you can take to save money and protect your investments.

WATCHES AND JEWELRY

Repairs to watch mechanisms and to valuable jewelry are best left to the professionals, but it's worth attempting some simple fixes to less-precious items to keep them looking their best.

I've scratched my watch face
Polish it back to perfection

A shallow scratch on your watch face needn't mean a trip to the jeweler's—polish it out yourself.
- For a glass-faced watch, try using a jeweler's cloth to polish out the scratch. If you don't have one, dab a little non-gel toothpaste onto the face and rub it in gently with a lint-free cloth. Wipe off with a damp cloth and buff with a dry cloth.
- If the cover is plastic, try dipping a cotton swab into nail polish remover (acetone). Rub it along the scratch in a circular motion and then remove any excess liquid. Check the watch against the light and repeat until the scratch has disappeared.

My necklaces are tangled
Sprinkle on some talc to unravel them

If your jewelry box looks like a bowl of spaghetti, take a little time to untangle your necklaces.
- Lay the tangled mass onto some newspaper. Sprinkle on a little talc to lubricate the chains and use two straight pins to carefully ease any knots apart. Once they are all separated, wash the necklaces in a mild detergent, rinse, and carefully pat dry.

To open a jump ring, grip it at each end with a pair of needle-nose pliers and carefully twist the ends in opposite directions. Stop once the gap is large enough to slip the jump ring over an adjacent ring or other fitting. Close the ring by twisting the ends back with pliers until the gap is closed.

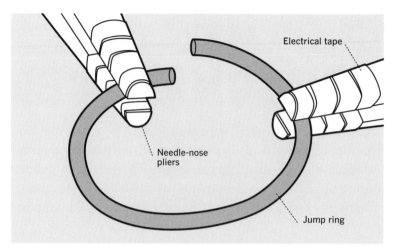

Electrical tape

Needle-nose pliers

Jump ring

The pendant has come off my chain
Repair the jump ring

Jewelers use jump rings to link together pendants, chains, and clasps. A jump ring is simply a metal ring with an opening that you can twist open and close tightly. Repairing a jump ring that has worked its way open is simple (see above). For added security, use a soldering iron (available from hardware stores) and lead-free solder to close up the gap in the jump ring.

Make it last JEWELRY

Clean your jewelry using a mild detergent (such as dishwashing liquid), warm water, and a soft toothbrush. Work in a plastic bowl, not over a sink, to avoid losing your jewelry down the drain. Don't use water on strings of beads—polish them with a soft, dry brush instead.

Never use harsh abrasives or strong cleaning agents as these may discolor certain stones. Be sure to remove your jewelry before you do your household cleaning.

Store your jewelry in its original box, which is usually lined with satin or velvet that keeps the piece safe from scratches. The box will also increase the value of the jewelry if you choose to sell it at a later date.

Regularly check for loose stones and weak links in chains. Fix them yourself or take them for professional repair before they fail—prevention is always better than cure.

GLASSES AND HEARING AIDS

You're lost without them, so when your eyeglasses or hearing aids break, you need a really quick fix. Loose screws are usually the problem with broken glasses, so it's worth investing in a set of tiny screwdrivers to tighten them up. The most common problems with hearing aids have to do with battery failure and blockages of earwax.

A screw has fallen out of my glasses
Make a temporary fix with fishing line

The hinges on the arms of your spectacles are held together by tiny screws. If one gets lost, there is a chance that the lens may not be held tightly in the frame and could drop out and break. Get a replacement as soon as possible, but in the meantime, make a temporary repair by cutting a short length of nylon fishing line. Put the glasses in their "open" position and thread the line through the screw hole with a pair of tweezers; loop the line through several times and then trim both ends so that only 2mm protrudes. Heat the tip of a knife over a flame, and touch it briefly to the free ends. This will melt them into small blobs, which will keep the line in place.

My glasses aren't level
Check the ear pieces

If your glasses sit askew, try bending their ear pieces to adjust their position. If you can't get a good grip with your fingers, use needle-nose pliers. Most opticians will adjust frames free of charge, but if you want to try your own repair, heat the metal of the frame in the steam from a teakettle to make it more pliable, then carefully, and little by little, bend the arms until they are straight once more.

The bridge has snapped
Soften the plastic and pin it back together

If your plastic-framed glasses snap at the bridge, carefully hold one snapped edge of the frame over the steam from a teakettle. When the plastic softens, insert a small needle into the broken edge so that half of it protrudes; allow the plastic to cool and harden around the needle. Now soften the other broken edge in the same way. Push the protruding pin fully into this softened section of the glasses, ensuring that the bridge is correctly aligned. Allow to cool before wearing.

WARNING !

Tiny screws, gemstones, and pieces of metalwork in jewelry can get lost very easily. Always work over a sheet of white paper so you can quickly spot anything you drop. Should a piece fall into the pile of your carpet, simply fetch your vacuum cleaner and stretch an old pair of nylon tights over the nozzle. Vacuum away, and the screw or stone will appear on the mesh of the nylon.

My hearing aid is not working
Check the settings and clean it up

Make sure the hearing aid is switched on. Then check that it is not set to pick up a hearing loop—it should be on the "microphone" setting for normal use.

- A dead battery is the most likely cause of a silent hearing aid. Try a replacement. Make sure that the battery is inserted the right way and that the compartment is fully closed. Some new batteries are supplied with one or both terminals covered with clear plastic film to protect them in storage—be sure to peel this off before use.
- If you have a behind-the-ear hearing aid, gently pull off the plastic tubing, wash it in soapy water, rinse, and leave to dry inside and out. Don't remove the elbow (the hooked part of the unit) or get the hearing aid itself wet—just wipe this part carefully with a soft, dry cloth. If the plastic tubing is brittle or cracked, buy a replacement.
- Clean an in-the-ear hearing aid by wiping it with a dry cloth—don't use water. Use the wax pick supplied with the hearing aid to clear any wax blocking the opening.

My hearing aid whistles
Adjust the volume

First, try turning down the volume setting on the device. If this doesn't work, remove and reinsert the hearing aid—a snug fit in your ear canal will help reduce the feedback and whistling.

- Some models of hearing aids give an audible warning when the battery is low, so check the battery and replace if necessary.

Make it last GLASSES

Use two hands to put your glasses on and to take them off—this helps prevent bending their arms.
Don't rest your glasses on their lenses, because they are likely to get scratched. Store them in a case that doesn't put any pressure on the frames or arms, or else they will get scratched. Don't store them in a case that is too small.

SHOES AND CLOTHING

Good-quality clothes and shoes can last for decades with proper care. What's more, well-made items fit well and look good, and become more comfortable with wear as they mold to your body shape. So rather than buying rounds of cheap clothes, invest in quality clothing and keep it looking great. Even some serious clothing disasters can be fixed with a little knowledge.

My sweater has shrunk in the wash
Try a little hair conditioner

Some garments are liable to shrink if you don't follow the manufacturer's washing instructions. There is a way to restore them to their proper size, but it's not guaranteed to work on all fabrics.
● Soak the garment in a bowl of warm water into which you have mixed a couple of squirts of hair conditioner or baby shampoo. Leave it for 20 minutes to let the fibers in the clothing relax.
● Pour out the water and gently press the garment between two towels to squeeze out most of the water; don't wring it out.
● Lay the garment out flat on a dry towel and carefully stretch it back into its original shape and size. Leave it to dry fully; you may need to replace the towel a couple of times as it gets damp.

A stray sock has turned my white clothes blue
Bleach and rewash

If your white cotton sheets pick up dye from a colored item in the wash, first try rewashing the load a couple of times at the recommended temperature with a powder detergent. If this doesn't work, you have one more option:
● Add a cup of bleach to a tub of cold water and soak the sheets in the solution for 10 minutes. Wash again as normal. Don't use bleach on fabrics made of wool or silk.

My clothes have wrinkled in the dryer
Smooth them out with a damp towel

Clothes should be removed from a dryer as soon as it has finished its cycle or they will wrinkle. If you've left them for too long, simply moisten a small towel, put it in with the load, and run the dryer again for a few minutes.

My coat is covered in dust
Improvise a lint remover

Picking hundreds of tiny fragments of lint off a dark wool coat is a tiresome task. Save time by rolling up a magazine and wrapping some wide packing tape around it, with the sticky side out. Roll the sticky edge along your coat to pick up the lint quickly and efficiently.

My dress is wrinkled
Give it a quick steam bath

When you're getting ready to go out and find that your dress is wrinkled, run a hot bath and hang the dress on an adjacent shower rod. The steam will quickly get rid of the creases.

My zipper has broken
The pull tag has come off

Zippers, buttons, and fasteners are the weak points of any garment. If the tab snaps off your zipper, you can make an emergency repair by threading a safety pin or paper clip through the hole in the slider. Some sliders don't have a hole, but the tab clamps into two slots on either side of the slider. Find an old item of clothing with a similar zipper: use a pair of pliers to pry off the tab and fit it into the broken zipper.

The teeth don't line up properly

When a zipper gets misaligned, it becomes impossible to close fully and the fitting will "gape." On a coat or other garment where the zipper opens completely, it's often easiest to replace a new zipper, but if the zipper is sewn into a dress or a pair of trousers or jeans, you may be able to save it.
● Using a pair of pliers, pull off the bumper (the metal stopper at the bottom of the zipper). You may need to use a bit of force to remove it. Open the zipper, stopping just one or two teeth from the bottom.
● Lay the garment on a flat surface and arrange the zipper's teeth symmetrically and straight. Close the zipper up halfway, making sure the teeth lock together correctly. Use a needle and thick thread to make a few stitches at the bottom of the zipper, where the bumper used to be. This will stop the slider from coming apart when the zipper is fully opened.

The zipper has caught on the fabric

Pull the garment taut along the length of the zipper. Ask someone else to pull the fabric out from under the slider; avoid pulling on the slider itself if at all possible—it may get damaged or stuck further.

WARNING

Don't hang woolen clothes or garments with a loose weave on wire coat hangers—they may get permanently stretched at the shoulders. Invest in some high-quality wooden hangers.

The zipper is jammed
Lubricate the teeth

A stuck zipper can be eased using one of many everyday products—be sure to apply the product above and below the point where the zipper is stuck.

● Rub a soft pencil along the teeth of the zipper—the graphite of the "lead" is an excellent lubricant.

● Run the edge of a bar of soap, some petroleum jelly, a cotton swab dipped in olive oil, or a stick of lip balm along the zipper.

● If none of the above works, try soaking the stuck section of the garment in a bowl of warm water into which you have added around 2 cups of dishwashing liquid. Give the concentrated soapy solution an hour or so to penetrate the teeth and slider.

DON'T WRESTLE WITH A STUCK ZIPPER—FREE IT QUICKLY WITH A BAR OF SOAP

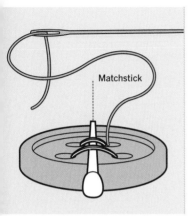

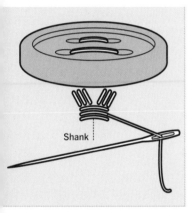

Use a matchstick as a spacer when sewing buttons onto thicker fabrics (top)—it'll help create a longer shank. Wind the thread a few times around the thread securing the button to the fabric to create a sturdy shank for the button (bottom).

My clothes get damaged in the wash
Prepare your garments for the machine

Delicate or expensive clothes need a little attention before you put them in the washing machine. First close any zippers, clasps, or hooks before cleaning—there's less chance of fine fabrics catching and being torn on their own fastenings. Examine the garment before washing; if you see any wear or tension in the fabric near the fastenings, consider washing by hand—the agitation in a machine is likely to result in a tear.

My buttons are always falling off
Brush the threads with nail polish

Life's too short to spend time sewing on buttons. Stop them from falling off in the first place by dabbing a little clear nail polish onto the threads on top of the buttons on a new garment. This will prevent the threads from fraying.

Sew them on securely

The mistake that most people make when sewing on buttons is to sew them flat onto the fabric. This leaves no room for the button to pass easily through the buttonhole and so creates tension in the threads when the garment is worn. The result—a lost button. The solution is to create a small stalk, or shank, to lift the button away from the fabric.

• Most buttons have four holes. When sewing on a button, sew the thread in two separate loops, rather than crossways between the holes. The stitching will lie flatter and be less prone to fraying.
• Start by sewing two loops on the button, but keep the threads loose at this stage.
• Slide a straight pin beneath the button, between the stitches you have made—this will elevate the button from the fabric. For thicker garments, such as jackets or coats, use a matchstick rather than a pin to create a longer shank (see left, top). Put in as many further stitches as you need to make the button secure. Remember not to sew across the holes.
• On the last stitch, push the needle through the material, but not through the button. Remove the pin and wind the thread a few times around the thread that secures the button to the fabric to create a shank (see left, bottom).
• Push the needle back down through the material and make a few stitches to secure the thread.

Seven ways to remove stains from clothes

Quick action is key to stain removal. Lightly dab—don't rub—the stain with cold water (or an appropriate solvent; see below) as soon as possible after the spill. Place the garment facedown on absorbent paper and apply the solvent from the back—this will push the stain out the same way it came in, rather than deeper into the fabric.

1 Tea, coffee, and fruit juice: dab the stain with a weak solution of white vinegar, then wash according to the manufacturer's instructions. If the stain has set, use an eyedropper to apply pure white vinegar to the back of the fabric, and press it through the garment into an absorbent towel with the back of a spoon before laundering.

2 Blood: rinse the stain in cold water, and soak it for 15 minutes in a cool solution of detergent. If the blood has dried, soak the garment overnight in a strong salty solution. In either case, wash as normal after treatment.

3 Red wine: blot the stain immediately with a clean cloth soaked in white vinegar or white wine. If this doesn't work and the garment is white, try a few drops of hydrogen peroxide (available from drugstore).

4 Sweat: crush two soluble aspirin tablets into a cup of warm water and rub the solution into the stain. Allow to rest for 2 hours before laundering. Sponging on a strong solution of salt and water can help to remove dried-on sweat stains.

5 Grass: dab the stain with isopropyl (rubbing) alcohol before washing.

6 Grease and oil: if there's a lot of grease on the surface, first sprinkle over some baby powder or corn flour, then scoop up the oily mess gently with a spoon. Blot away any excess oil, treat the stain with some shampoo, or spray it with WD-40 before laundering.

7 Lipstick: use your finger to work a little petroleum jelly into the stain, then launder on the hottest wash advised by the manufacturer.

> USE AN EYEDROPPER TO TARGET SOLVENT ON THE BACK OF A STAIN—THEN "LIFT" IT OUT OF THE FABRIC

TOOLS OF THE TRADE

Pencil eraser for suede shoes

To clean suede shoes, first loosen any dirt by rubbing the shoes with an old towel, then rub away any stubborn scuffs with a pencil eraser. Finish by brushing the shoes with a suede brush.

My shoes have white marks on them
Rub out winter salt with vinegar

The salt spread on icy roads and pavements in winter can leave a telltale white tidemark when it dries on your shoes.

● Wipe off the marks with diluted white vinegar and a paper towel or soft cloth—use roughly two parts water to one part vinegar. Work a small area at a time, buffing the shoes dry as you go, then polish them as normal. For suede shoes, use the same vinegar solution, but apply it with a clean toothbrush or suede brush.

The sole has come away from my shoe
Glue it back in place

For a long-term solution, a flapping sole needs to be repaired by a professional, but you can buy specialist shoe glue from a shoe repair shop for a temporary fix. Don't use a hot-glue gun or household adhesive unless it is an emergency—the fix won't last long.

● Clean and dry the area that needs repairing, then apply the adhesive according to the manufacturer's instructions. Wait for 10 minutes until the adhesive is tacky then carefully push the sole back into position. Hold the repair firmly together and use a hair dryer to warm the adhesive as it sets: this will help to prevent lumps from forming and will give you a much better and more watertight repair.

My son's sneakers stink
Make an odor absorber

If you need to keep a pair of shoes outside the house because they smell bad, it's time to try this simple tip.

● Cut off the feet and a little of each leg from an old pair of tights then fill the feet with baking soda. Tie a knot in each leg to seal the socks then pop them into the shoes overnight. You will need several boxes of baking soda, but your odor absorbers can be used again and again.

Gum is stuck to sole of my shoe
Freeze it away with ease

If chewing gum is embedded in the tread of your sneakers, it's a long job to scrape it out. Put the shoe into a plastic freezer bag and squash the bag onto the gum until it is truly stuck. Then put the shoe in the freezer. When the chewing gum is hard, pull the bag away from the sole—it should bring the chewing gum with it in one lump.

My laces have frayed
Use nail polish to extend their life

Frayed laces look untidy and are difficult to thread into the eyes on your shoes. You can neaten them up quickly and make an effective temporary repair by twisting the straggly threads and dipping them into clear nail polish.

My tennis shoes are dirty
Apply baking soda to remove stains

The rubber parts of sneakers and other sports shoes will pick up grass stains and other scuffs that are hard to remove. Dab a damp cloth into some baking soda and scrub away at the marks to make them look like new.

● When you buy a new pair of canvas shoes, give them a quick spritz with spray starch; this will prevent grime from working its way into the fabric.

I've run out of shoe polish
Improvise with some household favorites

A variety of chemicals can substitute for shoe polish: petroleum jelly, furniture polish, and hand lotion will all work well on leather. Dab a little on your shoes and work in with a soft cloth, then buff to a shine with a clean cloth. Patent leather can be brought to a shine with a soft cloth dipped in vinegar.

● When you're finished polishing, lightly spray the shoes with hair spray. The polish won't rub off so easily with this coat of protection.

My shoes are too tight
Try some stretching exercises

Those beautiful shoes that fit perfectly in the store now seem a little tight. First, try a gentle approach: put on a pair of thick socks and wear the (now even tighter) shoes indoors for a few days. This may be enough to stretch them into comfort.

● Spray the insides of the shoes with a 50:50 mix of isopropyl (rubbing) alcohol and water (test a small patch for color fastness first). Walk around in the shoes for 30 minutes; repeat the process a few times to improve comfort.

● Stuff the shoes with damp, balled-up newspaper and allow it to dry—this should ease the fit.

WARNING

Don't try to stretch expensive shoes yourself—it's an imprecise science and could result in damage. If you can't get a refund or replacement pair in a larger size, take the shoes to professional shoe repair where they can be stretched under more controlled conditions.

My clothes iron is dirty
Clean the base for a smoother press

Over time, the base of your iron will become coated with heat-fused dirt and grime. This will tend to make the iron drag, rather than glide, across your clothes and may even deposit gunk on your clean garments.

- Give the base a routine clean with a soft cloth moistened with white vinegar. If you need more cleaning power, dab a little baking soda onto the cloth. Never use a scouring pad on the base—you'll ruin the iron.
- For an even quicker clean, sprinkle coarse salt onto a cotton towel laid over your ironing board. Set your iron to its hottest setting, with the steam turned off, and run it over the salt.
- If the base is covered in waxy or oily deposits, set it to its maximum temperature and iron over some newspaper until the mess disappears.
- If the base has burnt-on marks, switch the iron off and allow it to cool. Use masking tape and newspaper to cover every part of the iron except the base. Wearing rubber gloves, take it outdoors and spray oven cleaner onto the base; allow it to work for a few minutes before wiping it away with a moist cloth.

My iron won't produce steam
Unclog the lime from its steam ports

Fill your iron with a 50:50 mixture of water and white vinegar. Turn on the iron and place it on a wire rack in a well-ventilated room. Allow the iron to steam for 15 minutes or until it runs dry. Refill it with water and repeat to clear the iron of vinegar.

My ironing takes forever
Boost your ironing speed and efficiency

Few people enjoy ironing. These simple tips and techniques will have you working through the clothes pile in short order.

- Take the cover off your ironing board and roll a layer of aluminum foil—shiny side up—over the surface of the board. Fold the foil neatly round the edges of the board, then replace the cover. The foil will reflect heat back up from the board, making ironing more efficient.
- Stop waiting for your iron to heat up and cool down to match the temperatures recommended for different fabrics. Start your ironing session with clothes that need a cool iron, and work up to those that need the highest setting.

- Iron shirts when they are still slightly damp—if they are too dry you'll work much harder to get rid of creases.
- When ironing pants, turn them inside out and lay them flat, one leg on top of the other, with the seams aligned. Fold the top leg back and iron the bottom leg. Repeat on the other leg.
- Always iron black or dark fabrics inside out to avoid putting an unwanted sheen on the garment.
- Iron to and fro, not in circular movements, which can scratch fabrics unpredictably.
- Always use boiled or distilled water to fill your steam iron—you'll reduce the deposits that can clog up the vents.
- When ironing shirts, start with the collar and cuffs. Follow the shirt's existing creases, and always hang up the shirt properly in your wardrobe as soon as you're finished.

Fitting aluminum foil beneath the cover of your ironing board will dramatically cut your ironing time.

4
Out
and About

CARS

GETTING AROUND

CARS

The complex electronic systems installed in today's cars undeniably make driving safer, more economical, and easier. However, they are a frustration for home mechanics who, in earlier years, could fix and maintain their cars with little more than a box of wrenches. While most repairs will need professional attention, there's still plenty you can do to improve your driving experience.

BEHIND THE WHEEL

Clear all-round visibility and a good driving position will help you to keep your attention focused on the road and make every journey more pleasant for you and your passengers.

The windshield keeps fogging up
Clear the condensation quickly

It is unsafe to drive with a foggy windshield; you should never set off until the glass is completely clear of condensation and ice. Rubbing with a soft cloth will soak up the moisture on the inside quickly, but at the cost of leaving smeary marks behind.

● To remove condensation without wiping, first set your car's ventilation system to "fresh" rather than "recirculate."

● Next, switch on your air conditioning to its coolest setting and turn the fan to maximum. As the air conditioning starts to dry the air within the car, you can slowly increase the temperature to make your environment more comfortable.

My windshield washer isn't spraying
Unblock the jets with a pin

The fine nozzles on your windshield washer are easily clogged by dirt. First check that there is fluid in the washer's reservoir; if there is, gently prod a pin into each nozzle to clear any obstruction. With the pin inserted into the nozzle, you can also change the angle at which the water sprays onto your windshield to ensure good coverage with washer fluid. Just move the pin to adjust the nozzle mechanism.

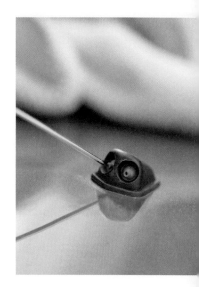

Wiggling a pin in the windshield washer nozzles is usually enough to clear any blockages.

The windshield is dirty
Make your own cleaning products

There's no need to pay for proprietary windshield-washing fluid. Make your own in a 2-liter bottle by mixing one tablespoon of dishwashing liquid with 10 ounces of isopropyl (rubbing) alcohol and top up with water. Use this solution to fill your car's windshield-washer reservoir.

● If your windshield is covered with dried insects, squirt a few drops of washing-up liquid into a bucket of warm water. Spread this over the screen with a sponge and then use a fine mesh bag (an onion bag, for example) to rub the bugs away.

● Wash your windscreen with a 75:25 mix of water and white vinegar applied with a microfiber towel; for a streak-free finish, rub over the glass with scrunched-up newspaper. Avoid domestic glass cleaning products—many of these contain ammonia, which can damage plastic and rubber surrounding the window.

The windows are iced up
Remove the ice with rubbing alcohol

If you don't relish scraping ice from your windshield in winter, fill a spray bottle with rubbing alcohol, spray the glass, and wipe the frost away. The solution will also help to free your frozen wiper blades.

● To prevent icing in the first place, wipe your windshield with pure white vinegar the evening before or cover the glass with rubber mats.

There's a fine scratch on the windshield
Polish your glass for better all-weather visibility

Using a good glass polish (bought from a auto supply store) will not just make your windows gleam, it'll remove fine scratches that contribute to glare and also help to bead water when it rains.

WARNING

Chips or cracks in a windshield should never be ignored because they can spread quickly, threatening your safety. Repairs are successful only for small cracks and chips (less than 1 1/2 in. across, at most) and involve injecting the area with a specialized resin. Auto stores sell kits that enable you to do this at home; if using one, follow the instructions carefully. If in any doubt, don't take a chance: contact your insurer or a windshield repair company as soon as you possibly can.

I suffer from glare when driving at night
Cut down on distracting reflections

At night, tiredness, a reduced ability to judge distance, and glare can impair our driving ability. It's impossible to eliminate glare completely, but you can reduce its effects and take defensive measures when driving after dark.

● Keep both sides of your windshield clean, and degrease your wiper blades with a paper towel dipped in windshield cleaner to reduce streaking. Using the same cleaning fluid, give your headlight glass a regular wipe and have your lights checked for alignment next time you have your car serviced. Repair any cracks or chips in the glass as soon as possible.

● If your car isn't fitted with a self-dimming rearview mirror, put the mirror into its night setting by flipping the tab at the base of the mirror—the lights of cars behind you will appear less bright.

● Make sure your sideview mirrors are correctly adjusted. Lean your head against the right-side window and adjust the driver's side mirror so you can just see the right rear corner of the car; lean over to the other side so that your head is centered in the windshield. Adjust the left-side mirror so that you can just see the left rear corner.

● Don't look directly into the lights of oncoming cars—look slightly away—and always slow down at corners so you're not surprised by the lights of an approaching vehicle. If you wear glasses, make sure they are clean and free from scratches.

The electric windows wobble
Smooth the movement with silicone spray

Slow or wobbling windows don't necessarily mean a failing motor. It's likely that the rubber lining on the window's guide rails has lost its lubricant coating, making the windows stick.

● Wind down the window and then apply some silicone spray or grease (available from all auto stores) right into the exposed window channel. Don't use oil-based lubricant—it'll work at first, but soon become gummed up.

My window switch is jammed
Vacuum away the debris

A small piece of grit can jam the mechanism of a window or door switch. Hold the tube of a vacuum cleaner, set to full power, over the switch and gently rock the switch back and forth to dislodge the particle.

To ease sticking windows, rub a bead of silicone grease into the window channels using the edge of a cloth.

The heating has stopped working
Check the fan and refill the coolant

If your heater isn't working, check that its fan still turns by listening for its whir. If not, try replacing its fuse in the cabin fuse box, which you'll normally find behind a panel at the end of the dashboard or beneath the steering column (see page 235).

● If the fan blows, but there's no warm air, you are probably low on coolant. Find the coolant tank under the hood and top it up to the "Max" indicator line with a 50:50 mix of coolant and water (you can usually buy this premixed at auto stores). You may have to drive a while for the coolant to make its way into the heating system.

My AC is weak
Run the system in winter to keep it lubricated

Recharge your car's air-conditioning system using one of the many kits available from auto stores. Be sure to buy one that includes a pressure gauge and follow the manufacturer's instructions closely.

● Run your AC for at least 10 minutes every week through the winter months. This will help lubricate the system's seals and keep them gas-tight for when you need cooling in the summer.

The car's radio won't work
Replace the fuse

The most likely cause of a silent sound system is a blown fuse.

● Consult your owner's manual to locate the fuse box. All the fuses are numbered and correspond to the numbers you'll see in your manual and on the fuse box itself (or the box cover). Remove the fuse marked "radio" and install a fuse of the same color (indicating its power rating) in its place. Many cars have spare fuses right in the box. If this doesn't work, the cables connecting the radio to the car's speakers may well have come loose and you'll need professional help to remedy the problem.

My GPS has no signal
Fit an external antenna

Some heat-reflective or heated windshields can interfere with GPS signals. You can fix this problem by fitting an external antenna to the GPS unit and securing the wire along the top, or in one corner, of the windshield where there's a gap in the heating mesh.

Running an external antenna from the GPS unit around the inner windshield can help to improve signal reception.

Use a pipe cleaner to clear out the drain holes on the underside of car doors— it will help to prevent rust from forming as a result of trapped moisture.

There's a bad smell in my car
Clean and deodorize

If you have spilled some smelly liquid inside your car, or if one of the children has vomited on the upholstery, first blot the excess moisture with a paper towel, then pick up the dried residue (if any).

● Sprinkle baking soda over the affected area and leave it to absorb any smells for an hour or so before vacuuming it up.

● Mix a liquid cleaner. For leather upholstery, make a paste of three parts baking soda to one part water; for vinyl and cloth, mix five parts warm water with one of white vinegar. Scrub the area using your cleaning agent and a lint-free cloth. Wet another cloth with warm water and rub again to remove the cleaning agent.

● Don't use too much water when cleaning your car's interior and leave the doors open after cleaning to let any moisture evaporate.

● Look on the underside of the car's doors. Some vehicles have small drain holes that allow any stray water to drain out. If your car has these, clear them periodically with a pipe cleaner to head off musty smells and (eventually) rust.

The plastic trim inside the car is scratched
Try a dab of petroleum jelly

Dangling keys or a loose seat-belt buckle can scratch the plastic molding of the car or the trim near the doors. The plastics used by different manufacturers vary greatly in composition, but scratches in hard plastics can sometimes be removed by applying a little petroleum jelly to the scratch with a fingertip, then buffing with a microfiber cloth.

● Don't add your car key to your bunch of house keys—keeping it separate will prevent scratching in the first place.

There's a rip in the seat
Use a patch kit

A small tear in your upholstery should be repaired as soon as possible—it will only get worse. If your seats are covered in cloth, your only choices are an iron-on patch or a needle and thread. Vinyl and leather seats, however, can be repaired almost invisibly using patch kits available from auto stores.

Ten tips for a comfortable drive

Driving puts many unnatural stresses on the arms and upper body. Following a few hints will help you arrive at your destination more safely and with fewer aches and pains.

1 Sit upright and well back in the seat. Raise or lower the seat so you can clearly see both the road and the instruments. Your knees should be level with your hips. Use a seat wedge (available from auto stores) if you are too low.

2 Slide the seat forward or backward so that you can fully depress the pedals without your back lifting off the seat back.

3 Adjust the angle of the seat back—it should be reclined from a vertical position by only 10–20 degrees.

4 Move the headrest so that it sits in the middle of your head—the center of the head rest should be closest to the tops of your ears.

5 Make sure that the head restraint is fully locked in place.

6 Tilt the seat cushion until it supports your thighs evenly and does not rub against the backs of your knees.

7 Move the steering wheel down and toward you so that you can place your hands comfortably on the wheel with your wrists straight at the 10 o'clock and 2 o'clock positions. Adjust its angle so that the air bag in the wheel faces your chest.

8 Remove your wallet from your back pocket—it causes your body to twist while driving.

9 Adjust your sideview mirrors (see page 224).

10 Don't place a cushion between yourself and the seat back, and avoid placing anything under the seats—objects can easily slide forward beneath the pedals.

NEVER MAKE ADJUSTMENTS TO YOUR SEAT POSITION WHILE DRIVING—YOU COULD LOSE CONTROL OF THE VEHICLE

BODYWORK

It's easy to neglect your car's bodywork. After all, you can still drive to work with that dent or scratch in your paint. Professional bodywork repairs can be costly, making them hard to justify. But it's possible to restore your car's dignity for very little money; try fixing a dent with a plunger or polishing your headlights with a tube of toothpaste.

A body panel is dented
Pull it into shape with a plunger

A rounded, smooth dent can sometimes be pulled out with a plunger. Moisten the plunger's rim, then press it into the center of the dent. Pull away sharply and the dent will (hopefully) pop out.

Use a hair dryer and a can of compressed air

If the dent is on a flat panel, away from any edges or creases, try this quick fix.
● Use masking tape to secure a square of aluminum foil over the dented area. This will protect the paintwork.
● Set a hair dryer to medium heat and use it to warm the dented metal for a minute or two. Switch off the hair dryer.
● Immediately take a can of compressed air (available from computer stores for dusting off components) and hold it upside down so that cold propellant is sprayed out. Squirt this onto the foil covering the dented area. The sudden and extreme change in temperature may cause the dent to pop out.

A shallow dent with no creases can often be pulled out with a kitchen plunger. Create as much suction as possible, then pull hard!

The chrome bumper has lost its shine
Polish it back with steel wool

Check if the surface to be cleaned is chromed steel or plastic chrome (a plastic substrate covered with a thin layer of chrome). Older cars may have bumpers and sideview mirrors made of chromed steel, while chromed plastic is often used for details on more modern cars. Apply a magnet to the bumper; if it sticks, it's chromed steel, if not, it's probably plastic.
● Chromed steel may appear dull or have rust spots, but can be restored by polishing vigorously with 0000 steel wool.
● Don't use steel wool on chromed plastic—instead rub it with a 2:1 mix of white vinegar and water, or use a specialist chrome polishing compound.

My car is filthy
Wash it without scratching

Most of us use automatic car washes for convenience, but if their spinning brushes are not well maintained, they could be scratching your paintwork. Cleaning your car manually will give you better results and save you money in the process.

Time needed **10 minutes**
You will need **car shampoo, hose, soft brush, microfiber cloths, two buckets, waffle-weave drying towel**

---

1 Park your car in a shady area—direct sunlight will cause water to dry into unsightly spots. Rub undiluted car shampoo over any stained areas, such as old bird droppings, to pretreat the stubborn marks.

2 Wash the wheels before the car body. Make sure they are cool, then spray them with water from a hose. Apply a little car shampoo with a microfiber cloth and scrub them with a soft brush; you can use an old toothbrush to reach smaller crevices. Rinse with water.

3 Wet the whole car using the hose. Half-fill one bucket with car shampoo, mixed according to the manufacturer's instructions, and another with water. Whip the shampoo up into a sudsy froth. Don't be tempted to use normal dishwashing liquid—you're more likely to get water spots as the car dries.

4 Soak a cloth in the sudsy water and rub it over the car, starting with the roof and working down.

Don't apply too much pressure as you'll risk scratching the car. Rinse the cloth in the bucket of clean water before reloading it with shampoo—this way, you'll rinse any grit off the mitt as you go. Keep wetting the car with the hose—don't allow it to air dry.

5 When you've cleaned the entire surface of the car, rinse it thoroughly with your hose.

6 Immediately dry the car using the drying towel or a chamois. This will help avoid water spots.

My headlights and taillights are dull
Give them clarity with toothpaste

Plastic headlight and taillight covers start to look dull over time, but can be revived with toothpaste. Put a pea-sized drop of paste on a clean rag, then firmly polish the light using a circular motion for 2–5 minutes. Wipe away the toothpaste, then use a clean cloth to rapidly buff the surface to a shine. For tough jobs, you can also use car wax to shine the lenses.

My alloys and trim are dull
Visit your auto store for the right products

Alloy wheels can get pitted by hot dust that comes off your brake pads. You can prevent this damage with a weekly wheel wash, but if it's too late, you can restore your alloys with one of the specialist compounds available from auto stores. Faded black plastic trim around windows and door frames can also be returned to its original finish with today's chemical treatments.

Non-gel white toothpaste is a mild abrasive, making it ideal for polishing out small scratches on headlight covers.

Car paint is made up of at least three layers—a base coat of primer, then a layer of color, and finally a thick topcoat of lacquer. Fine scratches (which often appear as circular swirls when seen under sunlight), water spots, and overall dullness are usually defects in the top lacquer coat and can be remedied by polishing. Deeper scratches and chips need different treatment (see below).

How do I get my paint job back into showroom condition?

Polish and wax your car

A car's paint job is subject to a daily battering of grit and stone chips, insects, and chemicals in the air as well as rainwater and ultraviolet light. Over time, the paint will become dull, covered in fine scratches and its color may even fade. Washing alone isn't enough to restore it to good condition. From time to time it will need polishing and—more often—waxing, which are very different processes. You should wax your car every few months to maintain a protective layer over the paint; polishing needn't be as regular.

Shine the body with polish

Car polish contains fine abrasives that remove a thin layer of the lacquer topcoat, so evening out the reflectiveness of the surface and making it look shiny. There are many polishing products on the market, each with its own instructions for use.

● Whichever product you choose, clean and dry your car before polishing. Work the polish onto the body with a microfiber cloth.

● Work on an area of about three square feet at a time, rubbing in the polish with a mix of circular and straight strokes. The polish will become more transparent as it is worked. Before the polish has completely dried, buff the polished areas to a shine with a chamois.

Protect the body with wax

Wax protects your car from the elements and gives it a high gloss. You should always wax after polishing a car, but you can top up the wax protection at any time. As with polish, there are hundreds of products available, from traditional waxes to advanced polymers. Liquid spray-on waxes are much easier to apply than harder waxes.

● Whichever wax you use, apply it in shady conditions, not direct sunlight. Closely follow the manufacturer's instructions—some waxes need to be applied to the paint, some via a supplied applicator.

Touch up deeper scratches

Scratches and chips that penetrate beneath the car's lacquer topcoat can't be polished out. If you run a fingernail over the scratch and it sticks, you'll need to buy a touch-up kit from your auto store and follow the instructions. For an exact match, find out the code number of your paint—it's usually printed on the driver's door jamb or under the hood. Some auto stores will match a paint color—take a portable part of the car (the gas cap, for example) with you.

BRAKES AND TIRES

Tires and brakes need careful monitoring and maintenance. Basic tasks, such as inflating your tires to the correct pressure, will keep you safe and save you money on fuel. Recognizing the various sounds that your brakes make can warn you of impending failure. Most repairs to these systems are best left to the professionals because of their key role in safety, but the tips below will at very least alert you to possible problems.

The brakes vibrate and grind
Listen carefully to diagnose the problem

Issues with brakes are more often heard than seen.
- Vibration under braking may be a sign of a warped brake disk, which will need replacement. Discs are usually replaced in pairs so prepare yourself for a bill from the garage.
- Grinding under braking usually results from brake pads that are worn down to nothing. With no pad, you'll hear metal scraping on metal and you'll need to replace the pads as soon as possible. Note that brand-new pads will grind a little, but the noise will stop once they have settled in.
- If your brake pedal feels spongy and it takes more effort than usual to stop the car, you may have a serious problem with your brakes. Don't wait, take your car to the repair shop today.

My tires are going flat
Check and adjust the pressure every two weeks

Even a properly installed, good tire will lose air pressure over time, and cooler temperatures will cause a drop in tire pressure. Filling tires to the proper pressure will keep you safe and save you money—consider that a tire's life span may be shortened by as much as 75 percent if it's inflated to only 80 percent of the optimum pressure.
- Know the correct pressure for your tires: you'll find this information in your owner's manual, printed on the inside ledge of the driver's door, or within the gas cap.
- Measure the pressure of each tire at least once a every two weeks using an accurate pressure gauge—most gas stations have combined gauges and air pumps. Your tires should be as cool as possible when you carry out the measurement, so avoid driving more than a mile or two to the gas station because friction will cause them to heat up. Don't forget to check the spare tire (if you have one).

Check the gauge as you're filling your tires with air and be careful not to overinflate them.

SEVERE UNDERINFLATION

OVERINFLATION

POOR ALIGNMENT

If the shoulders of the tire have worn more than the center (top), the tire is under-inflated. A bald strip in the center indicates over-inflation (center). One-sided wear (bottom) suggests incorrect wheel alignment or a suspension problem—have your car checked by a qualified mechanic.

My tires look worn
Decide if it's time for replacements

Most new tires have built-in tread-wear indicators in the main grooves of the tread. If the surface of the indicator bar is level or almost level with the tread, the tire is approaching its legal limit and must be replaced. You should also replace any tire that is more than 6 years old: you can tell its date of manufacture from the DOT number stamped on the sidewall: you will find the letters DOT, followed by a sequence of numbers ending in, say, 1509. Those last four digits tell you that the tire was made in the fifteenth week of 2009.

• Your tires may not wear evenly, which may indicate that they are under- or overinflated, or it may signal some other problem with the wheels and suspension (see left).

I've got a flat tire
Deal with a puncture on the road

A puncture needn't mean a new tire—you may be able to get a repair for a fraction of the cost of a replacement. Tires can be repaired as long as the puncture is in the main area of the tire's tread, and you haven't driven for long on the flat or part-deflated tire.

• If you suffer a puncture while driving, you may notice a flapping sound or your car pulling to the left or right. Pull over as soon as it is safe onto a firm, flat surface—don't be tempted to push on to your destination because you're likely to ruin the tire and damage your wheels.

• If your car has a spare wheel, you may want to call out your road assistance service or opt to change it yourself. If you change it yourself, you must follow the instructions in your car owner's manual.

• Many modern cars don't come with a spare tire, but are equipped with a can of sealant that you inject through the tire valve and then use a cylinder of compressed gas to reinflate the tire. This isn't a permanent repair—have the wheel inspected at a reputable tire center.

There's a nail in my tire
Get a repair as soon as possible

A screw or nail may get lodged in your tire without deflating it. Don't ignore the problem—the nail can move around while you're driving and cause a catastrophic blowout. Instead, drive as slowly as is safe to your local tire center and have them remove the nail. If the tire is sound, you'll have lost little; if there's a rush of air from the tire, you're in the best place for a speedy repair.

UNDER THE HOOD

When you lift the hood of a modern car, you're likely
to see an array of "black boxes" that house mechanical and
electronic systems. Finding and repairing most faults requires
special diagnostic equipment, and tinkering at home is
discouraged by manufacturers and may void your warranty.
However, there are still some simple tasks that you can carry out
to fix and maintain electrical, fluids, and mechanical components.

WHAT YOU CAN FIX YOURSELF

Basic under-the-hood maintenance includes checking and topping off
fluid levels, replacing electrical fuses, and checking battery levels and
connections. Be sure to secure your open hood with the prop arm before
getting to work on the engine. Note that layouts differ between makes and
models.

Windshield wiper–fluid reservoir
Replenish the fluid with a mix of
isopropyl alcohol, dishwashing
liquid, and water (see page 223).

Coolant tank
Top off the coolant if your car is
overheating. Remove the cap when
the engine is cool (see page 225).

Brake-fluid reservoir
Check the brake-fluid level
regularly—if it falls below the
indicated line, see a professional.

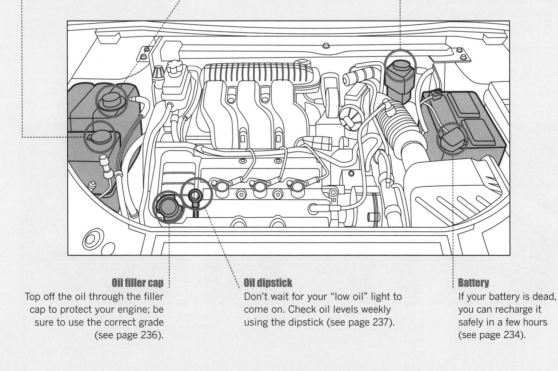

Oil filler cap
Top off the oil through the filler
cap to protect your engine; be
sure to use the correct grade
(see page 236).

Oil dipstick
Don't wait for your "low oil" light to
come on. Check oil levels weekly
using the dipstick (see page 237).

Battery
If your battery is dead,
you can recharge it
safely in a few hours
(see page 234).

My car won't start
Check the battery

If all you hear when you try to start the car is a dull click, the chances are your battery is flat and needs to be recharged. Some batteries have a small indicator on the top plate that warns of low charge.

● To recharge a battery, you'll need an inexpensive trickle charger, available at low cost from all auto stores. First, make sure the ignition is switched off. If possible, use a wrench to loosen the clamps on the battery posts, then remove them. Connect the red clip from the charger

My battery is dead and I'm in a hurry
Jump-start the vehicle

When you just can't wait for your battery to recharge, you can try jump-starting the car from another vehicle. It's always worth carrying a set of jumper cables (available from auto stores) in case you're stranded with a dead battery or need to give roadside assistance to another motorist.

Time needed **10 minutes**
You will need **a set of jumper cables**

1 Check that the two cars use batteries of the same voltage—most use 12V batteries. Park side by side so that the jumper cables reach between the two batteries. Turn off any nonessential electrical functions on both vehicles.

2 Attach the positive (red) cable to the donor car's positive battery post (below, left); attach the other end of the cable to the positive post of the dead battery.

3 Clip the negative (black) cable to the donor car's negative battery

post (below, center); clip the other end to a metal bracket on the engine of the dead car (below, right). Ensure that the cables are away from any moving parts.

4 Start the donor car and run it for two minutes; then try starting the dead car. If it starts, keep both cars connected for a few minutes, if not, call for auto assistance.

5 Disconnect the cables in reverse order to how they were connected.

to the battery's positive terminal (marked Pos or +) and the other
to the negative terminal (marked Neg or -). Don't let the metal
clips touch each other or any other metal. Once connected, plug the
charger into an electric wall socket and turn it on. Run the charger for
a few hours or, if possible, overnight. Unplug the charger, disconnect
its cables from the battery, reconnect the battery's cables to the battery
posts, and start the car.

● Corroded battery contacts may prevent your car from starting.
With a wire brush, vigorously clean both battery posts and inside
the connector clamps until you see nothing but clean metal. Reinstall
the connectors, tighten the clamps and try again.

● Some batteries are sealed units, but others can be topped up with
distilled water if the battery fluid level drops. To do this, unscrew each of
the (usually 6) plastic screw heads on the top plate of the battery. Look
inside using a flashlight—the metal plates within should be covered with
liquid; if not, top up with a little distilled water (not tap water).

● Have your mechanic check your battery in their garage, as outside
temperatures fall—cold weather can drain a battery because you make
more demands on it during winter as you run wipers, heating, and
headlights. Recharging or replacing your battery in good time means
you won't get stuck in the cold.

My lights don't work

Try installing a replacement bulb

A dead headlight or faltering brake light is dangerous and will soon
earn you a fine. The fixtures used to secure car bulbs vary greatly
between models—some are simple to replace, while others require
a trip to the mechanic. Check your owner's manual for instructions.
Replacement will usually mean gaining access to the back of the light
unit, so you may need to pull back some interior trim. Whenever you
install a new bulb, take the blown bulb to your auto store to help you
purchase an exact replacement. Always wipe the new bulb clean of
fingerprints after installing or wear latex gloves when handling it—the
oils on human skin may otherwise cause the bulb to blow.

Check your fuse box

If swapping your bulb doesn't solve the problem with your lights,
try the fuse. Every circuit in your car—from the lights to the AC—is
protected by a fuse. Many cars have two fuse boxes—one inside the
car and one—for high-power circuits—under the hood. Your owner's
manual will guide you to the location of a particular fuse. Replace it
with a fuse of the same rating (see right).

Car fuses are simple to
replace, easily slotting into
the fuse panel. Their color,
and often engraved markings
on their legs, indicate their
power rating. Always swap
like for like.

There's a knocking coming from the engine
Check your oil and fuel

If your engine is knocking, pinging, or chattering, you may need to look at your choice of fuel. Try a higher octane fuel—these are often sold under a name like "Premium" or "Super" and cost a little more than basic fuel. Low oil levels can also cause engine noise—check the level and top off if required (see opposite).

My engine squeals
Use soap on the belt for a quieter drive

Car engines use rubber belts—or more usually today, a single broad belt, known as the serpentine or poly-V belt—to supply power to systems such as the water pump and the AC. If this belt slips on its pulleys, it'll make a high-pitched squeal.
● Switch off your engine and allow it to cool. Press down on the top of the belt. If it is so loose that you can push it down by more than a half-inch, it needs to be tightened or replaced by a mechanic. However, you can temporarily silence the squeals.
● Use a knife to cut a thin slice from a bar of soap. Rub the soap on the inner surface of the belt along as much of its length as you can reach (having a thin slice of soap helps you reach further).
● Start the engine and check for squeals. Repeat the process if necessary.

My fuel consumption has risen
Economize your drive

There are many things that you can do to make your car run more efficiently, and so save yourself money on fuel.
● Have your car serviced at the correct, recommended intervals.
● Fill your tires to the correct pressure. Underinflated tires decrease fuel mileage dramatically.
● Make sure you are using the engine oil recommended for your vehicle—check the owner's manual.
● Avoid making multiple short journeys—try to combine them if at all possible.
● Don't carry excess weight: clear unnecessary items from your trunk, and remove bike racks and luggage racks if you don't need them.
● Drive smoothly, braking and accelerating in good time. Stick within the speed limits and change up a gear as soon as you can without laboring the engine.
● Turn off electrical systems, such as the AC and fan, if you don't need them.

Make it last CAR FLUIDS

The single most important thing you can do to add life to your car and prevent repairs along the way is to maintain the correct levels of all the fluids under the hood. It's good practice to check their levels once a month.

Check your oil by parking your car on a level surface. Turn off the engine and wait at least 15 minutes. Pull out the dipstick (which usually has an orange or yellow hooped handle), wipe it with a clean cloth and reinsert it completely. Wait 5 seconds, then pull it up again. Check the oil level relative to the MIN and MAX marks engraved on the dipstick. If the level is below MIN, find and unscrew the oil cap. Pour in the correct oil, a little at a time. Wait 30 seconds before checking the level with your dipstick again, as above. Stop before you reach the MAX mark—overfilling with oil could damage the engine.

Check your other fluids—coolant, brake fluid, windshield wiper–fluid, and other fluids under the hood are held in translucent reservoirs, marked with correct filling levels, so you easily see if they need a refill. Follow the manufacturer's instructions on topping off these fluids.

GETTING AROUND

We depend on equipment to get ourselves—and our belongings—from one place to another. Bags, suitcases, strollers, and wheelchairs take a lot of punishment over their lifetimes, but it's not difficult to restore them to perfect working condition when things do go wrong.

STROLLERS AND WHEELCHAIRS

Strollers are designed to carry our most precious cargo in comfort and style. Like wheelchairs, their weakest points lie in their moving parts—wheels, brakes, and folding mechanisms—which need regular attention to ensure efficient and safe transport.

The brake on my stroller isn't working
Adjust the brake cable

Stroller brakes can become clogged by dirt and debris, and they often need adjusting to maintain their stopping power.

● For stroller brakes that are activated by a brake lever (much like a bicycle brake), tighten or loosen the brakes with the adjuster nut, which is located where the cable enters the lever. If the cables have become kinked, you may need to buy and install a new cable.

● Some strollers have a cable adjuster (often shaped like a bullet) on the cable by the brake. Turn it, then check the brake's operation.

● For a foot-operated brake, check the brake assembly. Small stones or mud can become lodged in the teeth (located on the axle) that the brake locks onto—use an old screwdriver to clear the teeth.

My stroller clicks when I'm pushing it along
The brake isn't fully disengaged

The brake mechanism can catch against the wheel when in motion, causing a clicking sound.

● First, check that the brake lever is fully off.

● Next, check the brake cable (if your stroller has one). Tighten it (see above) if necessary, until the brake stops knocking.

● Finally, check all the brake's screws and bolts and ensure that the wheel's axle bolts are secure, tightening any that are loose.

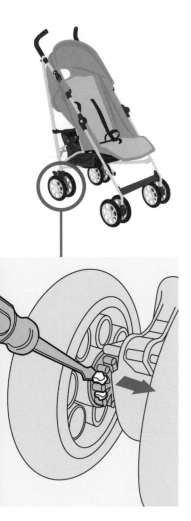

Stones or other objects lodged in a stroller's brake mechanism can be pried out with a screwdriver.

My collapsible stroller won't fold up
Remove obstructions, check for damage, and apply lubricant

A collapsible stroller that refuses to fold—or to stay in its folded position—is hugely frustrating.

● Make sure nothing is sticking out and stopping the sections of frame moving past one another—perhaps an object left in the basket beneath the stroller, or even the buggy fabric itself.

● Carefully inspect the catches and each section of the metal frame. Use pliers to straighten any bent metal catches; if the frame seems bent, open the buggy fully and try to bend the damaged sections back into shape.

● If you can't see anything stopping the buggy from folding, the joints and catches may have stiffened or seized (especially if you store it outside). Lubricate the joints with a squirt of aerosol lubricant or a silicone-based furniture polish.

WARNING

Do not attempt to force your stroller to collapse if you can't identify the obstruction—you risk breaking the stroller and could injure yourself on any splintered or broken parts. Take the unit back to the store where it was purchased for some expert advice.

I can't remove the stains on my stroller
Spruce it up with some quick cleanups

Snacks, drinks, mud, and worse will inevitably take their toll on the stroller's upholstery.

● Clean the seat area using the nozzle attachment of your vacuum to get into as many nooks and crevices as you can.

● If you can remove the seat covers and canopy, take them off and wash them on a gentle, cool cycle in your washing machine. Put the covers back on the stroller while they are still damp in case they shrink as they dry. Leave the stroller outside in a sunny spot to dry.

● If you can't remove the covers, clean them with warm, soapy water and a cloth. Use an old toothbrush to get into seams and corners.

● A nailbrush or stiff toothbrush dipped in warm, soapy water will dislodge the grime on webbing straps, which can be difficult to clean.

● Use antibacterial wipes to clean the frame and any plastic parts.

My stroller's fabric smells
Bring the freshness back

Food and drink spills can cause unpleasant odors to emanate from your stroller. Treat any smells with a liquid solution of baking soda and water: spray it onto the affected area using a clean, empty spray bottle, or apply it with a cloth, then wipe it off with another clean cloth. You can also use baking soda and just a little water mixed to a paste to scrub away stubborn stains.

My wheelchair tire is flat
Fix the leak and prevent future problems

A flat or poorly inflated tire will make moving the chair difficult, and is also likely to make it veer to one side.
- If your tire is flat, inflate it to the pressure indicated on the rim. If the tread is badly worn, the tire should be replaced.
- If the tire is punctured, you'll need to repair it. Follow the method for repairing a bicycle inner tube. It's worth keeping a couple of spare inner tubes handy so that you can get back on the road quickly (you can then fix the punctured tube at your leisure).
- If you suffer from repeated punctures, consider replacing your pneumatic tires with Kevlar-reinforced tires, foam-filled airless tires, or solid rubber tires. Ask your wheelchair supplier or repair shop for advice to suit your particular model. Alternatively, use tire sealant in the inner tubes to prevent punctures (see opposite).

My wheelchair needs a tune-up
Make sure the tires are inflated and unworn

Any adjustments to the setup of your wheelchair should be made in consultation with your health-care provider, but keeping the chair clean and in good repair are tasks that can be carried out at home with relative ease.
- Start with the upholstery. If your chair has a vinyl seat, wipe it down every week with a damp cloth and a gentle detergent. Every month, treat it with a fabric conditioner; this is sold in auto stores for use on vinyl car seats. Check the fabric for tears—a sagging seat will not just look bad, but it may contribute to pressure sores and poor posture.
- Wipe any metal surfaces weekly with a chamois, and treat chrome components with silicone-based car polish.
- The small casters on the front of the wheelchair can get clogged with hair, making the chair difficult to push. Remove the casters from their forks using an Allen wrench (also known as a hex key); pull the shaft out from the caster, taking care not to lose the washers. Pull out any accumulated hair and debris from the caster, and reassemble the unit; avoid overtightening the nuts.
- Check the wheels every week to ensure that they spin freely. Tighten the nuts holding the axle to stop any sideways movement or wobble of the wheels.
- Spray a small amount of bicycle lubricant on the moving parts of the chair, including the folding mechanism.

The hand grips keep slipping
Use a hair dryer to stick them in place

With use, the rubber grips on wheelchair handles often slip back on the metal frame, leaving a loose section of grip flapping behind the chair. The grips can be very difficult to push back over the handles, making the chair uncomfortable to push.

● Using a hair dryer on a warm setting, heat the grip along its entire length for a minute or two. The rubber will expand slightly with the heat, allowing you to push the grips back into place with just a little effort. They will contract as they cool to firmly grip the frame.

The battery is running out more quickly than usual
Check the tires and the battery

If the battery on your electric wheelchair doesn't seem to be lasting as long as it used to, check both the tires and the battery.

● Flat tires will not run as smoothly as fully inflated ones, putting extra strain on the motor that will drain the battery. Check that the tires are inflated to the correct pressure; pump them up or replace the inner tube if required.

● You can give your battery a boost with a conditioning recharge. Let it go completely dead then recharge it on the charger's lowest setting, sometimes called a "trickle charge." Let it charge for 24–36 hours.

● Wheelchair batteries need to be replaced roughly every two years. If a recharge doesn't help and the tires are not to blame, replace your battery as soon as you can.

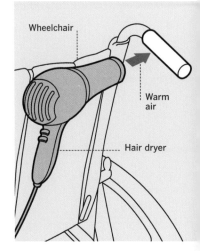

Wheelchair

Warm air

Hair dryer

Warm the hand grips evenly by moving a hair dryer along their length. Pull the grips back into place when they have relaxed.

Make it last WHEELCHAIRS

For electric wheelchairs, don't let the battery fall below 50 percent of its full charge. Invest in a voltmeter that will help you to keep track of the battery's charge.

Charge the battery overnight once every 2 weeks, even when not in use. If you're going away or know you won't be using the chair for a while, disconnect the battery.

To prevent punctures in pneumatic tires, inject a self-sealing compound (available from bicycle shops) into the inner tubes. Deflate the tire and unscrew the core of the valve, squeeze the sealant into the tube, then replace the valve core, and inflate the tire.

BAGS AND CASES

Suitcases and bags are a big investment, and it's easy to keep them looking their best with a handful of household items.

My handbag won't stay closed
Check the clasp and hinge

A metal clasp can bend through use until the two parts no longer clip together. Use pliers to bend each part gently back into shape, or press them together when closed. Stick insulation tape to the jaws of the pliers or cover the clasp with fabric to avoid scratches.

I've dented my hard suitcase
Heat it back into shape

Hard plastic cases can be dented by careless handling. Open the case and heat the dent with a hair dryer for about 10 minutes, moving the dryer to avoid "hotspots." If the dent doesn't spring back, push a block of wood covered in a cloth against the dent and tap it gently with a hammer.

There's a stain on my suede handbag
Act fast to spot-clean the bag

Suede is a delicate material that can be difficult to clean. The quicker you act, the greater your chance of removing any stains.
● For dry stains, gently rub a pencil eraser over the affected area.
● A slice of stale bread can be used to remove dirt stains. Remove the crusts, leave to dry out and harden, then rub the edge over the stain.
● Shift stubborn stains in suede by rubbing gently with a clean cloth dipped in a little white vinegar.

Make it last HANDBAGS

Make sure your handbag keeps its shape in storage by stuffing an empty bag with newspaper, tissue paper, or empty plastic bags.
If your bag came with a soft flannel storage bag, use it to keep the bag dust-free and protected from scrapes and scratches. Use a pillowcase instead if you don't have one.

The telescopic handle on my suitcase is stuck

Realign the release rods

Most wheeled suitcases or carry-on bags have a handle that is attached to the case through two telescopic metal tubes. The mechanism is prone to failure, leaving you with a handle that will no longer extend or retract. The fix is usually simple.

- Using a small screwdriver, remove the screws holding the handle onto the extending tubes. Keep the screws safe.
- Look into the exposed ends of the telescoping tubes. They are hollow and contain a thin metal rod. Its job is to transfer the movement of the release button on the handle of the case down the telescoping rods to the lock/release mechanism.
- Grab the end of one release rod and lift it out of the tube by about 8 inches or so. Then take the free handle piece and depress the release button. Looking into the open end of the handle, you should see a small hole that fits the end of the release rod. Push the rod firmly back into this hole. While holding it in place, repeat the process for the rod in the other tube.
- Holding both rods in place in the handle section, lower the assembly back down onto the telescopic tubes. Secure it back in position with two screws on the handle. Try the mechanism again—it should work!

The wheels on my suitcase are wearing out

Replace them with in-line-skate wheels

Worn or damaged suitcase wheels can be replaced with wheels for in-line skates, which are much more durable. You can buy the wheels in different sizes from skate shops or online. Be sure to match the size of the new wheels to the old.

- If the wheels are partially hidden, check to see if there is a fabric panel inside the case that can be lifted. Pry off any plastic wheel caps using a flat-head screwdriver. If the wheels are held on by rivets, you will need to take the case to a professional for repair.
- If the wheels are screwed in place, unscrew them with a screwdriver or Allen wrench. Some wheels are attached with bolts—use a wrench to remove them.
- Attach the new wheels by reversing the method above, taking care not to overtighten the screws or bolts.

To fix a stuck telescopic handle on your suitcase or carry-on bag, first remove the screws securing the handle to the telescoping tubes (top). Then, insert the thin metal rods within the tubes into their corresponding holes in the handle (bottom).

OUTDOOR ACTIVITIES

Even today's hi-tech outdoor fabrics and materials are vulnerable to damage from sharp objects, water, and sunlight. Waterproofing eventually becomes compromised, zippers jam, and chairs get moldy, so some knowledge of how to fix things in the field with improvised tools and readily available materials will make your trip that much more comfortable.

My hiking boots rub
Break in your boots to ensure comfortable walking

Some leather hiking boots are stiff and may require breaking in before you can hike long distances in comfort.
● Wear your new boots around the house while wearing your normal walking socks. Your feet swell in the afternoon, so this is the best time for it. Gradually increase the time spent wearing the boots.
● If the boots rub against a particular part of your foot, use a plaster or blister patch to protect the skin until the boot molds to your foot.
● Wear two pairs of socks—a liner sock under a thicker sock—to prevent blisters. The liner allows your foot to move inside the thicker sock, which also cushions it and prevents rubbing against the boot.

My zipper is stuck
Free it with an improvised lubricant

Zippers can become stuck when dirt or fabric gets trapped in their teeth. If you're out hiking or camping, try using any handy lubricant, such as bar soap, lip balm, or candle wax, to ease the teeth. If the zipper is metal, run a pencil along the teeth on both sides once it is free—the graphite in the pencil "lead" will help the zip to run smoothly in future.

I can't tighten my trekking poles
Reset and clean the mechanism

Trekking poles usually have a twist-lock mechanism that enables you to extend and collapse the pole and set it to a comfortable height. Sometimes, one section of the pole will turn without gaining any grip on the adjacent wider section, making the pole useless because it won't stay firmly extended.

If the zipper on your wet-weather gear gets stuck, and you're miles from home, see if anyone in your group has a stick of lip balm—it might just be the thing that keeps you dry.

- Pull the sections apart beyond the "Max" marking until the plastic expander just becomes visible below the collar of the wider section.
- Grip the expander with your fingers and turn the thinner section of the pole clockwise until you feel the expander start to grip. Push the pole back in and turn it as usual to lock.
- If this doesn't work, it may be that the surface of the expander is covered with dirt that stops it gripping the inside of the pole, or that the screw thread on the end of the pole is corroded, with the result that the screw cannot turn within the expander. In both cases, the remedy is to pull the narrow pole completely out of the wider one. Separate the expander from the screw by turning it counterclockwise. Clean the screw thread with some fine steel wool and lubricate it with a blob of bicycle grease (don't use a thin oil or WD-40). Use some fine sandpaper to scrub the outer face of the plastic expander—this will clean its surface and help it grip the inside of the pole. Reassemble the pole and try again.

My waterproof jacket gets wet
Treat it to a wash and dry

Modern waterproof jackets are usually made from a breathable, waterproof fabric coated with a layer of a specialist chemical called a Durable Water Repellent (DWR). This creates a layer of microscopic "spines" on the surface of the fabric; water drops sit on top of these spines, meaning that they cannot reach the fabric. With wear, the DWR becomes dirty and the spines become flattened, meaning that rain can form sheets on the fabric. This makes the outer surface of the fabric cold, with the result that sweat condenses on the inside of the jacket, making it feel wet.

- To revitalize the DWR, simply wash the jacket on a warm cycle in your machine. Use a specialist detergent (available at your local outdoors shop) added to the washer's detergent tray rather than regular soap powder. Never add bleach or fabric conditioner to the wash.
- Allow the jacket to air dry. You may wish to reapply a new coating of DWR, which is available in spray form from outdoors shops: you needn't do this after every wash—one application every year should be enough to keep your jacket fully waterproof.

Fix a loose trekking pole by pulling apart its sections (top) to reveal the expander— here, the green plastic component. Clean the screw thread with some fine steel wool (bottom).

There's mold on my outdoor chair
Freshen it up with a stiff brush

If your outdoor folding chair was damp when it went into storage for the winter, it might have developed mold and mildew. This is unsightly and can also destroy the chair's fabric. Use a stiff brush to remove the surface mildew, then scrub any black spots on the fabric with a solution of hot water and mild bleach. Let the bleach solution soak into the fabric so that it destroys any mold spores in the material. Rinse with water then leave to air and dry in the sun.

The needle of my compass is sticking
Wash away the static

The movement of a compass needle can be affected by static electricity that builds up in your clothes. Rub a little water over the compass case to disperse the electrical charge. This should free the needle.

My binoculars are foggy
Dry them out to remove condensation

Condensation on the inside of your binocular lenses cannot be wiped off and, if ignored, can lead to mold—a much harder problem to solve.
• Put your binoculars somewhere warm and dry for a day or two. This should evaporate any condensation.
• Alternatively, pop the binoculars in a large, airtight food-storage container or a freezer bag, along with a few cupfuls of rice or a desicant such as silica gel crystals (available from camera shops).

Make it last BINOCULARS

Put lens caps on your binoculars when they are not in use. This keeps dust off the lenses and protects against scratches.
Avoid touching the lenses as your fingers will leave oily prints that are difficult to clean off. To remove fingerprints, rub the lenses very gently with a special lens-cleaning solution and lens-cleaning paper.
Use a camera cleaner with a soft brush and an air blower to blow dust off the lenses—never wipe them with a paper tissue as you risk scratching the surface.

INDEX

mineral deposit removal, 15, 95, 100, 103, 159, 173, 177, 206
polishing aid, 217, 228
stain removal, 15, 100, 115, 190, 192, 215, 216, 242
unblocking toilet, 108
wicker tightener, 197
vinyl floor, 194
viruses, computer, 33, 57, 80–81

W

warning symbol, 9, 13
warranties, 10
washers
faucet, 94, 96, 97, 117
toilet, 109, 111, 114
washing machines
extending life of, 173
parts of, 168, 169
problems with
clothing damage, 214
DIY fixes for, 169
failure to clean clothes, 171
failure to fill up, 168
failure to spin, 171
failure to start, 168
leaks, 170–71
noisy vibration, 172
odor on clothes, 172
poor drainage, 173
slow filling, 170
watch face, scratched, 207
water emergencies. See also leaks
discolored tap water, 91
electrical safety and, 88
flooding, 88, 105–6
frozen pipes, 92
no water, 93
stopcock seized open, 90
water hammer, 113, 116
waterproof jacket, revitalizing, 245
water stains, 100
webcams, 75
websites, fake, 82–83
wheelchairs
extending life of, 241
flat tire on, 240, 241
low battery on, 241
slipping hand grips on, 241
tune-up for, 240

whetstone, as sharpener, 156–57, 159
white clothes, discolored in wash, 211
wicker seat, saggy, 197
Wi-Fi connection, 84, 85
Wii gaming system, 49
windows
broken, 143–44
car, 223, 224
condensation on, 145
cracked, 143
draft-proofing, 146
heat-leaking, 146
locks for, 145
passive shading and, 129
putty replacement on, 144
stiff, 143
stuck shut, 142
when to replace, 142
Windows operating system, 52, 53
window treatments, 186–88
windshield
chipped or cracked, 223
dirty, 223
fogged up, 222
iced up, 223
nighttime glare and, 224
scratched, 223
windshield washer, clogged, 223
wood-burning stove, lighting, 124–25
wooden floor
scratched or dented, 192, 193
stained, 192
wood saw, 12
wrench, 12
wrinkles, removing, 211, 212

X

Xbox, disk stuck in, 48–49

Z

zippers, 212, 213, 244

ACKNOWLEDGMENTS

Reader's Digest thank the following for permission to use theirs images.
The following abbreviations indicate the position of the image on the page:

a - above
b - below/bottom
c - center
l - left
r - right
t - top

2–3c Alamy Images: boostgraphics;, **2bl** Getty Images: SelectStock;, **3bl** Getty Images: Michael Bodmann;, **4tr** Alamy Images: Wavebreak Media ltd;, **5tl** Getty Images: fstop123;, **5tc** Getty Images: Image Source;, **5tr** Getty Images: Montreal_Photos;, **6t** Alamy Images: f:nalinframe;, **7tl** Getty Images: Stephan Zabel;, **7br** Getty Images: Blend Images - Jose Luis Pelaez Inc;, **8t** Alamy Images: Tetra Images;, **9cr** Alamy Images: Neil Fraser;, **10tl** Getty Images: Nick M. Do;, **11tr** Getty Images: Blend Images - Stellapictures;, **12tl** Getty Images: Stockbyte;, **12tr** Getty Images: Ziga Lisjak;, **12bl** Getty Images: Image Source;, **13cr** Alamy Images: Image Source;, **14cl** Alamy Images: Geo-grafika;, **14cr** Getty Images: Kevin Dyer;, **14bl** Getty Images: Burazin;, **15tl** Getty Images: px photography;, **15cr** Getty Images: Soubrette;, **15cl** Alamy Images: YAY Media AS;, **15br** Alamy Images: Elena Elisseeva;, **16tr** Getty Images: Joe Potato Photo;, **16cl** Getty Images: Jonathan Kantor;, **16c** Alamy Images: Volodymyr Semenchuk;, **16br** Alamy Images: Mouse in the House;, **17tr** Getty Images: Comstock;, **17cl** Getty Images: Nina Shannon;, **17cr** Alamy Images: Zoonar GmbH;, **17br** Alamy Images: Petro Perutskyi;, **18tl** Alamy Images: OJO Images Ltd;, **18br** Getty Images: Jeneil S;, **18–19c** Getty Images: Nikada;, **22bl** Alamy Images: Warren Mcconnaughie;, **24t** Getty Images: Rob Daly;, **30b** Getty Images: blackred;, **31r** Getty Images: DreamPictures/Shannon Faulk;, **32bl** Getty Images: Fotosearch;, **33tr** Alamy Images: Nalinratana Phiyanalinmat;, **38b** Getty Images: Newton Daly;, **58t** Getty Images: Fotosearch;, **59cr** Getty Images: JGI/Jamie Grill;, **62t** Getty Images: Johner Images;, **79tr** Getty Images: Tom Gufler;, **80bl** Getty Images: JGI/Jamie grill;, **81cr** Getty Images: Mark Bowden;, **83tr** Alamy Images: Brian Chan;, 85br Getty Images: Tetra images;, **86tl** Getty Images: Robert Daly;, **86br** Getty Images: SelectStock;, **86–87c** Getty Images: Michael Bodmann;, **92t** Shutterstock;, **93br** Getty Images: Sami Sarkis;, **107b** Getty Images: Comstock;, **115t** Alamy Images: Jochen Tack;, **116bl** Getty Images: nsj-images;, **117tr** Getty Images: Thomas Schneider;, **121t** Alamy Images: Juice Images;, **123br** Alamy Images: Parker Lee;, **124tr** Getty Images: MachineHeadz;, **127br** Alamy Images: Steve Teague;, **129t** Getty Images: mbbirdy;, **131tr** Getty Images: Carmen MartA-nez BanAs;, **132tc** Alamy Images: Jochen Tack;, **136b** Getty Images: Kentaroo Tryman;, **141t** Getty Images: slobo;, **142t** Getty Images: Jaap Hart;, **145t** Alamy Images: Peter Scholey;, **153t** Getty Images: Alex Wilson;, **154tl** Getty Images: John Dowland;, **154br** Getty Images: Paul Bradbury;, **153–154c** Alamy Images: Pollen Photos;, **159br** Getty Images: Steve Wisbauer;, **163t** Alamy Images: Everyday Images;, **165t** Alamy Images: Chris Rout;, **174b** Alamy Images: Robert Smith;, **176t** Alamy Images: Bon Appetit;, **178bl** Alamy Images: Chris Howes/Wild Places Photography;, 190tr Getty Images: Stephanie Horrocks;, **195c** Getty Images: Emrah Turudu;, **200bl** Alamy Images: PJB Images;, **203t** Getty Images: Martin Poole;, **220tl** Getty Images: beyond foto;, **220br** Getty Images: Denkou Images;, **220–221c** Alamy Images: StudioSource;, **222t** Getty Images: Andrey Artykov;, **225br** Getty Images: R. Nelson.

We are committed to both the quality of our products and the service we provide to our customers. We value your comments, so please feel free to contact us.

Trusted Media Brands, Inc.
Adult Trade Publishing
44 South Broadway
White Plains, NY 10601

Printed in China
1 3 5 7 9 10 8 6 4 2

WARNING

All do-it-yourself activities involve a degree of risk. Skills, materials, tools, and site conditions vary widely. Although the editors have made every effort to ensure accuracy, the reader remains responsible for the selection and use of tools, materials, and methods. Always obey local codes and laws, follow manufacturer's operating instructions, and observe safety precautions.